ZONDERVAN
Charts

CHARTS OF

PHILOSOPHY

AND

PHILOSOPHERS

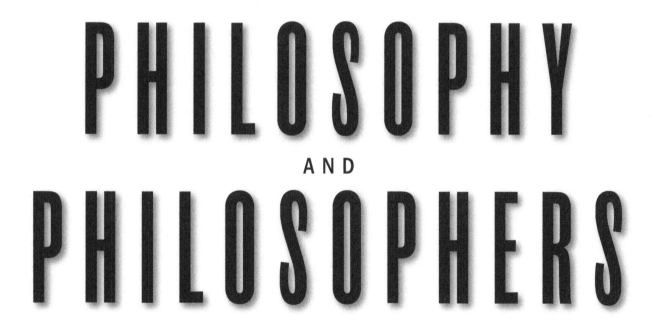

Books in the Zondervan*Charts* Series

Charts of Ancient and Medieval Church History (John D. Hannah)

Charts of Apologetics and Christian Evidences (H. Wayne House and Joseph M. Holden)

Charts of Bible Prophecy (H. Wayne House and Randall Price)

Charts of Christian Ethics (Craig Vincent Mitchell)

Charts of Christian Theology and Doctrine (H. Wayne House)

Charts of Cults, Sects, and Religious Movements (H. Wayne House)

Charts of the Gospels and the Life of Christ (Robert L. Thomas)

Charts of Modern and Postmodern Church History (John D. Hannah)

Charts of Philosophy and Philosophers (Craig Vincent Mitchell)

Charts of Reformation and Enlightenment Church History (John D. Hannah)

Charts of World Religions (H. Wayne House)

Chronological and Background Charts of Church History (Robert C. Walton)

Chronological and Background Charts of the New Testament (H. Wayne House)

Chronological and Background Charts of the Old Testament (John H. Walton)

Taxonomic Charts of Theology and Biblical Studies (M. James Sawyer)

Timeline Charts of the Western Church (Susan Lynn Peterson)

CHARTS OF

PHILOSOPHY

AND

PHILOSOPHERS

Craig Vincent Mitchell

ZONDERVAN®

ZONDERVAN

Charts of Philosophy and Philosophers
Copyright © 2007 by Craig Vincent Mitchell

Requests for information should be addressed to:

Zondervan, 3900 *Sparks Dr. SE, Grand Rapids, Michigan 49546*

Library of Congress Cataloging-in-Publication Data

Mitchell, Craig Vincent, 1958 –
      Charts of philosophy and philosophers / Craig Vincent Mitchell.
         p. cm. – (Zondervan charts)
      Includes bibliographical references.
      ISBN-13: 978-0-310-27092-8
      1. Philosophy – Introductions. 2. Philosophy – Outlines, syllabi, etc. I. Title.
BD31.M58 2007
   102'.02 – dc22
                                                                     2007006706

Interior design: Angela Eberlein

Printed in the United States of America

To my parents:

William Louis Mitchell, Betty Jean Baker, and Isaiah Liggins.

I thank the Lord for them because of the blessing that they have been to me and to everyone who has known them.

Contents

Introduction 13

Part 1: Classical Disciplines

Logic

1. Logic: The Science of Proper Reasoning or the Study of Arguments
2. Logical Terms
3. Informal Logical Fallacies
4. Laws of Logic

Metaphysics

5. Metaphysics
6. Property and Substance
7. Ontology
8. Idealism
9. Key Ideas of Universals
10. Universals
11. Particulars
12. Modality
13. Possible Worlds
14. Metaphysical Doctrines
15. Mereology
16. Mereological Principles
17. Cosmology
18. Persistence through Time
19. Teleology
20. Metaphysically Based Types of Realism
21. Types of Theories of Truth
22. Substantive Theories of Truth
23. Deflationary Theories of Truth
24. Axiology: Value Theory
25. Principles of Value Theory
26. Types of Value/Things That Have Intrinsic Value
27. Value Monism and Pluralism
28. The Fact/Value Dichotomy

Epistemology

29. Meta-epistemology
30. Perception or Metaphysics of Epistemology
31. Epistemology (According to David Hume)

32. Thomas Reid/Common Sense Realism
33. Epistemology (According to Immanuel Kant)
34. Modal Epistemology/Saul Kripke
35. Epistemology/Overview of Theories of Knowledge
36. Internalist Theories of Knowledge
37. Virtue Epistemology
38. Externalist Theories of Knowledge

Ethics

39. Meta-ethics
40. Metaphysics of Ethics
41. Moral Epistemology
42. Moral Psychology
43. Normative Ethics/Major Ethical Theories
44. Virtue Ethics
45. Internalist Moral Development (Cognitivism)
46. Linguistic Virtue Ethics
47. Non-Consequentialist Deontology
48. Kantian Deontology
49. Deontological (Rossian) Intuitionism
50. Act Utilitarianism
51. Rule Utilitarianism
52. Social Contract Theory (Contractarianism)
53. Social Contract Theory (Contractualism)
54. Aesthetics
55. Axiology of Aesthetics

Political Philosophy

56. Political Philosophy
57. Philosophy of Law
58. Economics
59. Salamanca School of Economics
60. Adam Smith (*The Wealth of Nations*)
61. Free Market Economics
62. Keynesian Economics
63. Socialism/Marxism
64. Western Followers of Marx

Part 2: Analytic Philosophy

History of Analytic Philosophy

65. Major Movements in Analytic Philosophy
66. Logical Realism
67. Logical Positivism
68. Ordinary Language Analysis
69. Post Postivists or Physicalists

70. Linguistic Essentialism
71. American Pragmatism

Philosophy of Language

72. The Linguistic Turn
73. Philosophy of Language
74. Reference and Referring
75. Theories of Meaning
76. Pragmatics
77. Speech Act Theory
78. Implicature
79. Donald Davidson's Truth Theory of Meaning
80. Direct Reference Theory
81. Metaphorical Meaning

Philosophy of Science

82. Philosophy of Science
83. Scientific Method
84. Scientific Realism
85. Scientific Realist Philosophers
86. Scientific Anti-Realism
87. Scientific Anti-Realist Philosophers

Philosophy of Mind

88. Philosophy of the Mind
89. Issues in Philosophy of the Mind
90. Cartesian Dualism
91. Materialism

Part 3: Continental Philosophy

Romanticism

92. Romanticism/Romanticists

Existentialism/Phenomenology

93. Existentialism
94. Continental Philosophers
95. Edmund Husserl's Phenomenology/Martin Heidegger's Phenomenology
96. Phenomenologists
97. Feminist Philosophy

Structuralism/Post-Structuralism

98. Structuralism
99. Post-Structuralism

Critical Theory

100. Critical Theory
101. Marxism/Freudianism

Hermeneutics

102. Hermeneutics

Part 4: Philosophy of Religion

History of Philosophy of Religion

103. 20th-Century Philosophy of Religion
104. 20th-Century British Philosophy of Religion
105. Process Theology
106. Neo-Thomism
107. Analytic Thomism
108. Reformed Epistemology
109. Alvin Plantinga

Religious Language

110. Religious Language Overview
111. Religious Language (According to Thomas Aquinas)
112. The Linguistic Turn in Philosophy of Religion
113. Arguments against the Verification Principle
114. Biblical Hermeneutics
115. Premodern Old Testament Hermeneutics
116. Premodern Biblical Hermeneutics
117. Modern Biblical Hermeneutics
118. Postmodern Biblical Interpretation

Philosophical Theology

119. Theological Essentialism
120. Doctrine of God
121. Doctrine of God/Creeds
122. God and Time
123. Divine Foreknowledge
124. Molinism or Middle Knowledge

Apologetics

125. Patristic Apologetics
126. Augustine's *City of God*
127. Medieval Apologetics
128. The Structure of the *Summa Contra Gentiles*
129. Reformation Views of Apologetics
130. Blaise Pascal: *Pensees*/Pascal's Wager
131. David Hume and Responses to His Arguments
132. Naturalistic Arguments against Miracles
133. Apologetic Methods
134. Classical Apologetics
135. Thomas Aquinas's Five Proofs for the Existence of God
136. Evidentialist Apologetics
137. Cumulative Case Apologetics
138. Epistemology Associated with Apologetic Approaches

Christian Ethics

139. Augustinian Virtue Ethics
140. Thomas Aquinas's (and Bonaventure's) Virtue Ethics
141. Divine Command Theory (Theological Voluntarism)/Divine Command Meta-ethics
142. Graded Absolutism (Hierarchicalism)

Part 5: History of Philosophy

Major Divisions in the History of Philosophy

143. Premodernity (Recorded History – 1600)

144. Modernity (1600 – 1950)

145. British Empiricists/Analytic Philosophers

146. The Continental Rationalists/Continental Philosophy

147. Postmodernity (1950 – Present)

148. Postmodernity/Cultural Postmodernity

Timeline Charts

149. Historical Overview

150. Pre-Socratic Philosophy

151. Classical Period (470 BC – 1 BC)

152. The Patristic Period (100 – 400 AD)

153. 5th – 9th Centuries

154. 10th – 12th Centuries (Medieval Philosophy)

155. Medieval Philosophy, 6th – 14th Centuries

156. 15th – 16th Centuries, The Salamanca School

157. 15th – 16th Centuries, Protestant Reformation

158. 17th – 19th Century European Philosophy

159. 17th – 18th Century European Philosophy

160. 19th-Century Continental Philosophy

161. Post-Humean British Empiricism

162. Franz Brentano and 20th-Century European Philosophy

163. 20th-Century Continental Philosophy

164. European Analytic Philosophy

165. Early American Philosophy

166. 20th-Century American Philosophy

167. Analytic Philosophy

168. Karl Barth and 20th-Century Theology

169. 20th-Century Evangelical Theology

170. 20th-Century British Philosophy of Religion

171. Process Theology

172. 20th-Century Thomistic Philosophy of Religion

173. Political Philosophy (Economics)

174. Political Philosophy (Free Market Economics)

175. Keynesian Economics

176. Classical Liberalism

177. Conservativism

178. Neo-Conservativism

Major Philosophers

Premodern Philosophers

179. Pre-Socratics

180. Plato

181. Plato's Philosophy/Example of Plato's Metaphysics

182. Aristotle

183. Aristotle's Philosphy

184. Aristotelian (Classical) Virtue Ethics

185. Stoics & Epicureans

186. Skeptics & Middle Platonists

187. Plotinus

188. Plotinian Metaphysics

189. Augustine

190. Augustine's Philosophy

191. Augustine's Hierarchy of Thought

192. Boethius & John Scotus Erigena

193. Anselm of Canterbury & Peter Abelard

194. Thomas Aquinas

195. Thomas Aquinas's Philosophy

196. John Duns Scotus & William of Ockham

197. Luis de Molina & Francisco Suarez

Modern Philosophers/Continental Rationalists

198. René Descartes

199. Blaise Pascal & Nicolas Malebranche

200. Baruch Spinoza

201. Gottfried Wilhelm Leibniz

202. Immanuel Kant

Modern Philosophers/British Empiricists

203. John Locke

204. George Berkeley

205. David Hume

206. Thomas Reid

207. John Stuart Mill

Index 229

Introduction

Whether people realize it or not, we are all philosophers. Some of us are good philosophers, and others are bad philosophers, but we are all philosophers. This is especially true in theological studies. Unfortunately, it is my experience that too many theologians know enough philosophy to be dangerous, but not enough to be competent. As a result, they try to combine Christian theology with incompatible philosophical systems. Theology is not an art, where one gets bonus points for creativity. There is a reason that tradition exists, and we should be very careful before we reject it and try something new.

Ever since William Ockham separated theology from philosophy, both disciplines have suffered. Consequently, most theologians and biblical scholars are woefully ignorant of their philosophical presuppositions. This ignorance results in various theological confusions that hurt the church. I am a firm believer that if our philosophical presuppositions take us to places that do not bolster our faith, then they are the wrong presuppositions. Scholarship is not an end unto itself. Christian scholarship exists to help the church of Jesus Christ and not to serve our own professional agendas.

Just as problematic as theologians who are not aware of their philosophical presuppositions are theologians who use philosophy badly. By this I mean that there are those who attempt to resurrect dead philosophical ideas that are dead for a very good reason. I am amazed and saddened whenever I see this happen. For an example, consider speech act theory, which died in 1967. It is all the rage right now, but eventually, theologians will smell the odor coming off of this corpse and move on to the next thing. Hopefully, the next thing will correspond with reality.

In 1998, Dr. Norman Geisler gave a very timely warning at the National Evangelical Theological Society. In his presidential address he encouraged biblical scholars to "Beware of Philosophy." Some were incensed at his speech, but others knew that what he was saying is true. I think that the advice that he gave is essential for evangelical scholarship. Some intellectual advice:

- Avoid the desire to become a famous scholar.
- Avoid the temptation to be unique.
- Do not dance on the edges.
- Steer right to go straight.
- Do not trade orthodoxy for academic respectability.
- Reject any methodology inconsistent with the Bible or good reason.

And some spiritual advice:

- Always choose lordship over scholarship.
- Do not allow morality to determine methodology.
- Do not allow sincerity to be a test of orthodoxy.

Dr. Geisler concluded, "We cannot properly beware of philosophy unless we be aware of philosophy."

It is to this end that I have written this book. My hope is that theology and biblical students will gain a better understanding of philosophy from this resource. It is also my hope that our work as Christian scholars will better serve the kingdom.

In His Service,
CRAIG VINCENT MITCHELL

PART 1
CLASSICAL DISCIPLINES

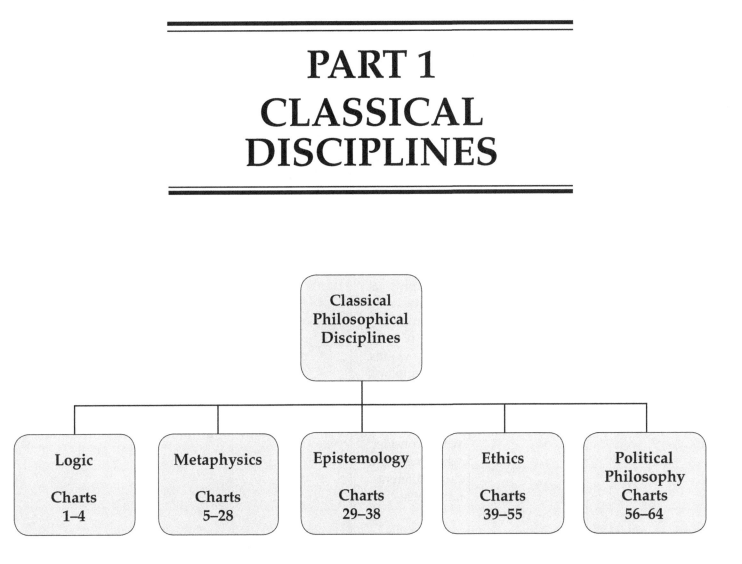

Logic is concerned with formal rules of argumentation and reasoning.

Metaphysics is about the nature of reality. This includes the study of ontology, cosmology, and theology.

Epistemology is the study of and or theory of knowledge. As a result, epistemology explores the nature of knowledge and how it is obtained.

Ethics is about the good, or how we should live. A closely related area is the study of aesthetics.

Political Philosophy focuses in on how people should live together and how they are governed. Consequently, political philosophy explores all of the positions of government. It also includes law and economics.

Logic: The Science of Proper Reasoning or the Study of Arguments

Argument–Two or more declarative statements. The last of these, the **conclusion**, follows from the others. The other statements, also known as **premises** or **propositions,** support the conclusion. **Inference** is the psychological process of drawing conclusions from premises.

Deduction Will have one or more premises and a conclusion. If the premises are true, then the conclusion will be as well. Consequently, deductive logic can provide a high level of certainty.	A **valid argument** will have the correct logical form. A **sound argument** has a valid form and all its premises are true.	**Symbolic logic**	Also known as formal logic. It includes a number of modern and traditional approaches to logic.	
		Mathematics	The study of quantities, magnitudes, and forms, generally with the use of numbers and symbols	
		Modal logic A logic based upon the concept of metaphysical necessity. It often employs the use of possible worlds. It also employs the use of **counterfactual arguments** which consider what one might do in different situations.	**Epistemic logic**	A kind of modal logic employed to ascertain what one should know in all possible worlds
			Deontic logic	A kind of modal logic employed to ascertain what one ought to do in all possible worlds. Necessity is replaced with ought.
Induction An argument tied to probability. As such, inductive logic cannot provide certainty.	A **strong argument** is well supported by evidence. A **weak argument** is poorly supported by evidence.	**Abduction**	An approach to logic developed by Charles Sanders Pierce to explain a set of data. This is also known as "inference to the best explanation."	
		Logic of explanation	Attempts to understand how or why something is the way that it is. This involves an examination of the possible causes for a given state of affairs.	
		Probability theory	A judgment based upon the mathematical likelihood of a given event.	

Chart 1

Logical Terms

Inference	The process of drawing conclusions from premises	
Paradox	A statement that is seemingly contradictory or opposed to common sense and yet is perhaps true	
Tautology	A trivially true statement	
Axiom	A statement that is universally accepted as true	
Logical fallacy	**Formal**	An argument that does not follow the rules of inference
	Informal	An error concerned with the content of the argument. It may also be concerned with the clarity of that argument.
Rhetoric	The art or science of using words effectively in speaking or writing	
Necessary	Essential, indispensable	
Sufficient	Equal to what is specified or required, enough	

Chart 2

Informal Logical Fallacies

There are at least thirty informal logical fallacies. The following list includes some of the more common ones.

Post hoc, ergo propter hoc	**Explanation**	Results from the false belief that one event necessarily causes another
	Example	The Raiders won the football game because I wore my lucky jersey.
Ad hominem	**Explanation**	Attack the person rather than presenting an argument to refute a position; one belittles or denigrates his opponent
	Example	His argument is wrong because he is stupid.
Ad ignorantiam	**Explanation**	The false belief that one's argument is right because his opponent cannot refute it
	Example	God must exist because you cannot prove otherwise.
Bandwagon appeal	**Explanation**	To argue that one is correct because everyone approves of his position
	Example	Of course I am right—everyone else thinks the same thing.
Begging the question	**Explanation**	When one's argument is based on the point that he is attempting to prove
	Example	Cats are bad because all catlike creatures are bad.
Testimonial	**Explanation**	When one employs an endorsement from a well known or well respected figure to prove his point
	Example	A famous scientist believes that this is true, so it must be right.
Semantic ambiguity	**Explanation**	A kind of confusion that results when a word or statement can be used in two different ways
	Example	I am going to the bank after work. *(Is the bank a financial institution or the side of the river?)*
False dilemma	**Explanation**	When one incorrectly assumes that there are only two possibilities to answer a given question
	Example	People are either football or baseball fans.
Slippery slope argument	**Explanation**	When one argues that many other bad decisions will result if a particular bad decision is made
	Example	If you allow this law to stand, then people will allow even greater evils to become legal.
Straw man argument	**Explanation**	When one substitutes a weakened argument for an opponent's real argument. This allows one to appear as if he has a better argument.
Hypothesis contrary to fact	**Explanation**	When one can claim to know with certainty what might have happened if circumstances had been different
	Example	My team would have won the game if the referees had done a better job.

Chart 3

Laws of Logic

(This list is not inclusive.)			
Law of non-contradiction	Something cannot be *A* and *Not A* at the same time and in the same way		
Law of the excluded middle	For any statement *P,* or *Not P* must be true and there is no other alternative		
Square of opposition	**Law of contraries**	A universal affirmative and a coincident universal negative predicate assertion are never both true. In other words, two propositions are contrary if they cannot both be true.	
		Example: "All cars are black" and "no cars are black" are never both true.	
	Law of contradictories	A universal affirmative predicate assertion is true if and only if a coincident negative assertion is not true. In other words, two propositions are contradictories if one is the denial or negation of the other.	
		Example: The statement "every car is black" is true if and only if the statement "not every car is black" is not true.	
	Law of subcontraries	For any particular affirmative and any coincident particular negative present-tense predicate assertion, it is always the case that at least one of them is true. In other words, two propositions are subcontraries when they cannot both be false, although they can both be true.	
		Example: **Proposition A**–Some wars are just. **Proposition B**–Some wars are not just.	
	Law of subalternation	When a universal affirmative present-tense assertion is true, any coincident particular affirmative present-tense predicate assertion is also true. In other words, whenever two propositions have the same subject and the same predicate terms and agree in quality but differ only in quantity, they are called corresponding propositions.	
		Example: **Proposition A**–All dogs are four legged animals. **Proposition B**–Some dogs are four legged.	

Chart 4

Metaphysics

Theology	Concerned with God's nature and existence as well as his relationship with all of reality. After William of Ockham, theology was separated from philosophy in general and metaphysics in particular.
Ontology	Concerned with existence, or being; it can also include such things as: free will/ determinism, substance, immortality of the soul. After William of Ockham, the term **ontology** is often equated with **metaphysics**.
Cosmology	The part of ontology concerned with time, space, and causation. The term **cosmology** can also be equated with **metaphysics**.
Metaphysical terms Andronicus of Rhodes coined the term "metaphysics." By metaphysics, he meant the writings coming after Aristotle's *Physics*.	• A **universal** is a general property that individual objects can possess. • **Predicates** express properties, kinds, and relations • A (concrete) **particular** is an object that instantiates a given property or relation • A **trope** is an instance of a property or relation conceived of as an abstract particular • A **bare particular** is a particular that does not instantiate a universal • A **proposition** is a statement about reality that is true or false • A **fact** is something in reality that makes a proposition true. A "truthmaker." • A **truthmaker** is a correspondent in the world in virtue of which a true proposition is made true • An **event** is a proposition about a specific time and place • A **state of affairs** is a statement about reality that may either obtain or fail to obtain. Those that obtain are facts. They also tie universals and particulars together. • For something to be **necessary** means that it must exist in any possible world • **Contingent**–Dependent upon something that is necessary for its existence • **Teleology** teaches that the world has a purpose and is in process to fulfill it. The branch of cosmology that deals with final causes.

Chart 5

Property and Substance

These ideas of properties and substance are defined by John Locke. Bishop George Berkeley (the subjective idealist) rejected the idea of substance.

Primary properties	These properties include things such as size, number, motion, extension, solidity, and figure.
Secondary properties	These properties have the power to create sensations. These properties include things such as heat, light, and sound.
Tertiary properties	These properties have the ability to alter the primary qualities of an object.
Substance	This is the bearer of a property. It is also that which is not a property.
Essence	That which makes something what it is, without which it would cease to be.

Chart 6

Ontology

	Universals	Particulars	The Mind	Types
Realism	Universals exist Universals are real	Concrete particulars exist	Universals and particulars exist independent of the mind	**Platonic realism:** universals exist in a separate world
				Aristotelian realism: universals exist in concrete particulars
Conceptualism	Universals exist	Concrete particulars exist	Universals exist only as a concept in the mind. Particulars exist independently of the mind.	
Nominalism	Universals do not exist	Only concrete particulars exist	Concrete particulars exist independent of the mind	**Moderate nominalism:** allows for states of affairs
				Extreme nominalism: does not allow for states of affairs
Idealism	Universals do not exist	Only concrete particulars exist	Concrete particulars exist but depend upon the mind	**Objective idealism:** is the only kind that allows for the existence of universals

Chart 7

Idealism

G. W. Leibniz coined the term "idealism" to explain that his metaphysical position was essentially the same as that held by Plato. It is difficult to define the term "idealism." Central to idealism is the thesis that reality depends upon the mind for its existence. Another idea associated with idealism is the rejection of materialism.

Type of idealism	Philosopher	Explanation
Objective idealism	Plato, Plotinus, Leibniz	What are most real are the forms. These forms are eternal, immutable, ontologically independent, and immaterial. The forms are beyond sensory experience and are known only through reason. Some argue that this is just metaphysical realism.
Subjective idealism	Bishop George Berkeley	Berkeley rejected the existence of material bodies and believed that only minds exist. God's mind makes all things appear to human minds.
Absolute idealism	G. W. F. Hegel	This approach to idealism involves a subject–object dualism in which the subject is the ground of reality. Absolute idealists reduce material bodies to phenomenal states within the mind. The "mind" is a universal self-consciousness that exists behind or outside of nature. Reality is nothing more than a universal "notion" (Begriff).
Transcendental idealism	Immanuel Kant	Kant believed that there is an external world (the noumenal world) that exists independently of the mind. His arguments against metaphysical speculation prevent one from actually knowing reality itself. All that one can actually know is the world of sensory appearances (the phenomenal world).
Critical idealism	Gottlieb Fichte, F. W. J. Schelling	A negation of Kantian transcendental idealism which makes the distinction between self and non-self. A forerunner to Hegel's absolute idealism, it asserts that the nature of reality is explained through mind-derived principles of beauty and goodness. Like absolute idealism, the mind is a universal self-consciousness that exists behind or outside of nature.

Chart 8

Key Ideas of Universals

Subject–Predicate Discourse
- **Predicates** express properties, kinds, and relations. They are universals.
- **Subjects** are concrete particulars.

Abstract Reference
Realists employ abstract singular terms to play the subject role. These abstract singular terms are used to refer to universals.

Principle of Instantiation
A universal must be instantiated (or exemplified) by a particular to exist. Platonic or extreme realists will reject this principle.

No Disjunctive (or Negative) Universals
The lack or absence of a property is not a property.

Indiscernability of Indenticals
Sameness of thing gives sameness of properties.
If concrete particular *a* is identical with concrete particular *b*, then *a* and *b* have exactly the same properties.

Identity of Indiscernables
Sameness of properties gives sameness of things.
If concrete particular *a* and concrete particular *b* have all of their properties in common, then *a* is identical with *b*.

Supervenience
Nonphysical universals are related to physical universals.
Entity **Q** supervenes on entity **P** if and only if every possible world that contains **P** contains **Q**. Some cases are symmetrical. For example: **P** and **Q** can supervene on each other.

Eliminativism–A reductionistic position that rejects predicates or abstract ideas as universals

Chart 9

Universals

	Nature of Universals	Type of Ontology	States of Affairs	Bare Particulars
Extreme realism (Platonic realism)	*Universalia ante res* (Universals before things)	Two or more world ontology, because more universals exist than are instantiated	Universals exist as states of affairs types	Rejects the existence of bare particulars
Moderate realism (Aristotelian realism)	*Universalia in rebus* (Universals in things)	One world ontology. Only those universals that are instantiated in particulars exist.	Universals and particulars exist as states of affairs	Rejects the existence of bare particulars
Moderate nominalism *Predicate nominalism* or *Concept nominalism* (Conceptualism) Universals exist as concepts of the mind. Properties are created by the classifying mind.	*Universalia post res* (Universals after things)	One world ontology	Universals and particulars exist as states of affairs	Rejects the existence of bare particulars
Extreme nominalism *Resemblance* or *class nominalism* A particular is connected to other particulars because of their resemblance or they are in the same class. (*See* **tropes**)	Only things exist	One world ontology	States of affairs are not required	Bare particulars exist

Chart 10

Particulars

	Nature	Attributes	States of Affairs	Objections
Aristotelian substance A realist position originally held by Aristotle	The concrete particular is the fundamental entity or substance. A concrete particular is the exemplifier of the universals associated with it.	Some universals are external to the essence of the particular and are only contingently identified by it.	Compatible with states of affairs	
Leibnizian substance	The concrete particular is the fundamental entity or substance. A concrete particular is the exemplifier of the universals associated with it.	Some universals are external to the essence of the particular and are only contingently identified by it. Allows for the existence of individual essences.	Compatible with states of affairs	
Substratum A nominalist position held by John Locke	Concrete particulars are complexes that have more basic entities as their constituents.	A substratum or bare particular	Not compatible with states of affairs	**1.** Incompatible with rigorous empiricism **2.** Contradictory claim that things that possess attributes (bare particulars) possess no attributes
Bundles A nominalist position held by the British Empiricists, including Berkeley and Hume	Concrete particulars are complexes that have more basic entities as their constituents.	A concrete particular is nothing more than a bundle of the empirically manifest attributes or collocated tropes.	In the case of moderate nominalists, it is compatible with states of affairs.	**1.** The identity of indiscernables **2.** There are no subjects, only predicates

Chart 11

Modality

Modality
Ideas that include the necessary, the possible, and the contingent. Modal semantics involve the idea of possible worlds.

Necessity
A requirement to exist in all possible worlds

Possibility
The concept that something may or may not exist, or occur

Contingency
Because things might possibly be otherwise, something may not exist in all possible worlds

De dicto Modality
Necessity or possibility ascribed to a proposition

De re Modality
The notion of a thing instantiating a property necessarily or contingently

Essentialism
That a thing has its properties necessarily or essentially

Haecceity
The unique individual essence of an existing thing

Modal Logic
A logical system that maps out the relations between modal sentences

Possible World
When a proposition and its opposite cannot exist at the same time and place. A possible state of affairs that is maximal.

Actual World
One of the possible worlds that is actual. It is the maximal possible state of affairs that obtains.

Book
A set of propositions that describe a world. The book on a world is that set of propositions true in that world.

Compossibility
A philosophical concept from Leibniz, employed by philosophers of religion. It asserts that various possible, but mutually exclusive, worlds can coexist within the mind of God. It is also used for the various possible, but mutually exclusive properties of God.

Chart 12

Possible Worlds

	Universals	Possible Worlds	Actual World	Particulars
Alvin Plantinga God is a necessary being. Plantinga uses possible worlds to explain freedom and evil.	**Extreme (Platonic) Realist** Employs possible worlds as one element in a network of concepts, i.e. properties, propositions, *de dicto* and *de re* modality	**Actualist possible worlds** Possible worlds are a maximally possible state of affairs	Actual world is a maximally possible state of affairs that obtains. The actual world includes the past, present, future, minds, and God.	**Haccieties (essentialism)**–An individual essence is a property that a thing has essentially and necessarily and is unique to that thing
D. M. Armstrong **Combinatorial Realism** Requires **Naturalism**–The doctrine that nothing at all exists except the single world of space and time	**Moderate (Aristotelian) Realist** States of affairs and simple properties are universals. Resemblances supervene on original properties.	**Actualist possible worlds** Any conjunction of possible atomic states of affairs, which are nonexistent recombinations of actual elements. Possible worlds are just constructs.	Possible worlds are alternatives to the actual world and to each other. Actual world is a maximally possible state of affairs that obtains.	**Leibnizian substances**–Individual essences. Subcribes to a type of hacciety.
G. W. Leibniz If God is omnipotent and omnibenevolent, he must create the best	**Moderate Nominalist** This view rejects naturalism	**Genuine possible worlds** Possible worlds are limited by their degree of orderliness and their variety or richness of phenomena	The actual world is the best of all possible worlds. The actual world includes the past, present, future, minds, and God.	**Leibnizian substances**–Individual essences. Only actual existing things in the world are concrete particulars.
David Lewis **Modal Realism** Nominalists cannot successfully carry out their project without possible worlds	**Extreme Nominalist** Possible worlds can provide a reductive account of a property, a proposition, *de re* and *de dicto* modality	**Genuine possible worlds** Possible worlds are equally concrete entities. No two of these worlds can be identical.	**Indexical theory of actuality** The actual world is not special. It is just another equally concrete entity.	**Bundle theory** A concrete particular is nothing more than a bundle of the empirically manifest attributes of collocated tropes

Chart 13

Metaphysical Doctrines

	Universals	Naturalism
Factualism	**Realism** Reality is independent of the mind and has a propositional structure. This position allows for the existence of God.	The totality of entities, or all that exists, is nothing more than the space–time system
Physicalism	**Nominalism** **Basic (Weak)** The only particulars that the space–time system contains are physical entities governed by nothing more than the laws of physics. This position still allows for the existence of God.	**Strong Physicalism** Everything that exists is governed by the laws of physics

Chart 14

Mereology

Mereology is the part of ontology that studies parts and how they relate to a whole. There are two types of **mereology**.
1. Classical Extensional Mereology–Extended **mereology** is concerned with spatial, temporal, or spatio-temporal, or for extended matter. Lesniewski developed the language and logic of mereology from his ontology. Leonard and Goodman developed the calculi of individuals.
2. Modal mereology is used to study the ontological dependence of objects on other objects.

Terms of Mereology

Overlap (XoY)–Two individuals overlap mereologically if and only if they have a part in common
Binary Sum (X+Y)–The mereological sum between two entities
Binary Product (X*Y)–If two individuals overlap they have one part in common
Difference (X-Y)–The mereological difference between two entities
General Sum and Product–These ideas cover problematic classes of individuals that cannot be resolved with a simple binary sum or product. This includes individuals with a common part in which the class is infinite.
Disjointness–Individuals are disjoint if and only if they do not overlap
Universe (U)–The sum of all objects whatever
Complement (U-X)–The difference between an entity and the universe
Atom–Something that has no proper parts. As such it is indivisible. Everything is made of atoms. It is questionable as to whether atoms actually exist.

Proper Parts Principles (PPP)	$X<<Y$ means X is a proper part of Y If $X=Y$ then X is an improper part of Y	A proper part is any portion of a given entity, regardless of whether it is attached to the remainder 1. Everything is part of itself 2. Two distinct things cannot be part of each other 3. Any part of any part of a thing is itself a part of that thing

Chart 15

Mereological Principles

Basic principles of mereology or ground mereology (M)	**Reflexivity**	Everything is a part of itself
	Antisymmetry	Two distinct things cannot be part of each other
	Transitivity	Any part of any part of a thing is itself part of that thing
	Mereological relations	**Overlap**–Two individuals overlap mereologically if and only if they have a part in common
		Underlap–The mereological difference between two entities
		Proper part–A proper part is any portion of a given entity, regardless of whether it is attached to the remainder
		Over-crossing
		Under-crossing
		Proper overlap
		Proper underlap
Supplementation principles	**Weak Supplementation (WSP)**	If an entity has a proper part, it has a proper part disjoint from the first. **M+WSP=Minimal Mereology (MM)**
	Strong Supplementation (SSP)	An entity which has a proper part needs other parts in addition to supplement this one to obtain the whole. **M+SSP=Extensional Mereology (EM)**
Closure mereology (CM)	**CM** / **GSP or GPP**	**CM+MM=Minimal Closure Mereology (CMM)** **CM+EM=Extensional Closure Mereology (CEM)**
	General Sum (GSP)	The mereological sum between two entities
	General Product (GPP)	If two individuals overlap they have one part in common
Fusion principles	**General Mereology**	**MM+Fusion=General Mereology (GM)**
	General Extensional Mereology	**EM+Fusion=General Extensional Mereology (GEM)**
Atomism	**Atom**	Something that has no proper parts. As such it is indivisible.
	Atomlessness	The assumption that atoms do not exist
	Atomicity	The assumption that atoms do exist **Atomistic Extensional Mereology (AEM)**

Chart 16

Cosmology

Time The temporal aspect of reality	**Perceptual**–Time as it appears to an observer	
	Conceptual–Time as it actually is	• **A theory**–A tensed view of time. This view allows for the past, present, and future. The only aspect of time that exists is the present. Rejects the idea of a space–time continuum. Also known as presentism. • **B theory**–A tenseless view of time. Relations of events are described as earlier than, or later than. Accepts idea of a space–time continuum. Also known as eternalism.
Space The spatial aspect of reality	**Perceptual**–Space as it is perceived by an observer	
	Conceptual–Space as it actually is	
Causation What relates one event in reality to another temporally	**First cause**–The cause of all other causes. Not Aristotle's idea.	
	Formal–The shape or "blueprint" to which an entity conforms	
	Material–The physical "stuff" of which something is made	
	Efficient–Forces or activities/agents produce an entity	
	Final–The purpose for which an entity exists	
Space–time continuum–An idea explained in Einstein's special theory of revelation. It asserts that space and time are tied together as aspects of a four-dimensional universe. There are three spatial dimensions and one temporal dimension.		

The Aristotelian Chain of Causes

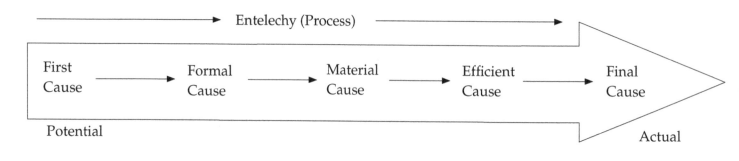

Chart 17

Persistence through Time

	Description	View of time	Arguments for
Perdurantism Compatible with David Lewis's position that all possible worlds are actual	Concrete particulars are four-dimensional beings because time is just another dimension on par with the three spatial dimensions. Concrete particulars have both spatial and temporal extension.	**B theory** According to J. M. McTaggart, this is a tenseless view of time. Relations of events are described as earlier than, or later than. All times and their contents are ordered by these relations. Accepts idea of a space–time continuum. Also known as eternalism.	**1.** Change in properties **2.** Change in parts **3.** Consistent with contemporary physics
Endurantism Consistent with Alvin Plantinga's actualism	Concrete particulars are only three dimensional entities that exist at different times	**A theory** According to J. M. McTaggart, this is a tensed view of time. This view allows for the past, present, and future. The only aspect of time that exists is the present. The past exists only as memory. Rejects the idea of a space–time continuum. Also known as presentism.	Consistent with Aristotelian substance theory

Chart 18

Teleology

That branch of cosmology (metaphysics) that is concerned with final causes. The word "teleology" is based on the Greek root *telos* which means "achievement, power, completion as a state, or perfection." Teleology also refers to the appearance of purpose in nature. As a result, teleology is compatible with **naturalism**.

Metaphysics	**Metaphysical realism**	Teleology is compatible only with metaphysical realism
Axiology	**Teleology in axiology requires metaphysical realism**	Teleology is compatible with value realism. Values are dependent upon metaphysics (ontology). The principle of organic unities is consistent with teleology. The principle of universality is also consistent with teleology.
Epistemology	**Teleology in epistemology requires metaphysical realism**	Teleology is compatible with epistemological realism as well as externalist approaches to epistemology. Only truth has intrinsic value in a teleological epistemology.
Ethics	**Teleology in ethics requires metaphysical realism**	Teleology is primarily concerned with the "good," rather than the "right." The good (*summum bonum*) has intrinsic value instead of the right. Teleology is consistent with moral realism. Virtue ethics and natural law are the only ethical theories compatible with teleology.
Aesthetics	**Teleology in aesthetics requires metaphysical realism**	Teleology is primarily concerned with beauty, because beauty is the only intrinsic value. Teleology is consistent with aesthetic realism.

Chart 19

Metaphysically Based Types of Realism

	Definition	Nominalism Semantic theory of truth	Idealism Coherence theory of truth	Anti-Realism Pragmatic theory of truth
Value realism Correspondence theory of truth	Objective values exist independent of the observer. Values supervene upon being.	Most nominalists reject this position because they believe that values are subjective	Most idealists are nominalists	Rejected because truth cannot be known. They do believe that all experience is value laden.
Epistemic realism Correspondence theory of truth	Knowledge is about an objective reality that exists independent of the observer. Knowledge (truth) supervenes on being.	Most but not all nominalists reject epistemic realism because they believe that metaphysics is about language rather than being.	Rejected because the world is dependent on the mind	Rejected because truth cannot be known. They believe that knowledge is subjective and is value laden.
Moral realism Correspondence theory of truth	Objective moral facts exist independent of the observer. Goodness supervenes on being.	Most nominalists reject this position. Empiricists base morality upon the passions and rationalists base morality upon reason; still others base morality upon naturalism.	Most idealists reject moral realism, because morality is created by the mind or the community	Rejected because truth cannot be known. They believe that morality is subjective and is value laden.
Aesthetic realism Correspondence theory of truth	Objective aesthetic facts exist independent of the observer. Beauty supervenes on being.	Some nominalists accept and others reject this position	Most reject this position	Rejected because truth cannot be known. They believe beauty is subjective and is value laden.

Chart 20

Types of Theories of Truth

While the concept of truth seems like a simple idea, it is actually a very complex one. Before the 20th century, there was only the correspondence and the coherence theories of truth. After the 20th century began, the number of theories expanded to solve epistemological, linguistic, and other problems.

Name	Description	Explanation
Substantive theories of truth	Truth has a distinct nature	Truth is either metaphysical, epistemological, or linguistic
Deflationary theories of truth	Truth does not have a nature	Truth is a much less important concept than many philosophers believe
Postmodern theories of truth	Truth is subjective	Truth is about power or disclosure
Truth and modality	Necessary truth	Something that cannot fail to be true. Something that is true in all possible worlds.
	Contingent truth	Something that can fail to be true. Something that is not true in all possible worlds.
	Actual truth	Something that is true in the actual world

Chart 21

Substantive Theories of Truth

Theory of Truth	Universals	Descriptions	Comments
Correspondence theory of truth	**Realist:** Truth supervenes on being. This position was held by Plato and Aristotle.	States of affairs are truth-makers. This theory is concerned with the metaphysics of truth.	**Traditionalist** approaches to the correspondence theory subscribe to metaphysical realism
			Minimalist approaches to the correspondence theory of truth attempt to avoid the subjects of universals and particulars
Coherence theory of truth	**Nominalist, idealist:** This position was held by the Continental rationalists	Truth results when there is a coherent set of beliefs. These beliefs may or may not have anything to do with reality. This theory of truth is primarily concerned with epistemology.	A coherence theory of justification (epistemology) is a necessary and sufficient condition for truth
			A coherence theory of justification is not a necessary and sufficient condition for truth
Pragmatic theory of truth	**Nominalist:** This position is held by pragmatists, who are radical empiricists and idealists. Some postmodernists hold this position.	Truth is made and not found. Truth is what works. This theory of truth is primarily concerned with epistemology.	**Pierce**–Truth is what is revealed at the end of scientific inquiry
			James–Truth is useful
			Putnam–Attempts to reconcile pragmatism with realism
			Rorty–The pragmatist can see little difference between truth and justification
Semantic theory of truth (Tarski's)	**Nominalist:** This position is consistent with the views of the British empiricists and by some Analytic Philosophers	This theory explains truth in a way that is consistent with science	There are no variants for this theory. This theory of truth is primarily concerned with philosophy of language.

Chart 22

Deflationary Theories of Truth

Explanation of deflationary theories of truth:

1. Truth has no nature
2. Truth is not even an important concept

Name	Philosopher	Description
Redundancy theory	**Frank Ramsey**	Ascription of truth to a proposition is apparent, but not actual. Ascribing truth is in reality doing nothing.
Performative theory	**P. F. Strawson**	To say that something is true is an endorsement of a proposition.
Disquotational theory	**W. V. O. Quine**	Truth is **disquotation**. Truth has crucial function within our language. Sentences rather than propositions are the primary truth bearers.
Prosentential theory	**Dorothy Grover, Joseph Camp, Nuel Belnap**	**Prosentences** are to sentences as pronouns are to nouns. The phrase "it is true" is a **prosentence** about truth predicates. Prosentential theorists assert that we are linguistically competent only if we have an ability to question and/or assert what is true.
Minimalist theory	**Paul Horwich**	Propositions, which are the contents of our beliefs, are the primary truth bearers.

Postmodern Theories of Truth

These theories of truth are subjective. They are similar to the pragmatic theory of truth, but they are not the same.

Theory	Philosopher	Explanation
Phenomenological theory of truth	**Martin Heidegger**	Truth is not correspondence or coherence, it is disclosure. The essence of truth is freedom. Untruth is concealment and errancy.
Structuralist theory of truth	**Michel Foucault**	Since there are no meta-narratives, there is more than one truth. Consequently, truth is ultimately about power.
Pragmatic theory of truth	**Richard Rorty**	Truth is what your friends let you get away with. There is no such thing as "the Truth."

Chart 23

Axiology: Value Theory

Value is concerned with what has worth and why. It is also concerned with how value motivates one to take action. Value theory has a history that goes back to Plato and Aristotle. Franz Brentano did much to explain value theory in the 19th century, especially his classic work *The Origin of Our Knowledge of Right and Wrong* (1889). Brentano's students Oskar Kraus and Alexius Meinong added to his work. G. E. Moore employed these ideas in his *Principia Ethica* (1903). Contemporary work in this field has been continued by Roderick Chisholm (*Brentano and Intrinsic Value*), Nicholas Rescher (*Introduction to Value Theory*), Noah Lemos (*Intrinsic Value*), Panayot Butchvarov (*Skepticism in Ethics*), and Elizabeth Anderson (*Value in Ethics and Economics*).

Definition of value	**Value**	A benefit oriented motivation for action. Values are ideals that have to do with the vision people have of the good life for the individual and his community. Values function both as constraints and as stimuli for action.
	Disvalue	A motivation for action that is not benefit oriented
	Intrinsic value	What is valued as "an end" or "for itself." The ultimate end value of a thing.
	Instrumental value	What is valued for the sake of something else. A value that is a "means" to an end.
Terminology of value	**Value object**	The object that is being evaluated
	Locus of value	An objective reason for value. **Example:** "Education is of great value for living the good life."
	Underlying value	Unstated values that are still important factors in decision making
	Value subscriber	A person who subscribes to a certain value or group of values
	Evaluation	A judgment regarding a value object
Value experience	**Brentano/Meinong value theory**	Franz Brentano developed a theory of value that is based upon emotion. All valuation can be described in terms of love or hate. Love and hate can have different levels or degrees. His student Alexius Meinong refined Brentano's theory by explaining other aspects of value realism.
	Value subject	The value subscriber who experiences
	Emotion	A positive or negative emotion (called the value feeling) regarding the value object
	Value object	That which is being evaluated
	Existence judgment	A judgment about the realization or the existence of the value object

Chart 24

Principles of Value Theory

	Realism	Nominalism
Principle of organic unities The opposite of principle of summation	The value of a whole must not be assumed to be the identical as the sum of the values of its parts	Rejects the principle of organic unities
Principle of summation The opposite of the principle of organic unities	Rejects the principle of summation	The value of every whole is merely a sum of the value of its parts
Principle of universality The opposite of the principle of conditionality	The part of a valuable whole retains exactly the same value when it is, as when it is not, a part of that whole	Rejects the principle of universality
Principle of conditionality The opposite of the principle of universality	Rejects the principle of conditionality	The intrinsic value of a fact is conditional on what other states of affairs obtain; that is, the value of a part of one whole can be different when it is part of a different whole
Principle of *bonum variationis*	Other things being equal, it is better to combine two dissimilar goods than to combine two similar goods. In other words, variety is intrinsically better than a lack of variety.	Rejects the principle of summation and supports the principle of organic unities
Principle of *bonum progressionis*	Other things being equal, it is intrinsically better to begin badly and end well than to begin well and end badly	Rejects the principle of summation and supports the principle of organic unities
Principle of existence	The existence of an intrinsic good is itself a good and is preferable to its nonexistence. The existence of an intrinsic evil is itself an evil.	
Principle of nonexistence	The nonexistence of an intrinsic good is not an evil and the nonexistence of an intrinsic evil is preferable to its existence and is not a good.	

Chart 25

Types of Value

	Realism	Nominalism
Intrinsic value An intrinsic value is something that is valued for its own sake	Value monism–The idea that there is one primary value. Value supervenes on being. Only universals such as properties, states of affairs, facts (states of affairs that obtain), intentional attitudes (such as happiness) have intrinsic value.	Value pluralism–The idea that there is more than one intrinsic value of an object. Intentional attitudes such as pleasure have intrinsic value.
Extrinsic or instrumental value An extrinsic value is something that is valued for the sake of something else	Only concrete particulars have extrinsic value	Some concrete particulars have extrinsic value

Things That Have Intrinsic Value

	Definition	Value Monism (Realism)	Value Pluralism (Nominalism)
Epistemology	The study or theory of knowledge. Knowledge is a universal.	Truth supervenes on being	Truth, belief, and justification
Morality	The study of the good or right action. The good is a universal.	Good supervenes on being	Consequences, rules
Aesthetic	The study of beauty, whether natural or artificial. Beauty is a universal.	Beauty supervenes on being	Beauty is subjective and is evaluated by some standard
Intentionality	A state of mind or special kind of belief that can be equated with a state of affairs	Happiness (*eudaimonia*) supervenes on being	Happiness, pleasure, and pain

Chart 26

Value Monism and Pluralism

(As explained by Elizabeth Anderson in *Value in Ethics and Economics*)

Value monism–Only one thing can have intrinsic value
Value pluralism–Many things can have intrinsic value
Agent neutral value–Something that everyone has reason to value

Monism These theories assume that states of affairs do have intrinsic value	**Naturalism**	"Good"can be compared to health or proper functioning. "Goodness"supervenes upon empirical properties of an object. This position is teleological. It is compatible with an Aristotelian metaphysical realism or with a moderate nominalism. Proper function is the sole signifying response.
	G. E. Moore's non-naturalism	"Good"is a simple and undefinable property that is known only by intuition. The "good"can be compared with the object of aesthetic liking. Any attempt to explain value in terms of natural is committing the naturalistic fallacy. Moore is a metaphysical (platonic) realist who argues for the principle of organic unities.
	Hedonism	Only what is pleasant qualifies as "good."Pleasure is the sole value signifying response. This position is compatible only with metaphysical nominalism.
	Rational desire theory	"Good"is what is rationally desired. Desire is the sole value signifying response. This approach to value is compatible with an Aristotelian metaphysical realism or with a moderate metaphysical nominalism.
Pluralism These theories assume that states of affairs do *not* have intrinsic value	**Consequentialism**	An egoistic moral theory that gives all agents the common aim of maximizing impersonal value. It assumes that all values are agent neutral. Practical reason demands that value be maximized. This is achieved by contrasting reason with emotions and social norms. This allows for a simple, precise, and determinate procedure of justification that employs objective calculations to overcome disputes.
	Expressive theory of value	Action is guided by norms described in terms of ideals and evaluative concepts like virtues or vices
	Pragmatic justification theory	This approach to value allows for the use of thick evaluative concepts which allows for a space of reasons, rather than thin concepts like good, bad, right, or wrong. This approach allows for common sense, intuitive reasoning. Comparative value judgments are evaluated by considering their functions, why people care about them, and what practices of evaluation serve these functions.

Chart 27

The Fact/Value Dichotomy

David Hume	*A Treatise of Human Nature*	• This dichotomy has its roots in Hume's fork. Truth is either analytic (necessary and deducible values) or synthetic (empirically verifiable facts). • It asserts that "One cannot derive ought from is." In other words, values (ethics and aesthetics) have nothing to do with metaphysics (ontology). • All supposed connections between ethics and metaphysics are based only upon induction • Values are based solely upon emotions • This dichotomy rejects teleology, natural law, and any idea of moral properties • This implies that values have no significance for science, economics, law, political theory, or psychology
G. E. Moore	*Principia Ethics*	He supported the fact/value dichotomy. Many analytic philosophers followed after Moore's ideas. He argued that if one attempts to base morality upon nature, then one has committed the naturalistic fallacy. The naturalistic fallacy is based on the fact/value dichotomy.
W. V. O. Quine	*"The Two Dogmas of Empiricism"*	Quine argued against the fact/value dichotomy. He asserted that the analytic/synthetic distinction is the basis for the fact/value dichotomy. He showed the analytic/synthetic dichotomy to be faulty. Consequently, the fact/value dichotomy collapsed with the analytic/synthetic distinction.
Aristotle	*De Anima*	Aristotle's position is contrary to the fact/value dichotomy. He argued that emotions are driven by reason. In other words, if one gets angry, he does so for a reason. Emotions, although sometimes faulty, are therefore judgments of value. Consequently, both facts and values are judged by reason.

Chart 28

Meta-epistemology

Metaphysics of knowledge	**Sources of knowledge**	**Empiricism**–Knowledge results from sensory experience
		Rationalism–Reason is the primary source of knowledge
		Intuitionism–Knowledge results from feelings or some unknown means
		Memory–Knowledge stored in the mind
		Testimony–Knowledge received from others
	Metaphysics	**Epistemic realism**–A position consistent with metaphysical realism and the correspondence theory of truth. Knowledge corresponds to the real world that exists independent of us.
		Epistemic irrealism–A position consistent with metaphysical nominalism or idealism. It is also compatible with the coherence, pragmatic, or semantic theories of truth. Knowledge is subjective and depends upon the observer.
		Objects of knowledge–What knowledge is supposed to be about
	Modal epistemology	Considers what can be known from possible and actual worlds
Ethics of belief (also known as normative epistemology) It is concerned with one's responsibility for knowledge	**Virtue**	Knowledge is teleological and is regulated by intellectual virtues. Knowledge results in *eudaimonia*.
	Deontology	One must believe only when a high level of certainty exists. To believe otherwise is wrong.
	Consequentialism	Knowledge results in pleasure. Knowledge results when the amount of certainty is greater than the amount of doubt.
Value of knowledge Concerned with what and how one is motivated to know	**Intrinsic value of knowledge**	**Value monists**–This position is consistent with the principle of organic unities and the principle of universality. Truth is the only intrinsic value of knowledge.
		Value pluralists–This position is consistent with the principle of summation and the principle of conditionality. Truth, belief, and justification all have intrinsic value.
	Instrumental value of knowledge	**Value monists** believe that individual bits of knowledge are instrumentally valuable
		Value pluralists believe that certain types of knowledge are more valuable than others

Chart 29

Perception or Metaphysics of Epistemology

	Source of knowledge	Metaphysics	Theory of truth	Skepticism
Extreme realism (position held by Plato)	Rationalism	Extreme realism	Correspondence theory of truth. Truth corresponds to the world of the forms (universals).	Skepticism is high, because the senses cannot be trusted
Common sense realism (position held by Aristotle, Thomas Reid, and G. E. Moore)	Combines empiricism with some rationalism	Moderate realism	Correspondence theory of truth	Skepticism is rejected because it conflicts with common sense
Contemporary realism (position held by David Hume)	Empiricism	Extreme nominalism	Semantic theory of truth	Results in extreme skepticsm
Epistemological dualism (position held by John Locke)	Empiricism	Moderate nominalism	Semantic theory of truth	Some skepticism must be accepted
Phenomenalism (position held by Immanuel Kant)	Combines rationalism with some empiricism	Moderate nominalism	Coherence theory of truth	Mitigated skepticism
Subjective idealism (position held by Bishop George Berkeley)	Empiricism	Moderate nominalism	Semantic theory of truth	Moderate skepticism
Relativistic idealism (position held by Friedrich Nietzsche)	Intuitionism	Extreme nominalism	Pragmatic theory of truth	Extreme skepticism

Chart 30

Epistemology (According to David Hume)

Explained in *An Inquiry Concerning Human Understanding*

All knowledge is:	Analytic	Synthetic
A priori Latin, meaning: Knowledge apart from sensory experience. This knowledge results from deduction.	Necessary truths Tautalogies Definitions Mathematics Cannot possibly be false **(Hume believed that all analytic truths are *a priori* and vice versa. He also thought that these truths are trivial.)**	
A posteriori Latin, meaning: Knowledge based upon sensory experience		Empirical truths Not true by definition Matters of fact **(Hume thought that all synthetic truths are *a posteriori* and vice versa. All significant knowledge results only from sensory experience.)**

Hume's fork	All knowledge is either a necessary truth or an empirical truth. All else is nonsense that must be rejected.
Hume's argument against causation	**1.** You can know that one thing follows another, but you cannot know that one thing causes another **2.** Knowledge of causes and effects is the result of sensory experience and not reason **3.** Thus, we cannot know that everything has a cause
Hume's argument against induction	Induction is based upon probability or past occurrences. Just because things have always worked a certain way before does not mean that they will continue to do so.

Conclusion: We can actually know very little.

Chart 31

Thomas Reid (Common Sense Realist)

1. The first principle of common sense is that perception, memory, as well as our other cognitive faculties are reliable
2. We have immediate knowledge of the reliability of our faculties
3. Reid allows for other sources for the reliability of our faculties, including track records and the uniformity of the laws of nature
4. Reasoning is not necessary for the immediate knowledge of the reliability of our cognitive faculties
5. Since we cannot get rid of our common sense beliefs, we should make our philosophical views fit these beliefs
6. Common sense beliefs have authority which makes them normative
7. Empiricism leads to skepticism

	Analytic	Synthetic
A priori	Necessary truth and common sense principles	
A posteriori		Empirical truth

Common Sense Realism

As held by Thomas Reid, G. E. Moore, and Roderick Chisholm

Principles of common sense	Some common sense propositions are known to be true
	Some common sense propositions are a matter of common knowledge
	Not everything that might be called a common sense belief or proposition is true or accepted
	It is more reasonable to accept common sense propositions or beliefs than to accept a philosophical theory that implies they are false
	Skepticism about the external world is to be rejected
	Some kind of **foundationalism** is essential to knowledge
	Epistemological particularism–Particular instances of knowledge can be used as data to assess and develop epistemological theories

Chart 32

Epistemology (According to Immanuel Kant)

Objections to common sense realism	Common sense lacks a criterion of knowledge or justification
	The reliability of one's cognitive faculties cannot be assumed

Types of knowledge	Analytic	Synthetic
A priori Latin, meaning that knowledge does not depend on experience	Tautology–A self-referential statement. *(ex. All bachelors are men)* Definitions **All analytic truths are a priori but not vice versa.**	Mathematics Logic God's existence **This is Kant's special category of knowledge**
A posteriori Latin, meaning that knowledge depends upon experience		Sensory experience **All a posteriori truths are synthetic but not vice versa.**

Kant's Transcendental Analysis of Mental Faculties

Mental Faculty	Synthetic *a priori*
Perception Or intuition	Space Time Causation
Understanding Enables people to understand facts about the world	Categories of understanding Mathematics
Reason	God The soul Freedom Morality

The World (According to Kant)

Phenomenal world	Noumenal world
The realm of sensory experience. According to Kant, one can only know what is in the phenomenal world.	The world as it actually is. Kant believed that one cannot really know what is in the noumenal world.

Chart 33

Modal Epistemology/Saul Kripke

As explained in *Naming and Necessity*

Types of Knowledge	Analytic	Synthetic
A priori Kripke argues that this idea does not entail necessity	**Conception** This involves some knowledge of the **actual world** as well as knowledge of **possible worlds.** This kind of knowledge is also susceptible to modal illusion.	
A posteriori Kripke argues that this idea does not entail contingency	**Conception** This involves some knowledge of the **actual world** as well as knowledge of **possible worlds.** This kind of knowledge is also susceptible to modal illusion.	**Perception** This involves knowledge of the **actual world** by means of properly functioning sensory and cognitive faculties

Terms of Modal Epistemology

Kripke argued that metaphysical ideas should not be confused with epistemological ones. There is no reason that one can or should know everything that is necessary or everything that is possible.

Metaphysical terms	**Necessity**	Concerns what exists in every possible world
	Contingency	Concerns what exists in only some possible worlds
Epistemological terms	***A priori***	Latin, meaning that knowledge does not depend on experience
	A posteriori	Latin, meaning that knowledge depends upon experience
	Necessary ***A posteriori***	Kripke argued that knowledge of the actual is sometimes prior to the possible. True identity statements like "I am Craig Mitchell" are examples of this type of knowledge.
	Contingent ***A priori***	Kripke argued that the knowledge of the possible is sometimes prior to the actual
	Conception	Knowledge of possible worlds via reason or intellection, and not imagination
	Modal illusion	The result of **conception** gone wrong. It is also known as misconception.
	Perception	Knowledge of the actual world via the senses

Chart 34

Epistemology/Overview of Theories of Knowledge

Theories of knowledge	Internalism– Knowledge is justified true belief The knower must know how he knows Skepticism is a significant problem A deontological approach to knowledge	**Foundationalism** • Suggests that knowledge is a structure in which one piece of knowledge rests upon another • The foundation of this structure of knowledge must be properly basic • Compatible with the correspondence and coherence theories of truth
		Coherentism • Suggests that knowledge is a structure in which each piece of knowledge depends on each other • Compatible with semantic, deflationary, and coherence theories of truth • Is actually another form of foundationalism
	Externalism– Knowledge is true belief produced by a reliable belief-forming process Does not require the knower to know how he knows Teleological approach to knowledge	**Naturalized epistemology** Knowledge results from natural processes. Reduces epistemology to psychology and cognitive science.
		Virtue epistemology Knowledge results from sensory experience, memory, and reason (both inductive and deductive). The intellectual virtues regulate belief-forming.
		Proper functionalism Knowledge results from the sensory and intellectual faculties operating properly in the proper environment and in accordance with their design plan.

The Gettier Problem

Edmund Gettier argued that knowledge is not **justified true belief**. He asserted that one can have a belief that is in fact true, in spite of the fact that he has sufficient but not the necessary justification. The result is that internalist epistemology has a difficulty that it has, as yet, not overcome. This is why externalist epistemology has gained more respectability.

Chart 35

Internalist Theories of Knowledge

Knowledge is justified true belief. Internalist theories require that one know how he knows in order to know. All internalist theories fail to solve the Gettier problem.

Noetic Structure	Explanation	Metaphysics of Knowledge	Ethic of Belief	Value of Knowledge
Classic (or extreme) foundationalism (position held by René Descartes and John Locke)	Beliefs form the basis of the noetic structure **Problem:** infinite regress	Metaphysical nominalism Semantic, pragmatic, or coherence theory of truth	Deontological justification The knower has a responsibility to not believe something unless a high degree of certainty can be attained	Value pluralism: justification, truth, and belief all have intrinsic value
Moderate foundationalism	Beliefs and sensory experience form the basis of the noetic structure	Metaphysical realism or nominalism Coherence, pragmatic or semantic theory of truth	Deontological or consequentialist justification	Value pluralism
Wholistic (or moderate) coherentism	Belief *A* receives positive epistemic status from playing an important role in a total system of beliefs	Metaphysical nominalism Semantic or coherence theory of truth	Deontological or consequentialist justification	Value pluralism
Linear (or extreme) coherentism An attempt to escape the infinite regress problem by using a circular structure	Belief *A* gets its justification from belief *B*. Belief *Z* gets its justification from belief *A*.	Coherence theory of truth	Consequentialist justification Justification is a matter of degrees. True beliefs are maximized and false ones are minimized.	Value pluralism

Chart 36

Virtue Epistemology

	Explanation	Internalism/ Externalism	Ethics of Belief	Value of Belief
Virtue consequentialism	Intellectual virtues provide justification by attempting to produce the highest aggregate of truth	**Internalist**	**Consequentialist** This process attempts to maximize true beliefs and minimize false ones	Value pluralism
Internalist virtue epistemology Linda Zagzebski	Intellectual virtues are necessary and sufficient habits for justification of beliefs	**Internalist**	**Deontology** One must use intellectual virtues to have knowledge	Value pluralism
Externalist virtue reliabilism, Perspectivism Ernest Sosa	Intellectual virtues are necessary but are not sufficient habits for knowledge	**Externalist** Compatible with naturalized epistemology or proper functionalism	**Virtue or broadly teleological**	Value pluralism Knowledge results in *eudaimonia*
Virtue reliabilism John Greco	Knowledge is true belief resulting from a cognitive virtue. Cognitive virtues give rise to knowledge if they are reliable and the reliability of the virtue is the result of responsible doxastic practices.	**Internalist**	**Virtue** Defective processes are identified as vicious	Value pluralism

Chart 37

Externalist Theories of Knowledge

All externalist theories dismiss skepticism. All externalist theories emphasize the importance of reliabilism. Reliabilism is the idea that knowledge results from true belief formed by a reliable process.

	Explanation	Metaphysics of Knowledge	Ethics of Belief	Value of Knowledge
Virtue reliabilism Ernest Sosa, Jonathan Kvanvig, Hartry Field	Intellectual virtues a part of a reliable belief-forming process	Metaphysical realism or nominalism Correspondence or semantic theory of truth	**Virtue warrant** Intellectual virtues are necessary but are not sufficient habits for forming knowledge	Value pluralism (justification, truth, and belief all have intrinsic value)
Naturalized epistemology W. V. O. Quine, Hilary Kornblith	Knowledge results from natural processes. Reduces epistemology to psychology and cognitive science.	Metaphysical naturalism Metaphysical realism or nominalism Correspondence, semantic, or deflationary theories of truth	**Teleological justification** Intellectual virtues are not necessary but are sufficient habits for forming beliefs	Value monism or pluralism
Proper functionalism Alvin Plantinga	Knowledge results from the sensory and intellectual faculties operating properly in the proper environment and in accordance with their design plan	Theistic or supernaturalist metaphysic Metaphysical realism Correspondence theory of truth	**Teleological warrant** Intellectual virtues are not necessary but are sufficient habits for proper functional belief-forming processes	Value monism (truth is the only intrinsic value)

Chart 38

Meta-ethics

The foundations of morality		
Metaphysics of ethics Investigates the nature of morality	**The status of moral facts**	Are there objective moral facts that exist independent of the observer? If not, then is there any objective value to morality?
	Free will/ determinism	Concerned with moral culpability. Is man free to act on his own or is man's action predetermined by God? Is there a mediating position?
	Moral language	Concerned with whether or not there is an objective moral reality and the nature of moral language
	Moral properties	Explores the existence of moral properties. It is also concerned with the nature of moral properties.
Moral epistemology Investigates how morality is known	**Cognitivism**	Moral knowledge is gained via a cognitive process
	Noncognitivism	Moral knowledge is gained via emotions. It assumes that there are no objective moral facts. Nonetheless, this position asserts that morality is still useful.
Moral psychology Investigates the nature of the moral self	**Moral motivation**	Explores the relationship between moral facts and moral motivation
	Moral development	Investigates how people develop morally
	Mental health	Explores the relationship between morality and mental health

Chart 39

Metaphysics of Ethics

<table>
<tr><td colspan="3">Studies the nature of morality</td></tr>
<tr><td rowspan="3">Moral facts</td><td>Realism</td><td>Moral facts are found and not made by men. They exist independent of the observer.</td></tr>
<tr><td>Irrealism (Anti-realism)</td><td>Moral facts are created and not found by men, but morality is useful for a successful society</td></tr>
<tr><td>Nihilism</td><td>Moral facts do not exist, and morality is not even useful</td></tr>
<tr><td rowspan="4">Moral properties</td><td>Naturalism</td><td>Moral properties are identical to natural properties</td></tr>
<tr><td>Eliminativism (Ethical Nominalism)</td><td>A reductionistic approach which asserts that science has no place at all for alleged moral properties or facts. It asserts that moral properties are nothing more than mythical entities.</td></tr>
<tr><td>Supervenience</td><td>Moral properties are relationally dependent upon other properties</td></tr>
<tr><td>Essentialism</td><td>A view of moral properties that is similar to naturalism, but it allows for the possibility of the supernatural. Moral properties depend upon the essence of a thing. It assumes that the essence of a thing carries an intrinsic and objective value.</td></tr>
<tr><td rowspan="2">Moral language</td><td>Emotivism</td><td>A view of morality developed by the analytic philosopher A. J. Ayer. He asserted that moral statements are nothing more than primitive, emotional noise. Moral statements are meaningless because there is no such thing as morality. There are only emotions.</td></tr>
<tr><td>Prescriptivism</td><td>A view developed by the analytic philosopher Richard Hare. Moral language has a logic of its own. Moral language is more than just primitive emotions. It is instead more of a command. For example: To say that stealing is immoral means "don't steal." Morality is thus about rules. These moral commands are universal, but they are not specific.</td></tr>
<tr><td rowspan="3">Moral responsibility</td><td>Freedom</td><td>The moral agent is morally culpable for his actions because he is free to do as he wishes</td></tr>
<tr><td>Compatibilism</td><td>The moral agent has limited moral culpability for his actions because his will is only partially free</td></tr>
<tr><td>Determinism</td><td>The moral agent does not have free will because of God, biology, or other external forces. Some hold that in this case the moral agent is still morally culpable; others assert that the moral agent is not morally culpable.</td></tr>
</table>

Chart 40

Moral Epistemology

		The study of how morality is known
Cognitivism Assumes that moral facts are found and not made. Morality is objective. Moral judgments express a belief. These beliefs can be true or false.	**Internalism** Moral knowledge is like other kinds of knowledge. Knowledge is justified true belief.	**Foundationalism**–Moral knowledge is dependent upon a foundation of knowledge that is properly basic
		Coherentism–Moral knowledge relies upon a system of coherent beliefs
	Externalism Moral knowledge is like other kinds of knowledge. Knowledge results from a reliable belief-forming process or mechanism.	**Naturalized epistemology**–Moral knowledge results from natural processes, perhaps a moral sense
		Virtue epistemology–Moral knowledge results from the use of virtues such as prudence
		Proper-functionalism–Moral knowledge results when a normal healthy person functions as he should. This may involve the use of **naturalized epistemology** or **virtue epistemology**.
Non-cognitivism Moral judgments do not express belief	**Projectivism** Moral judgments are nothing more than our projecting emotions into the world	**Emotivism** (A. J. Ayer)–There is no such thing as objective morality. Instead, morality is mere public opinion. To say that something is good is merely to mean that one likes that thing. To say that something is bad means that one dislikes that thing. Hence, morality is nothing more than emotional preference.
		Quasi-realism (Simon Blackburn)–Type of projectivism that seeks to explain and justify the realistic-seeming nature of our moral judgments
		Norm expressivism (Allan Gibbard)–A moral judgment expresses an agent's acceptance of norms
Moral skepticism	Assumes that even if moral facts exist we cannot know them	**Pyrhonian skepticism**–You cannot even know that you cannot know anything
		Hard empiricism–One cannot know morality because we have no moral sense
		The general belief that morality cannot be objectively known

Chart 41

Moral Psychology

Studies the nature of the moral self

Principle of Minimal Psychological Realism–A good moral theory is one which explains the character, motivation, and behavior of the average person

Moral motivation	**Internalism** Assumes that there is a connection between moral judgment and motivation	**Weak Internalism**–Recognition of a moral fact or obligation provides some motivation for moral action
		Strong Internalism–Recognition of a moral fact or obligation provides sufficient motivation for moral action
	Externalism	The rejection of **internalism**
	Altruism	**Rational altruism**–For an agent to act altruistically is to act in a way that is beneficial to his own well-being
		Psychological altruism–Human nature is such that an agent acts to promote the interests of others
		Ethical altruism–An agent ought to act in such a way as to promote the interest of others
	Egoism	**Rational egoism**–A moral agent has reason to act in a way that is consistent with his own self-interest
		Psychological egoism–Human nature is such that an agent acts only to promote his own self-interest
		Ethical egoism–An agent ought to act in such a way as to promote his own self-interest
	Welfarism	**Objectivism**–Asserts that the well-being of an agent is not a matter of the agent's attitudes or preferences. Instead, well-being depends upon some external standard.
		Subjectivism–Asserts that the well-being of an agent is a matter of the agent's attitudes or preferences
		Hybrid–Asserts that some aspects of an agent's well-being depend upon the agent's attitudes or preferences and some do not
Moral development	**Cognitivism**	An approach to moral development endorsed by **internalists** in which the moral agent regulates himself
	Non-cognitivism	A view of moral development held by **externalists** in which the moral agent is regulated by others
Moral health	**Welfarism**	Asserts that if one is healthy, he will recognize and be motivated by moral facts. It assumes that the moral man is a happy man.
	Positivism	Asserts that there is no connection between recognition of moral facts and mental health

Chart 42

Normative Ethics

Key Terms

Teleology These ideas come from Aristotle's *Metaphysics*	1. Morality depends on metaphysics (metaphysical realism) 2. Goodness depends on being 3. Pursuit of the good 4. The good depends on the nature of a thing 5. The good determines what is right
Deontology	1. Morality has no relation to metaphysics (metaphysical nominalism) 2. Rightness has priority over the good 3. Right determines what is good 4. Morality is only about obligations to rules or laws 5. Morality is subjective
Consequentialism Term coined by G. E. M. Anscombe in 1958	1. A type of deontology that seeks to maximize the good 2. Right action maximizes the good 3. British moral philosophy since the 17th century
Non-consequentialism	A rejection of consequentialism
Act	Rightness is determined by the action that one should take
Rule	Rightness is determined only by rules or laws

Major Ethical Theories

Teleology	Deontology	
Naturalism	**Act Consequentialism** Contractarianism Act utilitarianism Virtue consequentialism	**Rule Consequentialism** Contractualism Rule utilitarianism
Virtue Ethics	**Act Non-Consequentialism** Existentialism Situational ethics Moral particularism Linguistic virtue ethics	**Rule Non-Consequentialism** Kantianism Rossian intuitionism Divine command theory

Teleological virtue ethics requires **naturalism**, but **naturalism** does not require **virtue ethics**.

Both **moral particularism** and **situational ethics** suggest that moral principles and practical reasoning are insufficient to make good moral judgments. Each case is unique and should be judged on its own merits.

Chart 43

Virtue Ethics

Essential components	**Natural law**	A kind of naturalism that suggests that ethical properties are identical to natural properties. Right and wrong are based upon the nature of a thing. **Virtues** are what make a thing good. **Virtue ethics** are based upon human nature. Aristotle argued that the **natural law** is universal, rational, and objective. **Natural law** points to the existence of God, who establishes the created order. God also determines what is good and right.
	Doctrine of the mean	The idea that there is a continuum of behavior. Virtue is in the middle of this continuum. A deficiency of a virtue is a vice. An excess of a virtue is a vice.
	Perfectionism	Virtues emphasize human excellences
	Welfarism	To act in accordance with virtue is in a moral agent's best interest. The virtuous person is a happier person.
Types of virtue ethics	**Aristotelian virtue ethics (classical)**	A premodern system of ethics focused upon character and **natural law**. The man of character acts in accordance with the natural law. The virtues of man are determined by this natural law (or the nature of a thing). The virtuous man gains happiness (*eudaimonia*, happiness gained by self effort). One gains character by watching someone who already has character. One may also gain character by listening to or reading narratives.
	Augustinian virtue ethics	A premodern system of Christian ethics. The natural (cardinal) virtues are insufficient to provide true happiness (beatitude = happiness from God). Only the Christian can have hope of beatitude. The Holy Spirit infuses the theological virtues into the believer. The believer gains the cardinal virtues after the theological virtues.
	Agent based	A non-teleological system of virtue ethics developed by analytic philosophers. It is a system that has no place for natural law.
	Linguistic virtue ethics	A postmodern approach to virtue ethics developed by Alasdair MacIntyre and based upon the ideas of Ludwig Wittgenstein. It emphasizes the importance of narrative and community. It rejects moral, epistemological, and metaphysical realism.

Chart 44

Internalist Moral Development (Cognitivism)

Teleological Development

Aristotle

Aristotle assumes that humans have the ability to reason and communicate better than other creatures. He also assumes that humans are social creatures. Aristotle thought that how one thinks determines how one feels and behaves. He assumes that children begin life as egoists and grow more toward altruism. To grow in character one must observe a person who has prudence (practical wisdom). As a result, the moral agent learns to decide how to act in different situations by using their virtues.

The components of character	Desires	**Sense desires**–Desire for pleasure through the senses. These desires involve some sort of belief.
		Passional desires–Evaluate the situation in terms of positive or negative desirability
		Rational desires–Provide motivation for action based on moral judgments
	Goods	*Summum bonum*–The highest good
		Internal goods–Moral virtues
		Intrinsic external goods–These are goods to be pursued in and of themselves (for example, friendship)
		Extrinsic external goods–These are not goods to be pursued for themselves. They are instrumentally useful.
	Reasons	**Practical reason** connects sense desires and the passional desires with the conception of the good life. It is also concerned with the totality of goods.

Stage 4 Virtue	The person normally acts virtuously because he has a firm and unchanging character.
Stage 3 Self-control	The moral agent gains some control over his desires and sometimes acts in accordance with virtue. His character is still not firm and unchanging.
Stage 2 *Akrasia*	After observing a virtuous person the moral agent becomes aware that he has vices and decides to become virtuous. This decision results partly to please himself, and partly to please others. The moral agent begins to exercise the virtues. Lack of power or knowledge prevents him from being virtuous.
Stage 1 Vice	The moral agent must learn to be virtuous. He begins life concerned only with himself. His character is unformed.

Chart 45

Linguistic Virtue Ethics

This postmodern approach to ethics was developed by Alasdair MacIntyre. His most siginificant works are *After Virtue*; *Whose Justice, Which Rationality?*; and *Three Rival Versions of Moral Enquiry.* MacIntyre subscribes to Thomas Aquinas's list of virtues which combines the virtues of Augustine with the virtues of Aristotle. He was influenced by the thought of Ludwig Wittgenstein who rejected metaphysics and replaced it with linguistic analysis. Consequently, MacIntyre leaves no place for natural law or what he calls "metaphysical biology." Stanley Hauerwas has followed after MacIntyre's ethical theory. Proponents are also metaphysical nominalists, rejecting the existence of universals.

Meta-ethical presuppositions	**Metaphysics of morals**	**Moral irrealism**–Morality is important because of the community
		Free will–Man is morally culpable because he is free
	Moral epistemology	**Cognitivism**–Moral knowledge is gained through the virtue of prudence
	Moral psychology	**Motivation internalism**–Recognition of moral facts or obligation provides motivation for moral action
		Cognitivism–Moral motivation comes from within the moral agent
		Welfarism–It is beneficial to the moral agent to act morally
Theological virtues Augustine	**Love**	The love of God and the love of man for God's sake
	Faith	Grows out of love and gives one spiritual knowledge
	Hope	Grows out of love and causes man to look at eternity
Cardinal virtues Aristotle	**Justice**	The most important social virtue
	Prudence	Practical wisdom, a key to moral judgment
	Courage	The ability to overcome fear
	Temperance	Self-control
Community	The community is important because it determines meaning, truth, and morality. The individual must operate by the preestablished rules of the community.	
Narrative	Narrative is the key to learning of any type, especially for learning moral character	
Language	We are surrounded by language and cannot understand without it	

Chart 46

Non-Consequentialist Deontology

Divine command theory	This is a meta-ethical theory which argues that goodness is based upon God. It is also a normative ethical theory, in which the will of God determines what is right. It assumes that God's will is revealed. Some versions are compatible with only special revelation. Other versions are compatible with both special and general revelation.
Kantianism	This is a modern ethical theory that emphasizes universizability and equitability.
Rossian intuitionism	An approach to ethics developed by the analytic philosopher W. D. Ross. It posits a hierarchy of laws which must be obeyed.
Graded absolutism	An approach developed by Norman Geisler which posits a hierarchy of laws that must be obeyed.
Existentialism	Existentialism has only one rule: be true to yourself. Act in accordance with who you are

Deontology arose in the modern period following the ideas of William of Ockham. Because of his metaphysical nominalism, Ockham was a proponent of a type of divine command theory, which separated God's will from God's nature. Thus Ockham separated ethics from metaphysics to preserve God's freedom. Without a metaphysical foundation, morality, aesthetics, and epistemology became subjective. Morality is reduced to rules.

The **Continental rationalists** were metaphysical nominalists whose approach to ethics was exemplified by Immanuel Kant. He based morality on reason. The **Continental philosophers** who followed Kant were deontological as well.

The ethics of the **British empiricists** (also metaphysical nominalists) were exemplified by David Hume who argued, "You cannot derive ought from is" (the fact/value dichotomy). They based morality on the emotions (passions). Their ethics were deontological because they were divorced from metaphysics. Their ethics were also consequentialist, which means that right action maximizes the good. The term *consequentialism* was invented by G. E. M. Anscombe in her 1958 article, "Modern Moral Philosophy."

Chart 47

Kantian Deontology

This approach, developed by Immanuel Kant, argues that morality is based on *a priori* principles. These ideas are expressed in his *Groundwork for a Metaphysics of Morals, Critique of Practical Reason,* and *Metaphysics of Morals.* Kant invented the idea of autonomy. Autonomy suggests that men do not need any external authority to do right because reason provides sufficient motivation for moral action.

Meta-ethical presuppositions	**Metaphysics of morals**	**Moral realism**–Moral facts exist independent of the observer. Moral facts are found and not made.
		The good–An action done from a good will
		Free will–Man is morally culpable for his actions
	Moral epistemology	**Cognitivism**–Moral judgments express a belief. Morality is known through the use of practical reason alone. The Bible is not needed.
	Moral psychology	**Motivational internalism**
		Cognitive moral development
		Positivism–Virtue and happiness are not united in this life
Respect for persons	Because every person is endowed with the ability to think and choose, all men should be treated with respect	
Equality	Everyone should have an equal opportunity to attain whatever status they desire in a free society	
Universality	The laws of society should apply to everyone	
Hypothetical imperative	Hypothetical imperatives concern instrumental or extrinsic goods. These goods are a means to some other good or end. Intrinsic goods in contrast are an end in and of themselves.	
Categorical imperatives These are concerned with intrinsic goods and have two functions **Function 1:** to obligate the moral agent to obey **Function 2:** to act as a test of moral maxims	**1. Autonomy**	One should never act in such a way that he could not also will that his maxim should be a universal law
	2. Respect for persons	Act so that you treat humanity, whether in your own person or in that of any other, always as an end and never as a means
	3. Legislation for a moral community	All maxims that proceed from one's own making of law ought to harmonize with a possible moral community
Conclusions: Kant believed that virtue and happiness cannot be united in this life	1. God exists and we should worship him 2. There is objective right and wrong 3. There is an afterlife 4. There is a postmortem judgment 5. God will reward the good and punish the evil in the next life	

Chart 48

Deontological (Rossian) Intuitionism

W. D. Ross is primarily concerned with meta-ethics. He explained what he thought was the dominant ethical theory of the 19th century in *The Right and the Good*.

Meta-ethical presuppositions	**Metaphysics of morals**	**Moral realism**–Moral facts exist independent of the observer
		Good is unexplained
		Free will–The moral agent has free will and is morally culpable
	Moral epistemology	**Cognitivism**–Moral knowledge is intuited. Moral principles are self-evident.
	Moral psychology	**Motivational internalism**–Recognition of moral facts provides motivation for moral action
		Cognitivism–Moral motivation comes from within the moral agent
Other presuppositions	Moral principles cannot be reduced or unified into general principles	
	Moral principles are absolute	
	Ethics are deontological	
	Ethical conflicts are resolved through a hierarchy of laws	
***7 prima facie* duties**	**Promise keeping**–One must always keep his promises under any condition	
	Fidelity–One should always be loyal and true to their family and friends	
	Gratitude–One should always be thankful for what others have done for them	
	Good will–One's actions should always be motivated out of good will	
	Justice–One should always strive to act justly and see that justice is carried out	
	Self-improvement–One should never be content with their character and should always strive to improve	
	Nonmalificence–One should always strive to control their actions so that they do not act out of evil intent	

Chart 49

Act Utilitarianism

Jeremy Bentham took the utilitarianism of Francis Hutcheson and David Hume and modified it. It is a system that is teleological and consequentialist. It is a hedonistic (focused on pleasure) approach to ethics. Bentham believed that it is better to be a satisfied pig than a dissatisfied Socrates. Utilitarianism seeks to maximize utility or the good.

Meta-ethical presuppositions	**Metaphysics of morals**	**Moral irrealism**–Moral facts do not exist, but morality is useful
		The good is pleasure or happiness
		Free will–Men have free will and are morally culpable
	Moral epistemology	**Noncognitivism**–The passions (emotions) act as a moral sense
	Moral psychology	**Motivational externalism**–Recognition of moral facts or obligations do not provide motivation for moral action
		Noncognitivism–Moral motivation comes from fear of punishment
		Positivism–Happiness is equated with pleasure. There is no objective good to be united with virtue.
Greatest happiness principle	Act utilitarianism provides the greatest amount of happiness for the greatest number of people	
Explanation	An act is right if it results in as much good as any other alternative	
Calculus of happiness (hedonic calculus)	Decisions are based upon the total amount of pleasure to be gained minus the total amount of pain to be experienced	
	The number of people to experience the pleasure or pain	
	The certainty of the pleasure or pain	
	The intensity of the pleasure or pain	
	The duration of the pleasure or pain	
	The frequency of the pleasure or pain	
Political theory	A democracy is the best form of government because it is the most compatible to utilitarianism	

Virtue consequentialism is a type of consequentialism. It argues that virtues help maximize the good.

Chart 50

Rule Utilitarianism

John Stuart Mill developed this ethical system in response to the weaknesses of act utilitarianism. Mill believed that it is better to be Socrates dissatisfied than a pig satisfied. This system is deontological and consequentialist. Utilitarianism seeks to maximize utility or the good.

Meta-ethical presuppositions	**Metaphysics of morals**	**Moral irrealism**–Moral facts do not exist, but morality is useful
		Good is happiness (*eudaimonia*)
		Free will–Moral agents have free will and are morally culpable
	Moral epistemology	**Noncognitivism**–Moral judgments do not express belief
	Moral psychology	**Motivational externalist**–Recognition of moral obligation does not provide motivation for moral action
		Noncognitivism–Moral motivation comes from fear of punishment
		Welfarism–To act morally is beneficial
Happiness		Is more than pleasure. Happiness (*eudaimonia*) involves higher order pleasures such as intellectual and aesthetic enjoyments.
Definition of rule utilitarianism		The rightness of an act does not depend upon its consequences. An act is right if and only if it is required by a code of rules whose acceptance would lead to the greater utility for society than any available alternative.
Code of rules		These rules ensure that a minimally correct behavior standard is enforced and encouraged
Universality		The set of rules must apply to everyone

Chart 51

Social Contract Theory (Contractarianism)

This approach was developed by Thomas Hobbes and Jean Jacques Rousseau. Contractarianism is an ethical system that is deontological and consequentialist. It is both an ethical and a political theory.

Meta-ethical presuppositions	**Metaphysics of morals**	**Irrealism**–Moral facts do not exist, but morality is useful
		Good–Whatever brings peace and order. What is right to do depends on what rules it would be in everyone's interest for all to accept.
		Free will–Men are free moral agents who have free will. Consequently all men are morally culpable.
	Moral epistemology	**Noncognitivism**–Moral judgments do not express belief
	Moral psychology	**Motivational externalism**–Moral facts do not motivate a person to act morally
		Noncognitivism–People are motivated to act morally from fear of punishment
		Welfarism–To act morally is beneficial
Man's state of nature	According to Thomas Hobbes, "Man's natural state is a state of war of all against all." If left unto himself, man's life is "solitary, poor, nasty, brutish, and short." Man is free, equal, and rational, but he is also egoistic and antisocial.	
The solution	**The state**	A strong state is the only way to protect men from each other. Every citizen owes total allegiance to the state because the state offers men protection from each other. The state is legitimate as long as it can demonstrate itself capable of exercising power.
	Social contract	Men born into society are automatically enrolled in the social contract. This contract is something that all rational and competent agents would agree to. Men have no way to get out of this contract. As such, they must obey the state.
	Rights	Man has few rights and even these are subject to the needs of the state
	Rules/laws	People must forego the pursuit of their own interests to obey the rules that promote the interests of society as a whole

Chart 52

Social Contract Theory (Contractualism)

This position was developed by Immanuel Kant and most recently by John Rawls. Like contractarianism, it is a deontological and consequentialist ethical and political theory.

Meta-ethical presuppositions	**Metaphysics of morals**	**Realist**–Moral facts are found and not made
		Good–Is determined by what is right. All rational men can conclude what is right and will agree to it.
		Free will–Men are free moral agents who are morally culpable
	Moral epistemology	**Cognitivism**–Moral judgments express belief
	Moral psychology	**Motivational internalism**–Recognition of moral facts or obligation provides motivation for moral action
		Cognitivism–Moral motivation comes from within oneself
		Welfarism–It is in one's best self-interest to act morally
Man's state of nature	Men are rational and equal. At the same time, they are also antisocial and egoistic.	
The solution	**The state**	The state is agreed to by all competent rational individuals for the good of all
	The social contract	The social contract is a device used to reveal what is moral
	Rights	All men have equal rights
	Rules/laws	Are understood as something that rational individuals would agree to from a common perspective as one free and equal person among others
	Virtue	According to John Rawls, **justice** is the primary virtue. He asserts that justice is fairness.

Chart 53

Aesthetics

Meta-aesthetics		
Metaphysics of beauty Concerned with the nature of beauty	**Realism**	Aesthetic facts exist independent of the observer
	Irrealism	Aesthetic facts do not exist but are useful for appraising art
	Nihilism	Aesthetic facts do not exist and are not even useful
Aesthetic epistemology Concerned with how one knows beauty	**Aesthetic sense**	Aesthetic knowledge results from an aesthetic sense called taste (perhaps the passions)
	Reason	Aesthetic knowledge results from reason
	Intuition	Aesthetic knowledge results via some unknown means (perhaps the passions)
Value theory of beauty Concerned with the aesthetic experience	**Aesthetic experience**	What is the nature of the aesthetic experience and what causes it?
	Aesthetic development	How does one develop the ability to appraise an aesthetic experience?

Chart 54

Axiology of Aesthetics

Art			
The nature of art		Imitation	Art is a secondhand copy of reality
		Play	Art is an example of the creative process
		Escape	Art is an escape from the real world
		Expressionism	Art communicates feelings
Expressionism		**Romanticism (artist)**	Art should communicate the artist's feelings
		Object	The perceiver should recognize the emotion of the art object
		Appraiser	Art should evoke feelings in the appraiser
Subjectivism		**Cultural relativism**	Aesthetic experience varies with culture
		Postmodernism	Aesthetic experience is subjective and is determined by power
Objectivism		**Absolutism**	Aesthetic experience is objective and should be the same for everyone
		Educated observer	Aesthetic experience is the result of education

Types of Art	
Literature	Fine writing of a creative kind
Film	Motion pictures that tell a story in a creative way
Photography	Still pictures that emphasize the beauty of reality
Painting	A creative representation accomplished by covering the surface of canvas with paint
Sculpture	The art of representing real or imagined things in materials with three dimensions
Architecture	Concerned with the symbolic and artistic aspects of a building
Music	The art of combining vocal or instrumental sounds in varying melody
Dance	The work as a whole and the performance of it
Theater	Concerned with the art of plays, operas, and dramatic works

Chart 55

Political Philosophy

Morality and the state	**Welfarism**	The state has the function of looking after the welfare of its people
	Perfectionism	The promotion of human excellence is a primary factor in the evaluation of the political and social worth of a society. This assumes that there is a distinctive human nature.
	Positivism	Political philosophy has nothing to do with morality
Types of government (according to Aristotle)	**Benevolent monarchy**	According to Aristotle, this is the best kind of government
	Aristocracy	The rule of the best
	Polity	The rule of citizens
	Democracy	The rule of the many
	Oligarchy	The rule of the few
	Tyranny	The worst kind of government
Political positions	**Liberal**	**Classical liberals** emphasize personal freedom and individual rights. These rights include the right to life, liberty, and property. They desire to limit the power of the state.
		Modern liberals emphasize the freedoms of the French Revolution, specifically: liberty, equality, and fraternity. This position rejects social morality.
		Radicals desire dramatic and immediate change
	Moderate	Believe that the best position is one that avoids extremes
	Conservative	**Libertarians** are fiscally conservative but desire no interference from the government
		Communitarians emphasize the individual's duties to society
		Reactionaries believe that things have changed too much and desire to change things back
Philosophy of law	Concerned with the nature and purpose of law. Every society has some kind of legal system to resolve conflict and to make sure that justice is carried out.	
Economics	The study of wealth and poverty of societies and of individuals. Aristotle believed that economics comes prior to politics.	

Chart 56

Philosophy of Law

Theories of justice	**Retributive**	Ensures that those who violate the laws of society receive the punishment that they are due
	Distributive	The fair arrangement of goods, benefits, and responsibilities of a society
Legal theory	**Natural law**	The classical view of natural law is based upon metaphysical presuppositions that assert that there is a higher law that serves as a basis for civil law. The contemporary views of natural law are contrasted with legal positivism. Contemporary natural law theory asserts that there is a moral aspect to every law that should show the validity of that law. Natural rights are based upon the idea of natural law.
	Legal positivism	An idea of the 19th century that asserts that laws are only social constructs of a given society. They also assert that there is no connection between law and morality.
	Law and economics	Asserts that economic principles apply to every legal problem. This includes such things as family law, criminal law, and tort law.
	Postmodernism	This is concerned with how lawyers use language and how language relates to truth. This includes the study of feminism and the law, deconstruction, and pragmatism.
Areas of law	**Business law**	Includes such things as property law, contract law, and tort law
	Criminal law	Concerned with crime and punishment
	Constitutional law	Concerned with whether a given law is consistent with the constitution of a country
	International law	Concerned with resolving disputes of the laws between one country and another

Chart 57

Economics

Presuppositions	*Homo economicus*	A model of a rational economic human being. This model is egoistic and acts for its own self-interest. This self-interest causes *homo economicus* to be motivated by incentives.
	The allocation of scarce resources	Awareness of this scarcity combined with human self-interest causes changes in prices and behaviors
	Fair exchange	Results from people attempting to meet their own desires for scarce resources. Money is used to facilitate this fair exchange for goods and services.
Requirements for markets	**Property rights**	Based upon natural law. According to Aristotle, property rights are needed for virtue, for example: liberality and magnanimity.
	Law	Protects property rights and enforces voluntary agreements in contracts
	The state	The enforcer of the rule of law
Ethics and economics	**Positive economics**	The science that studies human behavior as it attempts to solve the problem of the allocation of scarce resources. It attempts to understand how economic activity is affected by changes in economic policy. It is not concerned with ethical judgments concerning the policy or the activity.
	Normative economics (or political economy)	Deals with the basic principles for the ethical advancement of the national economy by public officials. Thus, the formulation of economic policy is a normative activity.
Types of economics	**Macro economics**	Concerned with national economies
	Micro economics	Concerned with economics at the local level
Economic theories	**Capitalism**	An economic system in which all or most of the means of production are privately owned and operated for profit. This system assumes that a free market is essential.
	Chicago School of economics	Return to the principles set forth in Adam Smith's *The Wealth of Nations*. It is a rejection of the Keynesian approach to economics. This approach was proposed by Friedrich A. Hayek and adopted in America by Milton Friedman and is often referred to as the Chicago School of economics.
	Keynesianism	The economic system developed by John Maynard Keynes in his book *The General Theory of Employment, Interest, and Money*. It rejects the laissez-faire free market system that minimizes state intervention. It advocates government intervention to stimulate the level of demand. It also asserts that a small amount of inflation is acceptable to maintain full employment.
	Socialism	A system that developed in opposition to **capitalism**. It is a form of utopian liberalism that combines interest in social justice with economic reform. As such it emphasizes the importance of the worker. In many cases, socialism has been combined with **Marxism**, but it is not limited to any one political system.

Chart 58

Salamanca School of Economics

This group of theologians developed political and economic thought based upon the work of Thomas Aquinas. There were some members of this school from the Augustinian and the Franciscan orders, but they held a lesser influence on the development of these ideas.

Dominicans **University of Salamanca, Spain**	**Francisco de Vitoria (1480–1546)**	He was the founder of the Salamanca school. He wrote *De Indis et de Ivre Belli Relectione* which was concerned with international law as it related to commerce. He was an advocate of a worldwide free market. He also wrote *De Justitia*.
	Domingo de Soto (1495–1560)	He wrote *De Iustitia et Lure* which was concerned with monetary theory. He thought that money should imitate the natural law, by being always firm and fixed. As such, the value of money should not be changed by governments.
	Martin de Azpilcueta (1493–1586)	Also known as Navarrus, he wrote *Manual de Confesores y Penitentes*. He was concerned with extreme need and held private property in high regard.
	Tomas de Mercado (1500–1575)	Emphasized the importance of private property. He noted that self-interest cannot be separated from private property. He was also concerned with the theory of money.
Society of Jesus (Jesuits) **University of Coimbra, Portugal**	**Luis de Molina (1535–1600)**	Wrote *De Iustitia et Lure* about private property. He argued that private property existed even before original sin. He also wrote *La Teoria del Justo Precio* which was concerned with prices and proper wages.
	Juan de Lugo (1583–1660)	He was concerned with private property and with commerce
	Leonardo de Leys (1554–1623)	Also known as Lessius, his work influenced Hugo Grotius
	Francisco Suarez (1548–1617)	He emphasized the importance of natural law as it related to political and economic theory
	Juan de Mariano (1535–1624)	His work focused on the government and monetary theory. He thought that kings must act in such a way that they can damage the people without their consent. He also disapproved of currency debasement as a means of redistributing wealth.

Chart 59

Adam Smith (*The Wealth of Nations*)

In 1776, Adam Smith published his *An Inquiry into the Nature and Causes of the Wealth of Nations.* Many consider him to be the father of modern economic theory. His economic/political theory is based upon his ethical thought (utilitarian) in his book *The Theory of Moral Sentiments.* Adam Smith was primarily concerned with economic growth. Smith assumed that "men are not angels," that is, that we act in our own self-interest, not for the common good. He was concerned to create an economic system wherein there were incentives to act for the common good, because it benefited oneself.

The Results of Smith's System

Smith believed that a free market economy with a laissez-faire government rewards the virtuous with wealth and punishes the vicious with poverty. Smith was a firm believer in free trade. He also believed that a free market economy with free trade between nations would result in the wealth of all the countries that participate in it, thus making war less likely.

Laissez-faire government	The government should not interfere with the market. The exception to this principle is that the government should take whatever measures are necessary to ensure a level playing field for all who participate in the marketplace.
Free market	The market is the most efficient way to allocate scarce resources. This is because the prices for a good or service are determined by the demand for it.
Property rights	Smith emphasized the efficiency of privately owned property. Private ownership is thus beneficial to society as a whole. He also made clear the inefficiency of state-owned property.
Division of labor	Smith provided a systematic explanation of the division of labor and its consequences for an economy
Taxation	Smith asserted that taxation has a negative effect on the economy
	Tax money should only be spent on national defense, justice, and public works

Chart 60

Free Market Economics

David Ricardo	He wrote *On the Principles of Political Economy and Taxation*, in which he cried for free trade. Free trade is beneficial to everyone, while protectionism is harmful to everyone. Contrary to Adam Smith, he argued that labor should be the determinant of value.
John Stuart Mill	In his book *Principles* he argued for a proportional (as opposed to a progressive) income tax. He believed that the poor should be exempted from the tax and that inheritances should be taxed at a higher, more confiscatory rate.
Alfred Marshall	He turned economics into a discipline of its own that is separate from moral philosophy. He wrote *Principles of Economics*.
Carl Menger	The founder of the Austrian School of economics. In his *Principles of Economics* he argued that property ownership was natural for all men. He believed that property ownership is necessary for the survival of each individual.
Ludwig von Mises	A student of Carl Menger and an important figure in the Austrian School of economics. He emphasized the importance of free markets as an extension of free human action in his book *Human Action*. In his book *Socialism* he stood against socialism because it harms society by limiting productivity and freedom. In his *Critique of Interventionism* he argued against any form of government intervention in politics or the economic system.
Friedrich von Hayek	A student of von Mises, he emphasized the importance of the market. He argued that a free economy requires a free political system. His arguments are represented in his book *The Road to Serfdom*.
Milton Friedman	A student of Hayek and member of the Chicago School of economics. He stood against government intervention in economies. His solution for controlled economies is called "shock therapy." This involves no deficit spending, and free trade. He expressed his ideas in his books *Capitalism and Freedom* and later in *Free to Choose*.
Chicago School of economics	A group of neo-classical economists in the 1950s from the University of Chicago who were students of Frank Knight. Many were influenced by Hayek. The Chicago School emphasized the importance of markets and the choice of the individual. They also abhorred government intervention, believing that it always resulted in more harm than good.
Monetarism	A view of the economy in which the Federal Reserve Board (the central bank of the US) affects the economy via an accelerator (high money supply) and a brake (lower money supply). The Federal Reserve controls the money supply by controlling the percentage of deposits that banks can lend, by raising and lowering the interest rate charged to banks that borrow from it, and by buying and selling government securities. The Chicago School of economics supported this view of the money supply.

Chart 61

Keynesian Economics

John Maynard Keynes was a student of Alfred Marshall. Operating with the belief that the laissez-faire conditions that characterized the 19th century were dead, he created the field of macroeconomics and advocated a strong interventionist approach to the economy. As a professor at Cambridge University he wrote what many economists considered a work of genius, *The General Theory of Employment, Interest, and Money*. Keynes believed that the classical economic theory (Adam Smith), which served as the basis during the 19th century, was a special case which fit within his larger, general theory of economics. As a tireless enemy of communism, Keynes desired the creation of more wealth.

Government	Keynes believed that the economy was like a machine that can be controlled by the government. Consequently the four-part economic cycle can be stopped if the government takes the right approach. Keynes's system is compatible with socialism and with dependency theory (protectionism). It advocates government intervention to stimulate the level of demand. It also asserts that a small amount of inflation is acceptable to maintain full employment.
Monetary policy	The government can stimulate the economy by increasing or decreasing spending and by raising or lowering taxes when the economy slows down.
The market	Keynes viewed the market as dangerous. As such, it should not run free. Instead, the government needs to intervene in the market to ensure stability.
John Kenneth Galbraith	The popularizer of Keynes's views in the United States. As a professor at Harvard University he wrote three books that challenged the ideas of the neo-classicalist economists, including: *The Affluent Society*, *The New Industrial State*, and *Economics and the Public Purpose*. He also led Harvard University to become the main proponent of Keynes's ideas in the US.

Chart 62

Socialism/Marxism

Socialism

Socialism is about human welfare, but it is too diverse a movement to characterize. In general it stands opposed to capitalism, seeing it as inefficient and wasteful. Still, some more moderate socialists will embrace Keynesianism. Other moderate socialists might consider a Keynesian approach an empty reformism. Socialism is not necessarily committed to the atheistic, metaphysical materialism of Marxism. In much the same way, socialism is not necessarily committed to revolution, but to a democratic process.

Marxism

Karl Marx and Frederick Engels wrote the *Communist Manifesto* and *Das Kapital*. These works explain a political-economic philosophy that has held much of the world in slavery for the better part of the last century. There is no one agreed-to system, but rather a family of theories associated with Marxism. Today, these theories are viewed as a failure. There are a number of significant components to this family of theories. They are:

Atheism	Marxism subscribes to a metaphysical materialist viewpoint. In this position there is no God and religion is only an opiate of the masses.
Class struggle	Marx saw class struggle as an ongoing problem throughout history. Because he was influenced by Hegelian thought, he held a teleological view of history. He believed that history would culminate with the working class overthrowing the ruling class. This socialist revolution results in the complete liberation of man.
Theory of society	Marx provided a critical analysis of society. He concluded that economics is the foundation of society, and all else is superstructure. He believed that society would evolve from the primitive commune to the social class with a capitalist economy. The last stage of this evolution is a socialist revolution resulting in the elimination of private property and the division of labor.
Science	Marx claimed that this theory is scientific. That is, he believed that history progressed based on an inexorable law. At the end of history, socialist utopia was inevitable, as certain as the laws of gravity or the laws of motion.

Chart 63

Western Followers of Marx

Critical theory	**The Frankfurt School (Germany)**	Critical theorists recognize Freud as well as Marx as conceptual revolutionaries. They attempt to combine the ideas of both as a means of understanding and changing society. The Frankfurt School includes philosophers such as Max Horkheimer, Theodor Adorno, Herbert Marcuse, and Jürgen Habermas.
Marxist anti-humanism	**France**	This approach to Marxism involves a reaffirmation of the classical Marxism as well as a refusal of the problematic aspects of human nature (economic) or essence of man. It is a reaction to both critical theory as well as Sartre's Marxist humanism. This movement includes philosophers such as Louis Althusser, Etienne Balibar, Michel Pêcheux, Nicos Poulantzas, Barry Hindess, and Paul Hirst.
Marxist humanism	**France, Britain, North America**	An attempt to modify Marxism along the lines of a Sartrean existentialism.
Analytic Marxism	**Britain, North America**	An attempt to employ the methods of Anglo-American analytic philosophy to Marxist analysis of society. Analytic Marxism includes philosophers such as Jon Elster and Adam Przeworski.

Chart 64

PART 2
ANALYTIC PHILOSOPHY

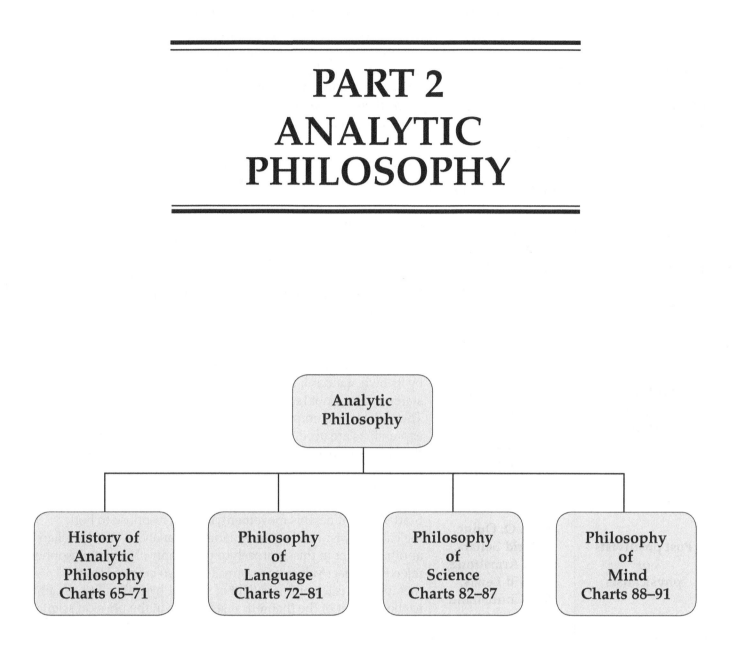

Contemporary Philosophical Disciplines

Analytic philosophy seeks to clarify the meaning of concepts. In many respects it attempts to be scientific. These areas of study have derived from the classical areas of study in philosophy. Most of these are sub-disciplines in metaphysics. Some are specialized aspects of metaphysics and epistemology.

Philosophy of language replaced epistemology in analytic philosophy because of the desire for clarity. It held the place of first philosophy for most of the 20th century.

Philosophy of science is another aspect of analytic philosophy. It is a combination of both metaphysics and epistemology. It explores the nature of science and helps to define scientific method.

Philosophy of the mind is a sub-discipline of metaphysics and is becoming first philosophy in 21st-century analytic philosophy. This is because philosophy of mind can provide solutions to problems that cannot be resolved by philosophy of language alone. Many of these problems center around the nature of intentionality.

Major Movements in Analytic Philosophy

The "linguistic turn" is about the movement from epistemology to philosophy of language. Philosophy of language is considered first philosophy in the study of analytic philosophy. The other branches of philosophy are understood in light of the changes in philosophy of language. According to Quentin Smith in *Ethical and Religious Thought in Analytic Philosophy of Language*, there are five major movements in analytic philosophy (see also Scott Soames's *Philosophical Analysis in the 20th Century*).

Logical realism	**G. E. Moore, Bertrand Russell**	These philosophers are metaphysical realists who assert that every word in a sentence correlates to a sense or meaning
Logical positivism	**A. J. Ayer, F. P. Ramsey, Moritz Schlick, Rudolf Carnap, Otto Neurath**	Carnap defined philosophy as the analysis of the language of science. This language of science is concerned with both scientific uses and everyday life. A key idea is the verification principle which argues that anything that is not empirically verifiable is meaningless. Proponents also emphasized the fact/value dichotomy.
Ordinary language analysis	**Ludwig Wittgenstein, J. L. Austin, Gilbert Ryle, R. M. Hare, P. F. Strawson, John Searle**	Started by Ludwig Wittgenstein, ordinary language analysts reject the verification principle because they argue that it is senseless by its own standard. These philosophers argue that philosophical statements are not tautologies or statements of equivalents. They are instead empirical generalizations about how ordinary expressions are used. These philosophers deduce conclusions from the linguistic thesis that the sense of an expression is its ordinary use.
Post positivists or physicalists	**W. V. O. Quine, Wilfrid Sellars, D. M. Armstrong, David Lewis, Paul Churchland**	Started by Quine, this movement arose in response to both logical positivism and ordinary language analysis. Wilfrid Sellars is another leader in this approach to philosophy. These philosophers rejected the fact/value dichotomy. They also believed that metaphysics is a legitimate field of study. Physical reality amounts to the referent of the theoretical sentences in the physical sciences.
Linguistic essentialism	**Saul Kripke, Alvin Plantinga, Robert Adams, David Brink**	This movement resulted from the ideas of Saul Kripke expressed in his work *Naming and Necessity*. By employing the use of possible worlds and necessity, the essentialists consider what is essential to trans-world identities. The Linguistic Essentialists (LE) agree with the Post-Positivist Physicalists (PPP) that metaphysics is a legitimate field of study.

Chart 65

Logical Realism

Correspondence theory of truth–A substantive theory that claims truth corresponds to reality		

Philosophers
G. E. Moore and Bertrand Russell and early Ludwig Wittgenstein

Presupposition
A logically perfect language free of the misleading tendencies of ordinary language is the goal of philosophy

Philosophy of language	**Definite descriptions**	A name is really a description of the material object that we are discussing
	Description theory	Sentences express thoughts, or propositions. Just as a sentence has a grammatical form, so the proposition expressed by the sentence has a logical form. Thus, a sentence can be represented logically.
	Semantic pragmatic minimalism	There is a minimal distance between what is said and the linguistic meaning of the utterance. Most hold that implicature is important but not part of what is said.
Epistemology	**Common sense realism**	• Some common sense propositions are known to be true • Some common sense propositions are a matter of common knowledge • Not everything that might be called a common sense belief or proposition is true or accepted • It is more reasonable to accept common sense propositions or beliefs than to accept a philosophical theory that implies that they are false • Skepticism about the external world is to be rejected • Some kind of **foundationalism** is essential to knowledge • **Epistemological particularism**–Particular instances of knowledge can be used as data to assess and develop epistemological theories
Metaphysics	**Metaphysical realism**	Abstract universals as well as concrete particulars exist
	Philosophy of religion	There is no God, so human life is meaningless
Axiology	**Value realism**	Human life has an ethical meaning. Goodness and beauty have intrinsic value. We know of them through intuition.

Chart 66

Logical Positivism

Redundancy theory of truth–A deflationary theory which suggests that the ascription of truth to a proposition is apparent, but not actual. Ascribing truth to a proposition is actually doing nothing.

Philosophers
A. J. Ayer, F. P. Ramsey, Moritz Schlick, Rudolf Carnap, and Otto Neurath

Presuppositions
1. Philosophy is the logical analysis of sentences of the sciences
2. One must study language to understand thought
3. Ordinary language is deceptive so it must be translated into an ideal or artificial language to prevent confusion
4. Something must be empirically verifiable for it to make any sense

Philosophy of language	**The function of language**	Language is used to express emotions about the arts or it is used to represent a scientific theory or proposition
	Humean skepticism	**Hume's fork**–All knowledge is either a necessary truth or an empirical truth. All else is nonsense that must be rejected.
		Hume's argument against causation–You cannot know that everything has a cause because knowledge of causation is only the result of empirical experience
		Hume's argument against induction–Induction is based only upon probability of past occurrences. Events may or may not continue as they have in the past.
Epistemology	**Verification principle**	Knowledge is based on what is empirically verifiable
Metaphysics	**Metaphysical nominalism**	Only concrete particulars exist
	The function of metaphysics	According to Rudolf Carnap, metaphysics should be regarded as an art
	Philosophy of religion	The verification principle renders the concept of God as senseless. Since there is no God, human life has no meaning.
Axiology	**Emotivism**	Facts have nothing to do with value. Ethical sentences have no truth value. The only function of ethical sentences is to express moral emotions. "Good" only expresses approval. Human life is ethically meaningless.

Chart 67

Ordinary Language Analysis

Wittgensteinian approaches to ordinary language analysis lead to postmodernity because of the focus on language and community

Performative theory of truth–A deflationary theory that suggests to say that something is true is only to endorse a proposition

Philosophers
Ludwig Wittgenstein, J. L. Austin, Gilbert Ryle, R. M. Hare, P. F. Strawson, and John Searle

Presuppositions
1. Philosophical problems are due to the misuse of language
2. Philosophers should focus on the subtleties of language use

Philosophy of language	**Use theory of meaning–** The meaning of a word is its ordinary usage	**Language games**–The context or the community determines the meaning of a word or sentence
		Speech act theory–Speech acts express ideas and encourage certain types of behavior
Epistemology		Philosophical theses are not empirical or synthetic, so they must be analytic (necessary and *a priori*)
Metaphysics	**Anti-metaphysical presupposition**	Ordinary language analysis seeks to rescue words from metaphysical usage and attempts to return them to ordinary usage
	Philosophy of mind	Language depends on intention. Intentionality is an important component of philosophy of the mind.
	Philosophy of religion	Ordinary language analysis is poorly suited to the task of philosophy of religion, because it is self-referentially incoherent and it fails to accurately describe ordinary usage of religious sentences. Human life is religiously meaningless.
Axiology	**Prescriptivism**	Ethical sentences are like commands in that they influence the actions of another. They are different from commands because ethical sentences are universizable. We do not know if ethical sentences have truth value or not. Morals are relative. Human life is ethically meaningless.

Chart 68

Post Positivists or Physicalists

Philosophers
W. V. O. Quine, Wilfrid Sellars, D. M. Armstrong, David Lewis, Paul Churchland

Post-positivist analytic philosophy is said to go beyond rationalism and empiricism. This movement began in the 1950s. Many, but not all post-positivists are also physicalists. Two of the most significant works in this movement are W. V. O. Quine's "Two Dogmas of Empiricism" and Wilfrid Sellars's "Empiricism and the Philosophy of the Mind."

Disquotational theory of truth—A deflationary theory which suggests that sentences rather than propositions are the primary bearers of truth

Presuppositions
1. Physical reality is the microscopic or macroscopic referent of the theoretical sentences in the physical sciences
2. Rejection of the views of the logical positivists
3. Rejection of the views of the ordinary language analysts

Philosophy of language	**Underdetermination of translation by data**	The class of all possible data for an empirical theory, in which the notion of meaning plays a central role, radically undermines the claims about meaning that it makes
	Indeterminancy of translation	The indeterminancy caused by an empirical theory, in which the notion of meaning plays a central role, cannot be resolved even if we have access to all of the physical facts
	Meaning	Meaning is not the center of philosophy. Donald Davidson developed a theory of meaning based on formal logic.
Epistemology	**Naturalized epistemology**	By rejecting the analytic/synthetic distinction Quine destroyed the rationalist form of foundationalism, while Sellars destroyed the empiricist form of foundationalism. Consequently, epistemology should be reduced to psychology or cognitive science.
Metaphysics	**Philosophy of mind**	The mind/body dichotomy is rejected because the concept of mind or spirit is rejected. Identity theory or functionalism are preferred ways of thinking about the nature of the mind.
	Philosophy of religion	Physicalism assumes everything that exists is governed by the laws of physics. As such, it is poorly suited for philosophy of religion. Only atheists are comfortable with this position.
Axiology	**Pragmatism**	Quine destroyed the fact/value dichotomy in his article "The Two Dogmas of Empiricism." He argued that all experience is value-laden. Ethics should be reduced to psychology or cognitive science.

Chart 69

Linguistic Essentialism

<table>
<tr><td colspan="3">Philosophers
Saul Kripke, Ruth Marcus, Alvin Plantinga, Robert Adams, David Owen Brink</td></tr>
<tr><td colspan="3">Correspondence theory of truth–Truth corresponds to reality</td></tr>
<tr><td colspan="3">Presuppositions
1. Intentional and modal logics constitute the formal basis for linguistic essentialism
2. A precise formulation of the distinction between logically necessary attributes, nontrivial essences, and trivial essences is crucial to linguistic essentialism</td></tr>
<tr><td>Philosophy of language</td><td>Rigid designator theory</td><td>Many locutions are rigid designators. These rigid designators can be used for modal logic and possible world semantics.</td></tr>
<tr><td>Epistemology</td><td>Naturalized epistemology</td><td>Knowledge results from natural processes</td></tr>
<tr><td rowspan="5">Metaphysics</td><td>Philosophy of mind</td><td>Allows for the existence of both the mind and the body</td></tr>
<tr><td rowspan="3">Ontology</td><td>Essential properties–A property is weakly essential just in case it is necessary to some object but not necessary to all objects. A property is strongly essential just in case it is necessary to some object but is contingently possessed by some other object.</td></tr>
<tr><td>Trivial and nontrivial essences–An Aristotelian essence is an example of a nontrivial essence. A trivial essence is one that is self-identical.</td></tr>
<tr><td>Platonic realism–Both abstract universals and concrete particulars exist. These concepts exist in different worlds.</td></tr>
<tr><td>Philosophy of religion</td><td>Human life has religious meaning</td></tr>
<tr><td>Axiology</td><td>Value realism</td><td>Human life has ethical meaning</td></tr>
</table>

Chart 70

American Pragmatism

American pragmatism is a mixture of empiricism and idealism. It holds that a theory is to be accounted true as long as it works. Pragmatists believe that all experience is value-laden. Much of American analytic philosophy was influenced by pragmatism. American analytic philosophers who subscribed to pragmatism include such figures as W. V. O. Quine, Hilary Putnam, and Richard Rorty. Some types of pragmatism (like Rorty's) lead to postmodernity.

Charles Sanders Pierce (1839–1914)	Founded American pragmatism. The purpose of pragmatism is to make ideas clear. He coined the term "pragmaticism" to differentiate his views from William James. He subscribed to metaphysical realism and rejected Cartesian certainty and methodological doubt.
	Three kinds of truth: **Transcendental truth**–The real character of a thing. What science attempts to ascertain. **Complex truth**–The truth of propositions **Logical truth**–The conformity of a proposition to reality. Experience can refute or affirm this kind of truth. Every proposition is either true or false.
	Pragmatic theory of meaning–The meaning of an idea is the sum of its practical consequences
William James (1842–1910)	James was influenced by Pierce. He viewed pragmatism as radical empiricism. Pragmatism is only a method to settle metaphysical disputes. He used pragmatism as a type of therapy.
	Pragmatic theory of truth–Truth in our ideas means their ability to work. Truth is the "cash value" of an idea.
	Pragmatic theory of meaning–The practical outcome of a belief is its true meaning
John Dewey (1859–1952)	Described his position as **empirical naturalism** or **naturalistic empiricism**
	Pragmatic instrumentalism–Knowledge is only for solving problems. This does not deny the objectivity of truth because it is not made relative to any individual.

Chart 71

The Linguistic Turn

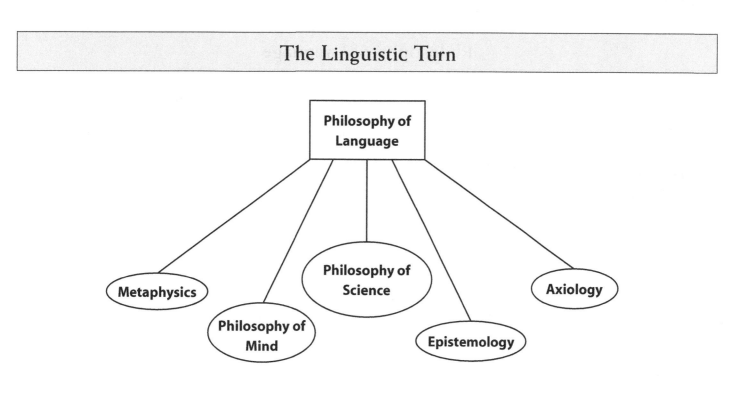

Philosophy of Language

The analytic philosophy movement is based around the development of philosophy of language. The "linguistic turn" is about the movement from epistemology to philosophy of language as first philosophy. Thus philosophy of language is the lens or the key to understanding philosophy.

The **Logical Realists (LR)** thought that language is essential to doing good philosophy. **The Logical Positivists (LP)** emphasized the importance of the verification principle. In other words, if something is not empirically verifiable then it is meaningless. The **Ordinary Language Analysts (OLA)** argued that there are no metaphysical problems. There are instead only language problems. The **Post-Positivist Physicalists (PPP)** disagree with the **OLA**. The **Linguistic Essentialists (LE)** agree with the **PPP** that metaphysics is a legitimate field of study.

Because intentionality is seen as a central feature of meaning, and intentionality is a feature of the mind, philosophy of language is merging with philosophy of the mind.

Chart 72

Philosophy of Language

The nature of language	**Grammar**	Concerned with the forms and structures of words. This includes the arrangement of words in sentences and phrases.
	Symbolic systems	Examines the range of things that can be communicated through symbols of various sorts
	Analyticity	Concerned with the priority of language to the mind (or vice versa)
	Theories of meaning	Concerned with what meaning is and what it is related to
Language and the mind	**Innate ideas**	Concerned with whether or not innate ideas provide a foundation of language and communication
	Private language	Concerned with the existence of language internal to the individual
	Intentionality	Explores the relationship between communication and intention of the communicator
Language and metaphysics	**The world**	Concerned with how language represents the world and our thoughts about the world
	Truth	What is the relationship between language and truth?
Semiotics	**Semantics**	The branch of linguistics concerned with the nature, structure, and development of the meanings of signs and symbols. Focuses on epistemology, as well as semantic theories and mental states.
	Pragmatics	The study of language which focuses attention on the users and the context of language use rather than on reference, truth, or grammar
	Hermeneutics	The art and science of interpretation
	Syntax	Concerned with the arrangement of words as elements in a sentence to show their relationship to one another

Chart 73

Reference and Referring

Meaning–The central question in philosophy of language. Meaning can be about linguistic expressions. Meaning can also be about the nature of linguistic meaning.		
Understanding–The grasping of what has been communicated or done		
Referential theory of linguistic meaning–Linguistic expressions have meaning because they represent some thing. Sentences mirror the states of affairs they describe.		
Definite descriptions	**Gottlob Frege, Bertrand Russell, early Wittgenstein**	A name is equivalent to the description of the referent. Sentences can be logically represented.
Description theory	**Bertrand Russell**	Sentences containing definite descriptions can be analyzed as triples of general statements
Direct reference theory	**John Stuart Mill, Ruth Marcus**	Flaccid designators are terms that represent different things in different worlds. Rigid designators are terms that do not change their referents in different worlds. Proper names are rigid designators.
Causal-historical theory	**Saul Kripke, Hilary Putnam**	An alternative to description theories

Chart 74

Theories of Meaning

Use theories	Ludwig Wittgenstein	**Language games**–Wittgenstein argues that the context or the community determines the meaning of a word or a sentence. Meaning is determined by how we use words or sentences.
	J. L. Austin, John Searle	**Speech act theory**–All communication is a social act that is either constitutive or regulatory. Constitutive speech acts must be obeyed for the act to be accomplished. Regulative speech acts encourage certain behaviors in the reader.
Psychological theories	**H. P. Grice**	A minimalist approach, based upon the speaker's intentions. Grice's system has two stages. In the first stage Grice reduces sentence meaning to speaker-meaning or semantics. In the second stage Grice reduces speaker-meaning to a complex of psychological states related to intentionality.
Verificationism	**A. J. Ayer**	A sentence only has meaning if it is empirically verifiable
Truth-conditional theories	**Donald Davidson**	Davidson suggests that a sentence's verification condition should be replaced with a sentence's truth condition. The truth condition consists of the requirements for the state of affairs expressed by that sentence to be true.
	Possible worlds	**Saul Kripke**–Definite descriptions do not explain proper names. An utterance is true if it agrees with the truth conditions of the actual world. A sentence's truth condition can be taken to be the set of possible worlds in which the sentence is true.
		Hilary Putnam–Meaning comes from the world in which we live. An utterance is true if it agrees with the truth conditions of the actual world.
	Intentional semantics	The speaker's intentions need to reflect the referent

Chart 75

Pragmatics

Semantic pragmatics Concerned with linguistic meaning or what is implicated	**Minimalists** Bertrand Russell, Gottlob Frege, Ludwig Wittgenstein, H. P. Grice	There is a minimal distance between what is said and the linguistic meaning of the utterance. Most hold that implicature is important but not part of what is said.
	Contextualists Wittgenstein, P. F. Strawson, J. L. Austin, John Searle	What is said is usually what is implicated by the utterance
Speech act theory Speech can be viewed as a social action that can be exemplified in a number of ways	J. L. Austin, John Searle Proponents assert that the basic unit of meaning is the speech act	**Locutions**–A locutionary act is one that expresses some proposition
		Illocutions–Every utterance has illocutionary force. An illocutionary act aims at the hearer's understanding. Illocutions have a communicative type of force that locutions do not.
		Perlocutions–Many utterances have perlocutionary force. Perlocutionary acts aim at achieving something other than understanding. A perlocutionary act generally implies that the hearer should take some form of action.
Implicature What is implied by the speaker's utterance	**H.P Grice** **Conversational implicature** asserts that hearers draw implications by making assumptions based on utterances from the speaker.	**Cooperative principle** is the primary norm involved in conversation. "Make your conversation such as is required, at the stage at which it occurs, by the accepted purpose or direction of the talk-exchange in which you are engaged."
		Conversational maxims–Corollaries that are summarized by the **cooperative principle**
	Relevance theory	Implications are the product of all-purpose cognitive processing that aims at efficiency of information transfer
	Conventional implicature	Implication results from the use of a special word

Chart 76

Speech Act Theory

Those holding this position include J. L. Austin and John Searle. They assert that the basic unit of meaning is the speech act.

Performative utterances	**Locution**	A locutionary act is one that expresses some proposition
	Illocution	Every utterance has illocutionary force. An illocutionary act aims at the hearer's understanding. Illocutions have a communicative type of force that locutions do not.
	Perlocution	Many utterances have perlocutionary force. Perlocutionary acts aim at achieving something other than understanding. A perlocutionary act generally implies that the hearer should take some form of action.
Rules	**Constitutive**	Violation results in the abortion of the speech act
	Regulative	Violation renders a speech act defective or infelicitous
	Borderline violations	**Example:** To give an apology in a jeering tone of voice
Truth value	**J. L. Austin**	Truth value is not very important. There are many ways in which utterances can go wrong without being false. Falsity is just another form of infelicity.
Meaning	**J. L. Austin**	Illocutionary force is a kind of meaning
Cohen's problem	**Jonathan Cohen 1964**	Cohen showed the problems of attempting to provide meaning without being concerned about truth

Chart 77

Implicature

H. P. Grice brought the **Ordinary Language Philosophy (OLP)** movement to an end in 1967 with his presentation at Harvard University **"Logic and Conversation."** According to Scott Soames (*Philosophical Analysis in the 20th Century*, vol. 2), by the time that Grice gave his lectures the ideas of **OLP** had run their course.

1. Grice critiqued the **OLP** movement by showing that there is more to philosophical problems than language problems (misusing ordinary expressions)

2. Grice also argued that **OLP** was in need of a systematic theory of meaning rather than the idea that meaning is use. A systematic theory of meaning would show that language use involves a system of conventionally encoded meanings and a system of rules that result in an efficient and rational exchange of information **(the cooperative principle)**. The result is **conversational implicature**, which is the proposition that the speaker asserts in the proper context. **Conventional implicature** is only a part of the information conveyed by an utterance of the sentence which does not require the cooperative principle.

3. Finally Grice attempted to resolve these issues by reducing linguistic meaning to psychology. He argued that sentence meaning is not always the same thing as the speaker's meaning **(the reduction project)**.

The cooperative principle	**Maxims of quantity**	1. Conversation contributions should be as informative as required 2. Conversation contributions should not be more informative than is required
	Maxims of quality	1. Speakers are obligated to speak as truthfully as is possible 2. Speakers should not say anything without adequate evidence
	Maxim of relevance	Conversational contributions should be relevant to the purpose of the conversation
	Maxims of manner	Speakers should: 1. Avoid obscure expressions 2. Avoid ambiguities 3. Be brief 4. Be orderly
The reduction project	**1st Stage**	Grice reduces sentence meaning to speaker meaning. A sentence's meaning is a function of individual speaker meanings.
	2nd Stage	Speaker meaning is explicated in terms of mental states
Conclusions	1. Speech act theory does even less than punctuation to explain intentionality 2. While speech acts exist, speech act theory is neither necessary nor sufficient to explain meaning 3. These philosophers moved from philosophy of language to philosophy of mind 4. **OLP** died as a movement	

Chart 78

Donald Davidson's Truth Theory of Meaning

Donald Davidson was a member of the **Post-Positivist Physicalists (PPP)** group of philosophers. He employed Tarski's theory of truth for a theory of meaning. Davidson believed that if it is possible for us to interpret the speech of another group then we have agreement with them.

Truth	**Tarski's or semantic theory of truth**	This type of theory of truth can be used for a natural language as a theory of meaning. Assertions can be verified by comparing the truth conditions of a sentence with what the speaker asserts to be true.
Extensional semantics	**Extension**	Truth value
	Semantic value	The truth value of a sentence; it may also include the propositional content or thought expressed by the sentence
	Compositionality principle	The semantic value of a sentence is a function of the semantic values of its constituents
	Substitutionality principle	In an extensional language, one co-referential expression can be substituted for another
	Extensional language	The substitution of an expression with the same extension doesn't change the extension of the whole
	Extensional context	A sentential context in which the substitution of co-extensional expressions may be performed
Intentional semantics	**Intention**	An expression's aspect of meaning which determines extension. It is an important concept for use with possible worlds. An expression's intention is the rule or function assigning its extension at each world.
	Intentional context	A sentence whose truth value would be changed if the expressions within it are substituted with expressions of the same extension
	Intentionality	The characteristic of mental states which consists in their being about something. This something may be an object or a state of affairs.
Conclusions (according to Scott Soames in *Philosophical Analysis in the 20th Century*)	1. Theories of truth are insufficient for theories of meaning 2. Interpretation of the speech of another group does not guarantee as much agreement between us and them as Davidson believed 3. We can make sense of big differences between ourselves and speakers of another culture 4. We have no reason to believe that there couldn't be speakers whose conceptual schemes are so different that we couldn't translate their speech	

Chart 79

Direct Reference Theory

Saul Kripke is a **Linguistic Essentialist** who wrote *Naming and Necessity.* In this work he argues that we should use possible worlds and essences to deal with the meaning of names. Rather than employ a semantic theory of truth, a disquotational theory of truth can be applied to meaning.

	Proposition	The thing expressed by a sentence. It is a bearer of truth and the object of belief.
Names	**Description theory of proper names**	**1.** Proper names have the same meanings as the descriptions associated with them
		2. Names are not synonymous with descriptions, but the referent of a proper name satisfies the descriptions that a speaker associates with it
	Meaning of names	While the meaning of a name can change over time, names are rigid
Rigid designators Two names have the same intention if they have the same reference in all possible worlds	**Modality**	Considers the effect of possible worlds
	Essentialism	The essence of a thing and its properties that would exist in every possible world
	Natural kinds	A kind of theoretical universal which requires a stronger metaphysical essentialism than an identity statement
	Necessary *a posteriori*	True identity statements (such as "I am Craig Mitchell") are examples of this type of knowledge. These type of statements involve a type of trivial essentialism.
	Accessibility relation	Possible worlds can be linked together in ways that allow for semantic rules of necessity and possibility
	Possible worlds	Rigid designators refer to the same entity across all possible worlds
	Transworld identification	A thing will have the same essence in every possible world. This essence allows that thing to be identified in every possible world.
	Types of rigid designators	**Persistent designators**–An expression which designates the same thing with respect to every possible world in which that thing exists
		Obstinate designators–An expression which designates the same thing with respect to every possible world
		Strongly rigid designator–A rigid designator of a necessary existent

Chart 80

Metaphorical Meaning

Key Questions about Metaphors:
1. What is metaphorical meaning?
2. How do hearers understand metaphorical meaning?

Donald Davidson	**Causal theory**	Metaphors mean what the words in their most literal interpretation mean, and nothing more.
		Objections: 1. If causal theory is correct, then one cannot misinterpret a metaphor 2. Metaphorical truth value is problematic 3. Because metaphorical utterances can have only literal meaning, consequently nothing can be used as a bearer of truth value
Aristotle and others	**Naïve simile theory**	Metaphors resemble similes in that both express comparisons. Some suggest that a metaphor is an abbreviated simile. Sentences have metaphorical meaning in addition to literal meanings.
		Objections: 1. It provides a shallow explanation for how metaphors relate to similes 2. This theory does not explain how metaphorical significance is communicated 3. Those aspects of similes that are similar to metaphors are often metaphorical
R. Fogelin	**Figurative simile theory**	A metaphor is just an abbreviated figurative simile
		Objections: 1. Some sentences can be either literal or metaphorical 2. Some metaphors are accepted as true long after the corresponding simile has proven false
John Searle	**Pragmatic theory**	Metaphor is a kind of indirect communication that involves a three-step interpretation: 1. Determine whether or not a nonliteral interpretation is needed 2. If metaphorical interpretation is needed, then the hearer must employ some system to generate a range of possible meanings 3. Another set of principles are employed to determine which system will most likely provide the right meaning
		Objections: Metaphors must be distinguished from other forms of indirect communication

Chart 81

Philosophy of Science

General assumptions about science	**Science involves:**	1. Collection of data 2. Formulation of hypothesis 3. Testing of the hypothesis 4. Refining of hypothesis, or 5. Elimination of the old hypothesis and reformulation of a new hypothesis
	Science assumes:	1. Regularity in nature 2. The results of tests are repeatable 3. Those who test and review tests will be objective and fair in their evaluations
	Nature of science	Science is an empirical inductive method for obtaining knowledge about the world
	Logic of science	**Abduction**–Inference to the best explanation. An approach developed by Charles Sanders Pierce to explain a set of data.
	Naturalism	Assumes that everything that happens can be explained by natural phenomena. One can be a naturalist without being a **physicalist**.
	Physicalism	Only that which is physical exists. There is no spiritual or mental.
Limits of science	**What science can and cannot do**	Science cannot claim to arrive at ultimate truth
		Science can provide confidence about a theory, but it cannot provide certainty
		Science requires testing
Scientific realism	**Metaphysics**	Scientific theories accurately model reality
	Epistemology	One can know that a scientific theory is true
	Axiology	Some argue that value has no place in science
		Others argue that science is value-laden like all of reality
Scientific anti-realism	**Metaphysics**	Scientific theories cannot and do not model reality
	Epistemology	One cannot know if a scientific theory is true
	Axiology	Some argue that science is as subjective as value

Chart 82

Scientific Method

Some question the existence of a scientific method. If there is a scientific method, then science is a discipline. If there is not a scientific method, then science is a sham.

Scientific realism Scientific theories accurately model reality	**Assertion:** There is a scientific method based upon falsification and reason	**Falsification**–Karl Popper argued that if science is an empirical-inductive activity, then scientific theories cannot be proven true; they can only be proven false through testing. When proven false, a theory must be discarded. With increased testing comes increased confidence in the truth of a theory. Scientific realists believe that there is a scientific method. Such as: **Hypothesis**–An unproved theory, proposition, or supposition **Theory**–A hypothesis that has passed every objective test, thus yielding greater certainty that it is true **Law**–A theory that passes every conceivable test, thus yielding the highest level of certainty that can be achieved
	Assertion: A scientific method is not needed for science to work	Some scientific realists argue that beauty is sufficient to prove the truth of a scientific theory. Hence, falsification is not necessary.
	Assertion: Scientific method does not need testing	**Bayes theory** is used to confirm a scientific theory based upon probability. It suggests that severe testing is a necessary but not a sufficient condition for achieving scientific knowledge.
Scientific anti-realism Scientific theories cannot and do not model reality	**Assertion**	There is not a scientific method because testing is not applied to all scientific ideas
	Proof: There are many examples that science does not follow any method	**Evolution**–Evolution cannot be tested or falsified. Consequently it should not be treated as a theory, but only as a hypothesis.
		Other minds–We cannot prove that other minds exist, but other minds are considered as a matter of fact
		Psychotherapy–There are at least 400 different approaches to psychotherapy
		Superstring theory–There is no way to test this theory but many assume that it is true
		Quantum theory–Science cannot explain the behavior of subatomic particles

Chart 83

Scientific Realism

The metaphysics of science	**Semantic realism**	Suggests that statements about theoretical entities are to be understood literally
	Reductionism	Suggests that theoretical entities are constructions out of more familiar materials
The epistemology of science	**Types of realism**	1. The best scientific theories are true 2. The best scientific theories are close to the truth 3. We are rationally justified to believe that the best scientific theories are true or close to the truth 4. **Minimal epistemic realism** asserts that it is logically possible to attain a state that warrants belief in a theory
The value theory of science	**Beauty**	A good scientific theory is beautiful
	Scientific virtues	A good theory must have scientific virtues in order to point to the truth. These include: simplicity, balance.
Scientific method	**Scientific realism requires scientific method**	**Falsification**–Karl Popper argued that if science is an empirical-inductive activity, then scientific theories cannot be proven true; they can only be proven false through testing. When proven false, a theory must be discarded. With increased testing comes increased confidence in the truth of a theory. Scientific realists believe that there is a scientific method. Such as: **Hypothesis**–An unproved theory, proposition, or supposition **Theory**–A hypothesis that has passed every objective test, thus yielding greater certainty that it is true **Law**–A theory that passes every conceivable test, thus yielding the highest level of certainty that can be achieved
	Scientific realism does not require a scientific method	Some scientific realists argue that beauty is sufficient to prove the truth of a scientific theory. Hence, falsification via testing is not necessary.
Argument for realism	**Success of science**	Applied science demonstrates the realism of scientific theories

Chart 84

Scientific Realist Philosophers

Philosopher	Book	Argument
Francis Bacon	*Advancement of Learning*	Scientific knowledge results from continuously experimenting. Observation and experimentation is the key to knowledge of the natural world.
Karl Popper asserts the growth of knowledge in science as a basic premise. The aim of science is finding true universal theories about nature. Science also seeks to eliminate false theories. Consequently, the best theory is the most testable.	*Conjectures and Refutations* and *The Logic of Scientific Discovery*	**The nature of science**–Science is empirical and thus requires testing for falsification. Science should require deduction rather than induction, because deduction results in certainty. Induction, which is tied to probability, can only yield uncertainty.
		Requirements for a good theory: 1. It is easy to find confirmation of its validity 2. Confirmation should only be considered if it results from a risky prediction 3. The more a theory forbids, the better it is 4. A theory that is not possibly refutable is a poor theory 5. Genuine tests of theories are attempts to refute them 6. The only good evidence is negative evidence
		Falsification–Karl Popper argued that if science is an empirical-inductive activity, then scientific theories cannot be proven true; they can only be proven false through testing. When proven false, a theory must be discarded. With increased testing comes increased confidence in the truth of a theory.
Paul Feyerabend	*Problems of Empiricism*	**Incommensurability**–A theory is incommensurable with the cosmos if it (the theory) suspends some of its (the cosmos's) universal principles
		The interpretation of a scientific theory depends upon nothing but the state of affairs it describes
		Theoretical pluralism–Science progresses through allowing a plurality of incompatible theories which contribute to progress by competition. Realism is desirable because it demands competing theories.
		The principle of testability–A good theory must at least be empirically adequate
Imre Lakatos	*The Methodology of Scientific Research Programs*	**A research program** has a central theory augmented by a set of auxiliary hypotheses that allow the data to be explained by the theory
		The history of science is explained not by successive paradigm shifts, but by competing research programs
		A good research program 1. Each new version of a theory preserves the unrefuted content of its predecessor 2. Each new version of a theory can predict some unexpected facts 3. These unexpected facts are verified through experimentation

Chart 85

Scientific Anti-Realism

Metaphysics of science	**Instrumentalism**	Suggests that scientific theories are only useful, but do not accurately model reality
Epistemology of science	**Constructive empiricism**	Suggests that science does not aim at truth. Instead, science only aims at empirical adequacy. In other words, it provides information that meets the scientist's purposes.
Value theory of science	**Pragmatism**	Science is not objective. Science is all about the subjective values of the scientific community.
Scientific method	There is not a scientific method because testing is not applied to all scientific ideas	There are a number of examples for which science does not follow any method. For example: evolution, psychotherapy, superstring theory, chaos theory, complexity theory, and others.
Other arguments for anti-realism	**Theory of underdetermination**	Theory underdetermines data. In other words, for any given set of data, there are an infinite number of theories that can account for it.
	Thomas Kuhn *The Structure of Scientifc Revolutions*	Argues that scientists are not objective or fair. They operate out of self-interest by preserving the status quo. Younger scientists challenge the status quo through experimentation and demonstrate that the current paradigm is wrong. This results in a paradigm shift.
	Natural ontological attitude	Well-confirmed scientific theories should be accepted as true. However, scientific realists make the mistake of adding metaphysical assumptions about the nature of truth.

Chart 86

Scientific Anti-Realist Philosophers

Philosopher	Book	Argument
George Berkeley	*A Treatise Concerning the Principles of Human Knowledge*	Causation is apparent but not actual. God is really behind all causation.
David Hume	*A Treatise on Human Nature*	**Hume's argument against induction:** Science is an empirical-inductive activity. Induction is based upon probability or past occurrences. One cannot assume that just because things have always worked out in a certain way in the past that they will continue to do so in the future.
		Hume's argument against causation: 1. You can know that one thing follows another, but you cannot know that one thing causes another 2. Knowledge of causes and effects is the result of sensory experience and not reason 3. Thus, we cannot know that everything has a cause
Thomas Kuhn	*The Structure of Scientific Revolutions*	Kuhn argues that scientists are not objective or fair. They operate out of self-interest by preserving the status quo. Younger scientists challenge the status quo through experimentation and demonstrate that the current paradigm is wrong. This results in a paradigm shift.
The later Paul Feyerabend	*Against Method*	Aesthetics and social factors play a more important part in the history of science than either rationalists or empiricists would like to admit
		There are no rules that cannot be done without in science, hence, there is no scientific method
Bas van Fraassen	*The Scientific Image*	**Constructive empiricism**–Suggests that science does not aim at truth. Instead, science only aims at empirical adequacy. In other words, it provides information that meets the scientist's purposes.
	Laws and Symmetry	There is no difference between laws and theories. Scientific method in general is of a questionable nature.

Chart 87

Philosophy of the Mind

Philosophy of the mind is really a sub-discipline of metaphysics. It is a domain that is explored by both philosophers and scientists. In the 21st century it has replaced philosophy of language as first philosophy. This came about when philosophers of language began to get stuck on a number of issues that can only be resolved in the philosophy of the mind.

Primary issues	1. What is the nature of the mind? 2. How does the mind relate to the brain and the rest of the body? 3. What are mental states? 4. How much can science tell us about the mind?
Cartesian dualism	Philosophy of the mind had its beginnings with René Descartes. He divided everything into either mind or body (spiritual or material). He argued that the mind and the body were united through the pineal gland. Cartesian dualism can take a number of different forms.
Materialism	This approach to philosophy of the mind assumes that the body or matter is all that exists. Proponents assume that the mind is nothing more than the brain. There are a number of forms of materialism.
Functionalism	Functionalists allow for the possibility of immaterial substances, but are still committed to materialism. This is the dominant view in cognitive science and psychology.
Eliminativism	The view that there are no intentional states, such as: reasons for action, beliefs, desires, or intentions

Personal identity	**Personal identity and time** Does the self change with time, or does one become another person?
	The self Concerned with the nature of the self
	Agency Concerned with the will and how decisions are made
Cognitive science	**Cognition** What is consciousness? How does it work?
	Emotion Concerned with the nature of the emotions and how they relate to cognition
	Action Concerned with individual acts and how they relate to cognition

Chart 88

Issues in Philosophy of the Mind

The mind/body problem	How does the mind interact with the body?	What is the mind? How does it relate to the brain?
Other minds	Do other minds exist?	You cannot prove that other minds exist
	Do animals have minds?	Once you define "mind," what other sorts of things have them? Do animals have minds?
	How do we explain social behavior?	Is there a human nature? How does one mind relate to another?
The external world	Perception	Is perception an accurate reflection of the real world?
	Knowledge	Is knowledge possible about an objective, external world? How much can one know about the external world? How certain can one be about the external world?
Consciousness	The nature of consciousness	What is consciousness? What are its attributes? What has consciousness?
	Sleep	What is sleep? How does it relate to consciousness?
Intentionality		How can our thoughts or beliefs be about something?
The self and personal identity	The nature of the self	What is the self?
	Personal identity	How does personal identity persist through time?
		Does personal identity persist after death?

Chart 89

Cartesian Dualism

René Descartes divided up the world between minds and material bodies.
Minds are: Thinking substances which are nonspatial, mental, and private
Material bodies are: Extended substances which are spatial, have material properties, and are public

Descartes believed that minds (or mental substances) can exist even after the demise of the body. He also believed that the mind and body interact and are united through the pineal gland. In the modern period many philosophers attempted to explain how the mind and body interact.

Nicolas Malebranche	**Occasionalism**	The mind and body do not interact. Mental and physical states are coordinated by God.
Bishop George Berkeley	**Idealism**	Only the mind exists. All that exists are our minds and the mind of God. The world is apparent, and not actual.
Baruch Spinoza	**Panentheism**	There is only one substance, the divine substance
G. W. Leibniz	**Parallelism**	The mind and body do not interact
Contemporary ideas	**Epiphenomenalism**	The mind is a by-product of the body. The mind has no powers of causation over the body.
	Property dualism	Only material substances exist, but there are two types of properties: spiritual and material
Arguments against dualism	If the mind is immaterial, where is it located?	
	Mental causation–How does an immaterial object like the mind interact with a material object like the body?	

Chart 90

Materialism

This approach to philosophy of the mind assumes that the body or matter is all that exists. Proponents assume that the mind is nothing more than the brain. There are a number of forms of materialism.

Behaviorism	**Philosophical**	This position assumes that Cartesian dualism is wrong because mental states are really to be understood in terms of behavior		
	Psychological	An empirical approach to the study of the mind. It is the science of human behavior. Human behavior can be studied, but the mind cannot. It assumes that Cartesian dualism is scientifically irrelevant.		
	Radical	The position held by B. F. Skinner. It rejects the idea of psychological behaviorism.		
Identity theory or physicalism	**Identity thesis**	Mental states are identical to brain states		
	Type identity theory	Every type of mental state is identical to some type of physical state		
	Token identity theory Not every mental state must be exemplified by a specific type of brain state	**Anomalous monism**–A position held by Donald Davidson		
		Functionalism– Allows for the possibility of immaterial substances, but is still committed to materialism. This is the dominant view in cognitive science and psychology.	**Black box**–The brain should be treated like a black box that responds to stimuli. The operation of the mind is not important to philosophers. The study of brain states should be left to psychologists and neurologists.	
			Computer–Assumes that the brain is a digital computer and that the mind is nothing more than a set of programs employed by the brain. The result is that mental states are nothing more than computational states of the brain. Some would argue that a computer with good artificial intelligence has a "mind."	
Eliminativism	A kind of reductionism that claims there are no intentional states, such as: reasons for action, beliefs, desires, or intentions. The belief in such things amounts to "folk psychology."			
Arguments against materialism	**Intentionality**–Materialism cannot explain intentionality			
	Consciousness–How can a material brain bring about consciousness?			
	Qualia–How can a material brain explain experiences like color, etc.?			

Chart 91

PART 3
CONTINENTAL PHILOSOPHY

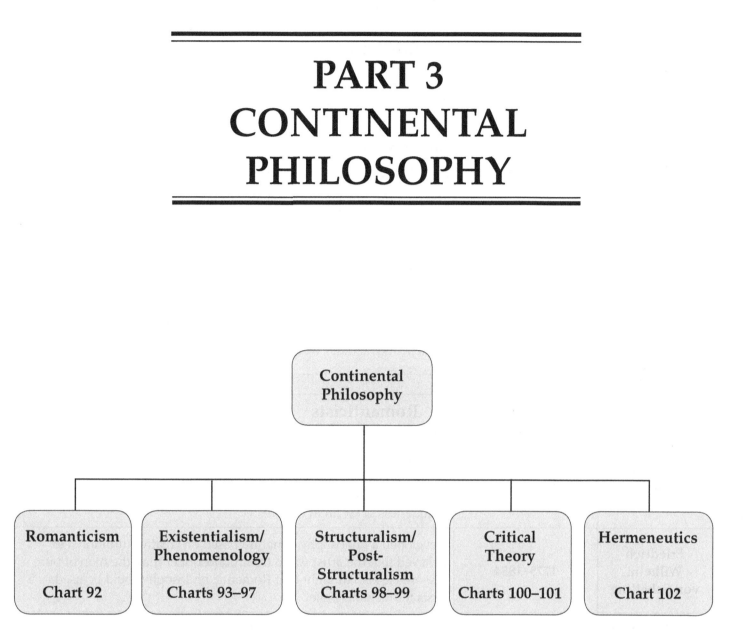

Continental philosophy attempts to understand the meaning of life, and how we ought to live. In some ways it attempts to solve problems that can only resolved by following after Jesus Christ and searching the Bible. As such, continental philosophy is a poor alternative to special revelation. Continental philosophy also seeks to deal with social/political concerns.

Existentialism is an idea that had its beginning in the works of Søren Kirkegaard and Friedrich Nietzsche.

Phenomenology is a non-empirical approach to psychology and epistemology that had its beginnings with Edmund Husserl. It is often combined with **existentialism**. **Feminist philosophy** is a variation of these ideas.

Structuralism/Post-Structuralism–Begun by Ferdinand Saussure, this is a linguistic approach to meaning that argues that power is found in the community.

Critical theory–This movement is based on the ideas of Marxism. It is also known as the Frankfurt School.

Hermeneutics–The art and science of interpretation, often equated with understanding.

Romanticism/Romanticists

Romanticism

Developed in Germany in reaction to the failure of the Enlightenment. It was a movement started by artists, musicians, and poets who emphasized a more holistic approach to knowledge. The romantics believed that nature reflects the forces used by the God of creation. They also believed that nature reveals the meaning of existence.

Sources of knowledge	Reason	Not a very significant source of knowledge
	Intuition	Knowledge results from means that we do not understand
	Feeling	The passions are a guide to what is true
Selfhood (results from a subjective process)	Subject (me)	Represents the inner life of the individual. The subject is involved in the creation of the phenomenal realm which appears to be objective. Because of the **subject's** involvement in the creation of this world it is actually a subjective world. The **subject** is involved with nature and the **objects** in it as a result of his sensory experience.
	Object (everything not me)	Represents the outer world of things

Romanticists

All Romanticist philosophers subscribed to idealism in one form or another

Johann Gottlieb Fichte	1762–1814	He combined Kant with Romantic thought. In his *Science of Knowledge* he employed Romanticism to support his German nationalism (metaphysical nationalism). He emphasized the uniqueness of German culture.
Friedrich Wilhelm von Schelling	1775–1854	Developed a philosophy of nature based on creative intuition. He believed that the artist was a truer philosopher than the man of pure reason. He also thought that Romantic philosophy could be used as a basis for religious belief.
Friedrich von Schlegel	1772-1829	Classified "progressive universal poetry" and all forms of post-Enlightenment artistic expression as "romantisch"
G. W. F. Hegel	1770–1831	History is moving to a state of freedom for mankind. The organic process by which this happens is the (Hegelian) dialectic. Reason is the way that the Absolute (knowledge) can be comprehended. Mind is the only reality.

Chart 92

Existentialism

(Existence Precedes Essence)		
Definition	Existentialism is not a system because it is not based on an ontology that includes any type of essence; instead, it does philosophy from the phenomenological perspective, that is, from the point of view of the individual. It is rather a set of ideas that result from a modern emphasis on the individual. Existentialism teaches that existence precedes essence, meaning that it denies that objective truth has the priority in philosophical thought.	
Themes	**Free will**	The rejection of determinism and fate
	Choice	Each individual is free to choose for himself how he should live. Each individual should choose for himself what is true/false or right/wrong.
	Authenticity	The individual should be true to himself. He should decide in accordance with his personality.
	Absurdity of life	Life is meaningless. As such, one is free to do whatever he decides.
	Anxiety or angst	The sense of complete responsibility which belongs to the person who must choose for himself
	Responsibility	The individual must take responsibility for his life and his situation. To reject responsibility is to act in "bad faith."
Truth	**Subjectivity**	Something is not "true" until you appropriate it for yourself. Truth is dependent upon experience.
Morality	**Subjectivity**	Existentialist ethics are deontological and non-consequentialist. The rule of existentialist ethics is "be true to yourself." In other words, do not let others constrain your actions.
Types of existentialism	**Christian**	Existentialism began with Søren Kierkegaard. He attempted to move the church toward an experiential faith. He was followed by neo-orthodox theologians such as Karl Barth, Rudolf Bultmann, and Emil Brunner.
	Atheistic	**German existentialists.** Friedrich Nietzsche began this approach to existentialism, followed by Martin Heidegger, who combined existentialism with phenomenology.
		French existentialists followed Martin Heidegger. They include Maurice Merleau-Ponty, Jean Paul Sartre, Albert Camus, and Simone de Beauvoir.

Chart 93

Continental Philosophers

Ludwig Feuerbach	**1804–1872**	Feuerbach believed that "Man is the true God and Savior of Man." He also rejected the Christian belief in immortality. Feuerbach also attacked the hypocrisy of the clergy. Feuerbach rejected Hegel's abstract idealism. He also interpreted Hegel's thought as a type of pantheism.
The Young Hegelians		These are followers of Feuerbach, who include: David Friedrich Strauss, Bruno and Edgar Bauer, August von Cieszkowski, Moses Hess, Karl Marx, Friedrich Engels, Max Stirner, Arnold Ruge, and Karl Schmidt. Most of these men had studied to become biblical theologians. While they had disagreements over the details, the Young Hegelians believed that Hegelian theory should be used to establish a new world order.
Søren Kierkegaard	**1813–1855**	Kierkegaard developed his philosophy in reaction to Hegel's. He believed that Hegel was so concerned with the community that he left no room for the individual. As the father of existentialism, Kierkegaard emphasized a subjective view of truth and faith. He also focused on themes of authenticity and angst. Kierkegaard believed in making decisions without reference to the past, the future, or the community.
Karl Marx	**1818–1883**	Marx was a disciple of Feuerbach. Marx applied Hegelianism to political-economic theory. An atheistic materialist, Marx believed in a teleological view of history in which the working class would overthrow the ruling class.
Arthur Schopenhauer	**1788–1860**	An atheistic idealist with a Kantian epistemology. At the same time, Schopenhauer rejected Kant's ethics. He believed that the world of appearances is a facade that hides the "will." The will is a destructive force that always desires more. Central to his philosophy is the existing individual.
Friedrich Nietzsche	**1844–1900**	Nietzsche was influenced by reading Schopenhauer. He was an atheist who argued that there is no objective truth or morality. He explained the concept of the "will to power," the idea that people attempt to force their will and values upon others. The Superman is unrestricted in his use of the "will to power."

Chart 94

Edmund Husserl's Phenomenology

An **idealistic** and **Romantic** approach to epistemology developed by Edmund Husserl, it attempts to relate acts of consciousness with their objects. It differs from empirical psychology because it is a philosophy that deals with the essence of consciousness.

Acts of consciousness	Objects of consciousness
Analyzing, judging, imagining, remembering, and willing	They need not actually exist in reality, but only in the consciousness

Phenomenological reduction
1. Get rid of reality 2. Isolate the **objects of consciousness** and the **acts of consciousness**. There are different types of each. 3. The **transcendental ego** (a self behind the self, the starting point of all knowledge) is the foundation of the **objects of consciousness** and **acts of consciousness**. Husserl equates the **transcendental ego** with **absolute being**. The **transcendental ego** produces the sense that reality exists.

Meaning–Arises from interior consciousness

Martin Heidegger's Phenomenology

While Heidegger said that Husserl gave him the eyes to see, he took a whole new approach to phenomenology. Heidegger moved from Husserl to Aristotle to develop his view of phenomenological existentialism. In his work *Being and Time*, Heidegger used phenomenology to understand *Dasein* (human existence). He did not see phenomenology as a science; instead Heidegger rejected all philosophical theories.

Heidegger rejects:	**Science**	Phenomenology is not a science because *Dasein* is not best approached in scientific terms
	Husserl's central concepts	Heidegger rejects the transcendental ego, reduction. Consciousness is not the way to understand the connection between humans and the world.
Phenomenology is:	*Dasein* (human existence)	Phenomenology is able to understand *Dasein* from within the concrete particularity of a lived life
	Intentionality	Heidegger agreed with Husserl that intentionality is the defining characteristic of all lived experiences. He disagreed with Husserl that intentionality is the nature of consciousness.
	Alethia (truth)	Truth, according to Heidegger, is disclosure; meaning that the nature of a thing is revealed in our interaction with it
	Hermeneutics	Heidegger fused phenomenology with hermeneutics. He tied *Dasein* to interpretation because all of our experience is about interpretation. Hermeneutics are about disclosure. Assertion and questioning are key parts of disclosure. Questions can be problematic.

Chart 95

Phenomenologists

Edmund Husserl	**1859–1938** German	Student of Franz Brentano. Thought of phenomenology as a science of consciousness and essences, which provides a foundation for all scientific knowledge.
Martin Heidegger	**1889–1976** German, atheist	Student of Edmund Husserl. His most famous work was *Being and Time.* Combined phenomenology with existentialism.
Hans Georg Gadamer	**1900–2002** German	He applied Heidegger's ideas on phenomenology to hermeneutics. His most famous work is *Truth and Method.* Hermeneutics is an ongoing process of understanding. He argued that language is the medium of hermeneutic experience. Philosophy is about understanding or hermeneutics.
Hannah Arendt	**1906–1975** German, Jewish	Influenced by Rudolf Bultmann, Martin Heidegger, and Karl Jaspers. She emphasized the ideas of existence and being in the world. Her most important work was *The Human Condition: A Study of the Central Dilemmas Facing Modern Man.* She applied phenomenology to political philosophy.
Emmanuel Lévinas	**1906–1995** French, Jewish	Argued that ethics precedes metaphysics. He did not have an ethical theory, nor did he delve into meta-ethics. Instead, he focused on the meaning of ethical relations. He wrote *Totality and Infinity: An Essay on Exteriority.* He rejected Heidegger's phenomenology and emphasized an escape from Being. He also developed an ethical transcendental philosophy and hermeneutics.
Jean Paul Sartre	**1905–1980** French, atheist	He studied both Husserl and Heidegger. He rejected Husserl's transcendental ego. His most famous work, *Being and Nothingness,* emphasizes human freedom. Much of his work involved political commentary and analysis.
Maurice Merleau-Ponty	**1908–1961** French	In his *Phenomenology of Perception* Merleau-Ponty explained our being in the world from a phenomenological standpoint. He employed Husserlian phenomenology in an attempt to uncover the roots of rationality. Much of his work involved political commentary and analysis.
Jacques Derrida	**1930–2004** Algerian, Jewish	Postmodern influenced by Heidegger. He argued that there is no world outside of the text. He developed deconstructionism.

Chart 96

Feminist Philosophy

Feminist philosophy attempts to correct the problem of patriarchy and male oppression. Many of these ideas have their foundation in Martin Heidegger's phenomenology.

Subject	Philosopher	Ideas	Book
Political philosophy	Simone de Beauvoir	Women have always been subordinated to men, but this does not have to be the case. As such, women should try to improve their social and political position.	*The Second Sex*
	Kate Millett	Argues that patriarchy is evident in every aspect of society. As such, women are not treated justly.	*Sexual Politics*
Epistemology	Ann Garry, Marilyn Pearsall	Knowledge and science in general employ masculine models	*Women, Knowledge, and Reality*
Ethics	Carol Gilligan	A psychologist who argued against the ideas of Lawrence Kohlberg (moral development). When understood from a feminine perspective, ethics are grounded in the maintenance of interpersonal relationships. The feminist view of ethics emphasizes personal moral responsibility.	*In a Different Voice*
Economics	Esther Boserup	Rejects classical economic theory because it fails to take women into account. Feminist economists come from many different perspectives. Feminist economists attempt to understand what is happening to women. Women have special insights about economics that are gained from the informal sector. Women are not regarded as significant factors in economics.	*Women's Role in Economic Development*
Hermeneutics	Elisabeth Schüssler Fiorenza, Phyllis Trible	Women have special insight into truth and knowledge. Consequently, only women can interpret the Bible properly.	

Chart 97

Structuralism

Ferdinand Saussure 1857–1913		
Sign	**Signified** **Signifier**	The **signified** is what the sign represents The **signifier** is the word that represents the signified
Arbitrariness	There is no natural connection between the signified and the signifier. Meaning is assigned by the community.	
La langue (language)	The whole linguistic system	
Parole (speech)	*Parole* must be evaluated by *la langue*. Each speech act can be compared to a move in a game of chess. In other words, the **structure** of the game determines the significance of a move in the same way as the **structure** of a language gives meanings to a speech act.	
Linguistic relativism	The rejection of both metaphysical and epistemological realism. These are instead replaced with the belief that we can only know the system of concepts generated by the arbitrary structures of language.	
Community	The individual does not have the power to change a sign once the community has determined it	
Semiology	Saussure's study of signs. It includes the study of linguistics and social institutions.	

Other Primary Figures	
Claude Lévi-Strauss (1908–)	Applied Saussure's system to anthropology. He asserted that universal truth is found at the level of structure. So he studied social structure in the same way that Saussure studied language.
Roland Barthes (1915–1980)	A literary critic who developed Saussure's science of semiology. He combined **structuralism** with **existentialism.** He concluded that the author is dead.
Jacques Lacan (1901–1981)	Applied structuralism to psychoanalysis. He also applied structuralism to sociology and literary criticism. He is also known as a **post-structuralist** because he challenges the assumption that language is stable.
Michel Foucault (1926–1984)	A philosopher/historian who combined **structuralism** with **phenomenological existentialism.** He spent most of his work examining the social relationship between the normal and the abnormal.

Chart 98

Post-Structuralism

Post-structuralism is a movement away from structuralism. Post-structuralists find structuralism too limiting. Post-structuralism is a postmodern idea that argues that there is no objective truth or reality. Post-structuralists reject the concept of meta-narratives.

Roland Barthes	**1915–1980**	A literary critic who developed Saussure's science of semiology. He combined **structuralism** with **phenomenological existentialism.** He concluded that the author is dead.
Jacques Derrida	**1930–2004**	Postmodern influenced by Heidegger. He argued that there is no world outside of the text. He developed deconstructionism. Deconstruction plays with the inherent instability of meaning in a text. It allows the reader to develop new meanings because the author is dead and has no rights concerning the meaning of a text.
Michel Foucault	**1926–1984**	A philosopher/historian who combined **structuralism** with **existentialist phenomenology**. Foucault was influenced by G. W. F. Hegel and Martin Heidegger. He spent most of his work examining the social relationship between the normal and the abnormal.
Jean-Francois Lyotard	**1924–**	A French philosopher who was influenced by phenomenology, Marxism, and psychoanalysis. He was also influenced by Deleuze's philosophy of desire. Lyotard rejects meta-narratives, the idea of a grand scheme that explains everything.
Julia Kristeva	**1941–**	Kristeva's work involves linguistics, French literature, and psychoanalysis. She is also a novelist.
Gilles Deleuze	**1925–1995**	A philosopher who commented on a wide variety of things. He considered philosophy as a self-referential process to create concepts. He emphasized a philosophy of desire.

Chart 99

Critical Theory

The followers of Karl Marx assert that Marxism is a meta-narrative (an all-embracing theory of everything). Marx's theory of society provides a true knowledge of society. In fact, Marxist theory provides a correct analysis of all cultural phenomenon. Thus critical theory is a worldview that has also been called an alternative metaphysics.

Key Components of Critical Theory

1. Critical theory produces enlightenment and freedom, thus allowing self-determination
2. Critical theory is a form of knowledge
3. Critical theories provide knowledge because they are reflective. Natural sciences, on the other hand, provide knowledge because they are objectifying.

The Frankfurt School	The **Frankfurt School** is a group of German philosophers who subscribe to critical theory. The members of the Frankfurt School recognize Freud as well as Marx as conceptual revolutionaries. The Frankfurt School seeks to validate reflection as a legitimate kind of knowledge.	
Max Horkheimer	**1895–1973**	Horkheimer was a communist who developed a new type of philosophical investigation of societal and theoretical concepts. He argued that positivism and modern ontology are the main currents of contemporary thought. These forces reinforce the power of the status quo. He asserted that only critical theory can help the individual to understand society and justice.
Theodor Adorno	**1903–1969**	Heavily influenced by Heidegger, Adorno started the Frankfurt School with Horkheimer. He emphasized a self-reflecting, conscious life. He rejected speculative metaphysics as well as Hegelianism.
Ernst Bloch	**1885–1977**	He developed a metaphysic of history in which the superstructure is determined as the basis of the future. He also emphasized the idea of Utopia as the ideal for any society.
Herbert Marcuse	**1898–1979**	A philosopher, social critic, and political activist. He combined Marxist thought with Heidegger's phenomenology.
Walter Benjamin	**1892–1940**	A Marxist, Jewish theologian and philosopher, who also influenced Adorno
Jürgen Habermas	**1929–**	Began as Theodor Adorno's assistant. His approach to critical theory focused on a reconstruction of historical materialism. He rejected capitalism because of the problems that result from it. His theory of communication is a key to critical theory.

Chart 100

Marxism

Karl Marx and Friedrich Engels wrote the *Communist Manifesto* and *Das Kapital*. These works explain a political-economic philosophy that has held much of the world in slavery for the better part of the last century. There is no one agreed-to system, but rather a family of theories associated with Marxism. Today, these theories are viewed as a failure. There are a number of significant components to this family of theories. They are:

Atheism	Marxism subscribes to a metaphysical materialist viewpoint. In this position there is no God and religion is only an opiate of the masses.
Class struggle	Marx saw class struggle as an ongoing problem throughout history. Because he was influenced by Hegelian thought, he held a teleological view of history. He believed that history would culminate with the working class overthrowing the ruling class. This socialist revolution results in the complete liberation of man.
Theory of society	Marx provided a critical analysis of society. He concluded that economics is the foundation of society, and all else is superstructure. He believed that society would evolve from the primitive commune to the social class with a capitalist economy. The last stage of this evolution is a socialist revolution resulting in the elimination of private property and the division of labor.
Science	Marx claimed that this theory is scientific. That is, he believed that history progressed based on an inexorable law. At the end of history, the socialist utopia was inevitable, as certain as the laws of gravity or the laws of motion.

Freudianism

Sigmund Freud is the father of modern psychology. His legacy is the theory and practice of psychoanalysis.

Atheism	There is no God. As such, the concept of God is produced by the mind because it is what we human beings have need of.
Naturalism	Human existence is the result of natural forces and not of supernatural intervention. Evolution explains many aspects of the workings of the human mind.
The unconscious	Many of our desires and drives are repressed and are played out in our unconsciousness in the form of dreams
Moral constraint and guilt	Guilt results from tension between the ego and the superego. Guilt and shame are useless emotions that are harmful to the well-being of the individual.

Chart 101

Hermeneutics

F. D. E. Schleiermacher	**1768–1834 German**	A Romantic theologian who is known as the father of modern hermeneutics and classical liberalism (theology). He extended hermeneutics beyond the domain of the Bible to ordinary speaking and writing. He divided hermeneutics into two categories: the historical/grammatical category and the psychological/technical category. Schleiermacher emphasized the importance of authorial intent for understanding a text.
Wilhelm Dilthey	**1833–1911 German**	Dilthey's hermeneutic attempted to understand authors better than they understood themselves. He employed hermeneutics to interpret not only texts, but history as well. He emphasized a linguistic historical approach to interpretation because it could easily be used in historical analysis.
Martin Heidegger	**1889–1976 German**	Heidegger's ideas on hermeneutics were influenced by Dilthey. Heidegger fused phenomenology with hermeneutics because he wanted to explore the ontology of interpretation. He also tied interpretation to *Dasein* because all of experience is about interpretation. Interpretation is also about disclosure. Assertion and questioning are key parts of disclosure. Questions can be problematic because they can distort our understanding.
Hans-Georg Gadamer	**1900–2002 German**	He applied Heidegger's ideas on phenomenology to hermeneutics. His most famous work is *Truth and Method.* Hermeneutics is an ongoing process of understanding. He argued that language is the medium of hermeneutic experience. Philosophy is about understanding or hermeneutics.
Paul Ricouer	**1931–2005 French**	Ricouer's phenomenological hermeneutics are influenced by Husserl rather than Heidegger. He defines hermeneutics as the "art of deciphering indirect meaning." Ricouer also employs some ideas of structuralism in his system. Thus language is an unconscious system of structures deeper than the intentional subject. Ricouer's hermeneutics employ both suspicion and affirmation. Absolute knowledge is impossible, so hermeneutic truth is a wager and not a possession.

Chart 102

PART 4
PHILOSOPHY OF RELIGION

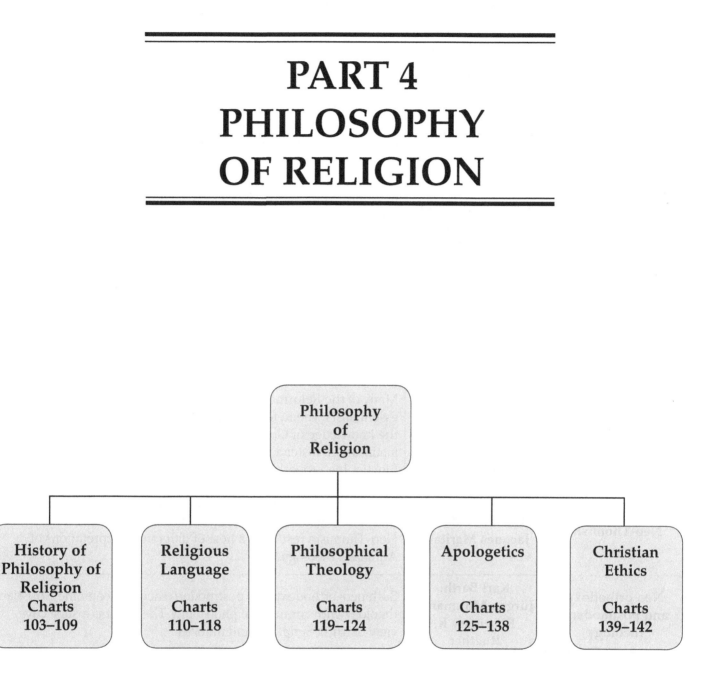

Philosophy of Religion

| History of Philosophy of Religion Charts 103–109 | Religious Language Charts 110–118 | Philosophical Theology Charts 119–124 | Apologetics Charts 125–138 | Christian Ethics Charts 139–142 |

Contemporary philosophy of religion has been dominated by **religious language**, which is a part of **philosophy of language**. Because of the **verification principle** of the **logical positivists**, philosophy of religion lost respectability. Philosophers like **Ludwig Wittgenstein** and **W. V. O. Quine** dealt logical positivism a death blow. Religious language also includes the study of biblical hermeneutics.

Philosophical theology is the part of metaphysics that is concerned with the nature of God. It is also concerned with how God relates to creation. Believers should take an Anselmian approach to the subject, meaning that philosophical theology should be done in light of the Bible and the creeds. **Alvin Plantinga's** *Nature of Necessity* gave philosophy of religion a new respectability among **analytic philosophers** that it did not have before in the 20th century.

Religious epistemology is concerned with how we know of God's existence. **Apologetics** is a primary concern in this area of study.

Christian ethics explains how Christians are to live and act.

20th-Century Philosophy of Religion

	Philosophers/ Theologians	Explanation
British philosophy of religion	**Basil Mitchell, Richard Swinburne**	This group was united only in their desire to respond to the verification principle of the logical positivists. Each of these philosophers of religion took different approaches to theology.
Process philosophy/ theology	**Alfred Whitehead, John Cobb, Charles Harsthorne**	Process philosophy was originally developed as a way to do naturalistic philosophy that was based upon the latest scientific understanding. Before 1923 scientists subscribed to a steady-state universe. This theory argued that the universe had always existed and would always exist. Process theology adapts these and other ideas to theology.
Theological essentialists	**Alvin Plantinga, Robert Adams, Thomas Morris, William Craig**	The theological essentialists employed the idea of metaphysical essentialism to theology. This results in "perfect being theology." There are both Protestants and Roman Catholics who subscribe to this kind of philosophy.
Reformed epistemology	**Alvin Plantinga, George Mavrodes, Nicholas Wolterstorff, William Alston**	Many of the Reformed epistemologists are also linguistic essentialists. The Reformed epistemologists also believe that the knowledge of God is not the result of reason, requiring justification. Instead, the knowledge of God is the result of functioning properly.
Neo-Thomism	**Etienne Gilson, Jacques Maritain**	Neo-Thomism got its start with Leo XIII. With the *Aeterni Patris* (1879) he urged a return to Aquinas for Roman Catholic theology. Neo-Thomism results in a host of different interpretations of Aquinas's theology.
Neo-orthodoxy and postmodern theology	**Karl Barth, Jürgen Moltmann, Rosemary R. Ruether**	Both neo-orthodoxy and postmodern theology combine Christian theology with continental philosophy. The result is a subjective view of truth, Scripture, and miracles.

Chart 103

20th-Century British Philosophy of Religion

This group was united only in their desire to respond to the verification principle of the logical positivists. These philosophers of religion took different approaches to theology.

Oxford University	**Nolloth Chair (Oriel College)**	**C. C. J. Webb (1865–1954)**–An Anglican layman who was also a philosopher of religion. He subscribed to personal idealism (a theological version of absolute idealism). He asserted that God is a personal being who relates to human creatures.
		L. W. Grensted (1884–1964)–He was a psychologist rather than a philosopher
		I. T. Ramsey (1915–1972)–He employed ordinary language philosophy to defend and explain the meaningfulness of religious language
		Basil Mitchell (b. 1917)–An Anglican layman who developed a cumulative case approach to apologetics. He was also a moral philosopher.
		Richard Swinburne (b. 1934)–One of the most significant philosophers of religion of the 20th century. He employs both metaphysics and epistemology in his defense of theism.
		Brian Leftow (b. 1956)–Noted for his work on God and time
	Trinity College	**Austin Farrer (1904–1968)**–Concentrated his work in the area of theistic metaphysics. His work was largely Aristotelian and Thomistic.
	Christ Church	**Eric Mascall (1905–1993)**–He taught philosophical theology in the Thomistic tradition at Christ Church, Oxford and then at King's College, London
	New College	**Hastings Rashdall (1858–1924)**–A moral philosopher and philosopher of religion who subscribed to **personal idealism**. Rashdall believed that God is a personal being. He also argued that an idealist proof of God's existence provided the ultimate basis for theism. He attempted to combine a utilitarian view of ethics with Christian theology.
Edinburgh University		**Thomas F. Torrance (b. 1913)**–A philosophical theologian who is confessional and Christ centered. He attempted to integrate faith with science.
Cambridge University		**John Polkinghorne (b. 1930)**–An Anglican priest and member of the Royal Society in Physics who attempts to reconcile faith with science

Chart 104

Process Theology

Process philosophy was originally developed as a way to do naturalistic philosophy that was based upon the latest scientific understanding. Before 1923 scientists subscribed to a steady-state universe. This theory argued that the universe had always existed and would always exist. Process theology adapts these and other ideas to theology.

Pierre Teilhard de Chardin	**1881–1955**	A Roman Catholic cardinal, Chardin attempted to unite process philosophy with Catholic theology. He asserted that everything was moving to its *telos* in the **omega point**.
Henri Bergson	**1859–1941**	Bergson's process philosophy resulted from his attempt to reconcile philosophy with contemporary views in physics. Bergson focused primarily on time.
Alfred North Whitehead	**1861–1947**	Whitehead was a mathematician and a philosopher, not a theologian. He attempted to correlate philosophy with the prevailing view in science. Many physicists subscribed to a steady-state universe, believing that the universe was always in existence. As such, the universe is uncreated and eternal. Instead, Whitehead believed, the universe as well as everything in it is always in the process of becoming. Thus Whitehead followed the ideas of the pre-Socratic Heraclitas. Heraclitas argued that you cannot step into the same river twice, meaning that everything is in the process of constant change. Whitehead did not accept many of the traditional Christian beliefs regarding the Godhead or Jesus Christ.
Charles Hartshorne	**1897–2000**	Agreeing with Whitehead, Hartshorne rejected Christian orthodoxy. He attempted to unite process philosophy with Christian theology. He taught for many years at the University of Chicago Divinity School.
John Cobb	**1925–**	Cobb is a theologian who combined Christianity with Buddhism and process philosophy. He is the primary force behind the process theology at the Claremont Graduate School.
Bernard Loomer	**1912–1985**	A process theologian at the University of Chicago Divinity School

Chart 105

Neo-Thomism

Neo-Thomism got its start with Leo XIII. With the *Aeterni Patris* (1879) he urged a return to Aquinas for Roman Catholic theology. Neo-Thomism results in a host of different interpretations of Aquinas's theology. There are two phases in neo-Thomism. The first phase began with *Aeterni Patris* and lasted until 1917. During this first phase, Thomism was equated with Aristotelianism. The second phase of neo-Thomism began in 1917 and lasted until the second Vatican Council. Neo-Thomism came to an end with Vatican II because Pope John XXIII embraced philosophical pluralism.

Pope Leo XIII	**1878–1903**	His encyclical *Aeterni Patris* concerned "the Restoration in Catholic Schools of Christian Philosophy According to the Mind of the Angelic Doctor Saint Thomas Aquinas"
Cardinal Désiré-Joseph Mercier	**1851–1926**	A leader in the first phase of neo-Thomism. He helped institute the revision to the *Code of Canon Law* which recommended that professors of philosophy and theology teach in accordance with the doctrines and principles of Thomas Aquinas.
Jacques Maritain	**1882–1973**	Along with Etienne Gilson he was one of the most significant Thomists in the 20th century. Maritain emphasized that Thomism required metaphysical and epistemological realism. He attempted to replicate in the 20th century what Aquinas had done in the 13th century. He taught for many years in the U.S.
Etienne Gilson	**1884–1978**	Along with Maritain, Gilson was one of the most significant Thomists in the 20th century. Gilson, like Maritain, emphasized that Thomism requires both metaphysical and epistemological realism. Gilson sought as accurate a knowledge of Aquinas's teaching as was possible. Among other things, he founded the Pontifical Institute for Medieval Studies in Toronto.
Frederic Copleston	**1907–1994**	A Thomist philosopher/historian noted for his nine-volume work on the history of Western philosophy
Austin Farrer	**1904–1968**	Concentrated his work in the area of theistic metaphysics. His work was Aristotelian and Thomistic.
Eric Mascall	**1905–1993**	He taught philosophical theology in the Thomistic tradition at Christ Church, Oxford and then at King's College, London
Analytic Thomism	**1950s to present**	Peter Geach and G. E. M. Anscombe founded this movement at Cambridge University in the 1950s. They were followed by Anthony Kenny.

Chart 106

Analytic Thomism (neo-Thomism cont.)

Ludwig Wittgenstein	**Cambridge University**	A leader in the **ordinary language analysis** movement in analytic philosophy. He became a Roman Catholic as an adult. He began to apply analytic philosophy to present the ideas of Aquinas.
G. E. M. Anscombe	**Cambridge University**	A student of Ludwig Wittgenstein and wife of Peter Geach. She urged a return to premodern philosophy and ethics. She converted to Roman Catholicism as an adult and started the movement.
Peter Geach	**Cambridge University**	A student of Ludwig Wittgenstein and husband of G.E.M. Anscombe. He became a Roman Catholic as an adult. He began applying the approach of analytic philosophy to the study of Thomas Aquinas.
Anthony Kenny	**Cambridge University**	A student of Peter Geach, he wrote among other works *Aquinas (Past Masters Series)*
Brian Davies	**Oxford University**	He wrote, among other works, *The Thought of Thomas Aquinas*
Eleonore Stump	**St. Louis University**	She coedited with Norman Kretzmann *The Cambridge Companion to Aquinas*. In addition, she also coedited with Scott MacDonald *Aquinas's Moral Theory*. She also wrote *Aquinas*.
Anthony Lisska	**Denison University**	He wrote, among other works, *Aquinas's Theory of Natural Law*
John Haldane	**University of St. Andrews**	He coined the term **Analytic Thomism** in the 1990s

Chart 107

Reformed Epistemology

Many of the Reformed epistemologists are also linguistic essentialists. The Reformed epistemologists also believe that the knowledge of God is not the result of reason, requiring justification. Instead, the knowledge of God is the result of functioning properly. The following individuals were among those who wrote articles in *Faith and Rationality*, which explained the main ideas of Reformed epistemology.

Alvin Plantinga	**1932–**	Professor emeritus at the University of Notre Dame, Plantinga has written a trilogy that explains his ideas with regard to epistemology in general, and the knowledge of God in particular. This trilogy includes: *Warrant: The Current Debate, Warrant and Proper Function,* and *Warranted Christian Belief.* His method, known as proper functionalism, is consistent with his metaphysical realism.
Nicholas Wolterstorff	**1932–**	Professor emeritus at Yale University, he taught philosophy with Alvin Plantinga at Calvin College. His approach to epistemology is heavily influenced by the writings of Thomas Reid. His ideas on epistemology led him to write in the field of hermeneutics.
William Alston	**1921–**	He taught philosophy at the University of Michigan with George Mavrodes and influenced Alvin Plantinga. An analytic philosopher who has written extensively in the fields of philosophical theology, epistemology, and philosophy of language. His approach to epistemology attempted to combine some sort of foundationalism with reliabilism. He served as first president of the **Society of Christian Philosophers**.
George Mavrodes	**n.d.**	Professor emeritus at the University of Michigan, where he taught philosophy of religion. He served as president for both the **Society of Christian Philosophers** and the **Society of Philosophy of Religion**.

Chart 108

Alvin Plantinga

As a theological essentialist and a Reformed epistemologist, it can be argued that Alvin Plantinga is the most significant philosopher of religion of the last century. He made theism a respectable position within analytic philosophical circles. A founding member of the Society of Christian Philosophers, Plantinga led a movement that resulted in approximately one third of all philosophers holding to some kind of theism.

Subject	Books	Ideas
Philosophy of language	*The Nature of Necessity*	Plantinga follows the linguistic essentialism of Saul Kripke and Ruth Marcus; consequently he employs the ideas of possible worlds and essentialism.
Metaphysics	*The Nature of Necessity*	Like Kripke, Plantinga employs modal logic and considers the significance of possible worlds. This leads to metaphysical realism and essentialism.
Epistemology	*Warrant: The Current Debate, Warrant and Proper Function, Warranted Christian Belief*	Plantinga rejects the idea that knowledge is justified true belief. He argues that justification is deontological and consistent with metaphysical nominalism. His approach to epistemology is consistent with his metaphysical realism and essentialism. He advocates a teleological approach to epistemology known as proper functionalism. This position is consistent with his Reformed epistemology.
Evil	*The Nature of Necessity* *God, Freedom, and Evil*	Plantinga develops what is called **the free will defense**. He employs possible worlds, essentialism, and middle knowledge to show that the best of all possible worlds must have a certain amount of evil if men are to have free will.

Chart 109

Religious Language Overview

Pseudo Dionysius the Areopagite	*c. 500*	God can only be known through created symbols. The divine is inaccessible to men, thus symbols are the only way to encounter God. Symbols both reveal and conceal the truth about God. Consequently, he argues for the *via negativa* (way of negation) in his *On Divine Names* and his *On Mystical Theology*.
Anselm of Canterbury	**1033–1109**	The father of scholasticism whose interest in the relationship between language and reality is expressed in his *De Grammatico, De Veritate,* and his *Philosophical Fragments*. He viewed language as a system of signs. As such, he was concerned that grammar and grammatical form can be misleading.
Moses Maimonides	**1135–1204**	*Via negativa* (way of negation). In his *Guide for the Perplexed* he argues that religious language can only communicate the experience of ultimate reality or the divine.
Thomas Aquinas	**1224–1274**	Religious language is **analogical.** In other words, religious language communicates truth, but not literal truth.
John Duns Scotus	**1264–1308**	*Via negativa* (way of negation). Religious language is **univocal** or **equivocal**. Ultimate reality can only be understood by negating or denying all words.
Meister Eckhart	**1260–1327**	*Via negativa* (way of negation)
David Hume	**1711–1776**	**Hume's fork**–Truth must be empirically verified or based on reason. Anything not in line with these ideas must be consigned to the flames. Consequently it does not make sense to speak about God or religious truth.
Alfred Jules Ayer	**1910–1989**	The **verification principle**–It does not make sense to discuss anything that is not empirically verifiable. The **logical positivists** used **Hume's fork** as the foundation for this principle.
Ludwig Wittgenstein	**1889–1951**	**Word games**–Religious language makes sense in light of the religious community
Ian Thomas Ramsey	**1915–1972**	He employed ordinary language philosophy to defend and explain the meaningfulness of religious language

Chart 110

Religious Language (According to Thomas Aquinas)*

Aquinas was explaining why human speech is inadequate to speak of God		
Key terms	**Univocal language**	Using two words with exactly the same meaning
	Equivocal Language	Using two words with completely different meanings
	Analogical language	1. Using two words with some meaning in common 2. A perfection term is predicated of God "neither wholly univocally nor purely equivocally. Instead it is predicated analogously, which is the same as proportionally."
Arguments against univocal language	**Epistemological argument**	**The empiricist view of language** 1. All knowledge comes from sense experience 2. God is not an object of our sense experience 3. Knowledge of God is mediated to human creatures indirectly 4. Human language cannot be used of God and creatures univocally
	Metaphysical argument	**Divine transcendence** We inadequately resemble our creator; as a result we cannot fully understand him
	Conclusion	No language applies univocally to God and creatures
Equivocal language	**Arguments against**	1. Equivocal language goes against our proofs of God 2. Equivocal language goes against what Scripture says about our natural knowledge of God 3. Equivocal language goes against the perfection of God's knowledge for us 4. Equivocal language goes against established linguistic practice
Analogical language	**Analogy of proportion**	One word may be used of two things because each of them has some order or relation to a third thing
	Analogy of proportionality	One word may be used of two things because of the relation the one thing has to the other

*With thanks to Greg Welty

Chart 111

The Linguistic Turn in Philosophy of Religion

The **linguistic turn** occurred early in the twentieth century. The turn was about the movement from epistemology to language as first philosophy. The **linguistic turn** followed the **epistemological turn**, which began with the arrival of the modern period (about 1600 AD). The **epistemological turn** represented the movement from metaphysics to epistemology as first philosophy.

Philosophy	**Analytic**	This movement began with G. E. Moore and Bertrand Russell (**logical realists**). Many of the analytic philosophers attempted to make philosophy compatible with science.
	Continental	Martin Heidegger led the **Continental philosophers** in the linguistic turn when he combined existentialism with phenomenology. He argued that meaning is found in being.
Theology	**The effect of analytic philosophy**	The **logical positivists** were motivated by the belief that there are no metaphysical problems. As a result, they developed the **verification principle**, which argues that if something is not empirically verifiable then it does not make sense to talk about it. Theology is not empirically verifiable, so most theologians largely avoided most types of analytic philosophy.
		The **Ordinary Language Analysts** (philosophers) argued that meaning is found within a community. As a result, religious language makes sense within the community of believers.
	The effect of Continental philosophy	Because **Continental philosophy** does not reject theology, many theologians embraced it. Hans Georg Gadamer, Paul Ricouer, Emmanuel Levinas, and others have been very influential with theological hermeneutics.

Chart 112

Arguments against the Verification Principle

The Verification Principle

According to this principle, it does not make sense to discuss anything that is not empirically verifiable. The **logical positivists** used **Hume's fork** as the foundation for this principle. The result was that metaphysicians, ethicists, and theologians were cut out of philosophical discussion unless it was from the standpoint of history or **Continental philosophy**.

Logical positivists		This group includes A. J. Ayer, Morris Schlick, Otto Neurath, and Rudolf Carnap. They believed that philosophy is about the analysis of scientific language.
Ludwig Wittgenstein	*Philosophical Investigations*	Wittgenstein argued for word games, the idea that meaning is determined by the community that one is part of. Hence, in religious circles discussion about God is completely sensible.
W. V. O. Quine	"Two Dogmas of Empiricism"	Quine argued that the verification principle is referentially incoherent. In other words, the verification principle cannot even meet its own standard **(Hume's fork)**.
Karl Popper		Popper argued that science does not attempt to verify a hypothesis. Instead, science attempts to falsify one. He did not believe that the falsification principle should extend beyond science.
Conclusion	The verification principle does not provide sufficient or necessary justification to prevent theologians to discuss God or religion	

Chart 113

Biblical Hermeneutics

Premodern assumptions Hermeneutic of trust Correspondence theory of truth	**The author of the Bible**	**Divine**–The author of the Bible is God
		Human–God uses human instruments to communicate his truth
	The reader	Believes in miracles and the supernatural
	Dominant method of interpretation	**Historical-grammatical interpretation**–An attempt to understand what the human author wrote
		Allegory–Meanings that the human author did not intend
Modern assumptions Hermeneutic of doubt Coherence theory of truth	**The author of the Bible**	**Human** authorship is assumed; there is no room for supernatural authorship
	The reader	Employs an anti-supernatural bias because science can explain everything
	Dominant method of interpretation	**Historical-critical methodologies**–Assumes that the history of the Bible is unreliable. It attempts to interpret the Bible from a scientific standpoint.
Postmodern assumptions Hermeneutic of suspicion Pragmatic theory of truth	**The author of the Bible**	**Human** authorship is assumed, but the possibility of supernatural authorship is not denied
	The reader	Does not believe that science can provide the answers. Allows for the possibility of the supernatural.
	Dominant method of interpretation	**Socio-critical methodologies**–An interpretative method based upon the power of the interpretive community. It asserts that truth is what is good for the community.

Chart 114

Premodern Old Testament Hermeneutics

Premodern assumptions	**Authorship**	The Torah is divinely inspired. Hence, God is the author of the Torah.
	Correspondence theory of truth	Truth is what corresponds to reality. The Torah describes reality. The Torah contains the entire truth of God.
	Hermeneutic of trust	Because of its divine inspiration, the Torah can be trusted
		Inerrancy–The Torah is true without any mixture of error
		Authority–The Torah has authority for every area of life
		Sufficiency–The purpose of interpreting the Torah is to gain instruction for our lives. Nothing else is needed.
Method of interpretation	**Categories of Hebrew interpretation**	**Peshat**–Literal exegesis comparable to the historical-grammatical method of interpretation
		Allegory–Extended metaphor. Meanings that the human author did not intend.
		Midrash–Commentary or explanation of the Bible bounded by the community and its traditions
		Pesher–Eschatological fulfillment in the contemporary situation
	Apostolic exegesis	**Typology**–Using ideas in the Old Testament as types that are found in the New Testament
		Historicizing–Viewing the text in terms of prophecy and fulfillment
		Reorientation–Finding Christ in the Old Testament

Chart 115

Premodern Biblical Hermeneutics

According to Augustine in *De Doctrina Christiana* (*On Teaching Christian Doctrine*) Augustine believed that Christians must interpret the Bible in a way that is consistent with our faith. He also believed that the Holy Spirit is needed to interpret the Bible.

Premodern assumptions **Ethic of interpretation** The right way to interpret the Bible is in accordance with the traditional faith of the Christian community. The reader must depend on the Holy Spirit for illumination.	**Authorship**	There are two authors for the Bible: the first is divine, the second is human. Thus the Bible is inspired (God breathed). Interpretative methods must take both authors into account.
	Correspondence theory of truth	Truth is what corresponds to reality. The Bible describes reality.
	Hermeneutic of trust	Because of its divine author, the reader can trust in the truth of the Bible
		Inerrancy–The Bible is true without any mixture of error
		Authority–Because of its divine author, the Bible provides guidance to the church
		Sufficiency–Because of its divine author, believers do not need anything else as a guide for faith and practice
Method of interpretation The Holy Spirit illumines the Word of God	**1st level of interpretation**	**Historical-grammatical method** is used to obtain the human author's intent. This allows for the use of **lower critical methodologies** such as: textual criticism, form criticism, and rhetorical criticism.
	2nd level of interpretation	**Allegory**–Is used to obtain meanings that the human author did not intend
Limits on interpretation Only those within the Christian community can give valid interpretations of the Bible	**Creeds** Only those who subscribe to the creeds are within the community	**Nicea** explains the deity of both the Father and the Son
		Constantinople explains the deity of the Father, the Son, and the Holy Spirit
		Chalcedon explains the nature of Christ
	Theological virtues Are given by the Holy Spirit to guide and empower the Christian	**Love**–Valid interpretations are consistent with the love of God and the love of man for God's sake
		Faith–Valid interpretations are consistent with Christian faith
		Hope–Valid interpretations are consistent with Christian hope

Chart 116

Modern Biblical Hermeneutics

Modern Assumptions	**Authorship**	The Bible has a human author only. Consequently, there is no room for the supernatural.
	Coherence theory of truth	Truth results from a coherent set of belief without contradiction. The Bible does not describe reality.
Ethic of interpretation The only right way to interpret the Bible is in a way that one (the individual) can be absolutely sure of the truth of the interpretation. This means in accordance with scientific principles.	**Hermeneutic of doubt**	The Bible cannot be trusted for accuracy of any kind. The meaning of the text can be arrived at by scientific means.
		Inerrancy is rejected because proponents claim: 1. Inerrancy is a philosophical concept that is alien to the Bible 2. We do not have the original manuscripts 3. The Bible does not claim to be inerrant 4. An inerrant Bible requires an inerrant hermeneutic Modernists may sometimes argue for limited inerrancy, meaning that the Bible is inerrant in matters of faith and practice, but not for issues of science or history
		Authority–The Bible has less authority than science and human reason
		Sufficiency–The Bible must be supplemented by science to meet the needs of people
Method of interpretation Proponents employ scientific approaches to interpretation. These approaches suggest that the Bible must be interpreted like any other book. These approaches have an inherent anti-supernatural bias.	**Historical-critical method** Developed by Baruch Spinoza in his *Political Theological Treatise*. Further developed by F. D. E. Schleiermacher (the father of modern hermeneutics and classical liberalism).	**Higher criticism**–An approach to biblical interpretation that questions the Bible's veracity. It attempts to use "scientific methods" to understand the Bible.
		Source criticism–Assumes that the authorship of each book is in question and seeks to find the original sources of the text
		Form criticism–Assumes that the form of the text was influenced by the style and form of other cultures
		Redaction criticism–Attempts to find what was added by others after the text was first written
		Lower criticism–Attempts to look at the text critically without questioning the veracity of the Bible
		Textual criticism–Seeks to catalog and analyze textual variations to determine which text is the best
		Rhetorical criticism–Examines the structure of the text. Rhetoric helps find the primary meaning of the human author and shows the unity of a text.

Chart 117

Postmodern Biblical Interpretation

Postmodern assumptions **Ethic of interpretation** The only right way to interpret the Bible is in a way that is advantageous to one's community	**Authorship**	The Bible has a human author
	Pragmatic theory of truth	Truth is what works or is useful. The community determines what is true based on what is good for them. The Bible may or may not be useful depending upon which community one is in.
	Hermeneutic of suspicion	The reader operates with the belief that the writer is attempting to force his values on the reader
		Inerrancy—It all depends on if your community agrees on the Bible's inerrancy
		Authority—The only authority that the Bible has is what an individual or a community may give to it
		Sufficiency—The sufficiency of the Bible is dependent upon one's community
Method of interpretation All of these approaches to the Bible employ a neo-Nietzschean will to power over the text. Meaning does not reside with the text or with the author.	**Socio-critical methods** Approaches to interpretation that are based upon a community. They assert that knowledge is determined by a community.	**Liberation theology** asserts that only the poor are capable of understanding the Bible. The wealthy are incapable of coming to a knowledge of the truth. The right interpretation is one that benefits the poor. Gustavo Gutiérrez is a leader in this hermeneutical/ethical method.
		Feminist theology asserts that only women are capable of understanding the Bible. A correct interpretation is one that benefits women. Rosemary Radford Ruether is a leader in this hermeneutical/ethical method.
		Black theology asserts that only black people can understand the Bible. A correct interpretation is one that benefits black people. James Cone is a leader in this hermeneutical/ethical method.
	Narrative criticism	Asserts that truth is best communicated through the use of narrative
	Reader response	An approach to interpretation that asserts that meaning is determined by the reader
	Structuralism	A movement led by Claude Lévi-Strauss, Roland Barthes, Jacques Lacan, and Michel Foucault that replaced existentialism. Also known as semiological analysis.
	Post-structuralism	A movement away from structuralism led by Michel Foucault and Jacques Lacan
	Deconstruction	A type of post-structuralism developed by Jacques Derrida. Takes advantage of the inherent instability of meaning in a text and attempts to find novel and/or interesting meanings instead. All of this is done for purposes of play.

Chart 118

Theological Essentialism

If God is a necessary being, then he has essential properties. This means that in every possible world, a divine being must possess these properties.

Alvin Plantinga led this movement (in his book *The Nature of Necessity*) by following in the footsteps of Saul Kripke's *Naming and Necessity*. The theological essentialists applied the idea of metaphysical essentialism to theology. This results in "perfect being theology." There are both Protestants and Roman Catholics who subscribe to this philosophy. Plantinga argued that God as a necessary being has an essential nature. Plantinga also deals with the problem of pain, evil, and suffering.

Perfect being theology		A perfect being has essential attributes that will be found in any possible world. The idea of God as a perfect being was first explained by Anselm of Canterbury. God must possess certain attributes perfectly. God's perfect attributes are the same as his essential attributes.
Communicable attributes	**Omnipotence**	God is perfectly powerful. This means that he can do anything that he purposes to do or anything that is consistent with his nature. Some argue that omnipotence entails the other attributes. God has the maximal set of compossible great-making powers.
	Omniscience	God has perfect knowledge, meaning that he knows anything that can be known that is not in conflict with his nature
	Omnipresence	There is no place from which God is spatially distant
	Omnibenevolence	God is perfectly good. God is the source and standard of good.
Incommunicable attributes	**Simplicity**	God's essence is identical with his existence. As such, his perfections and properties are identical. God is not some composite that can be reduced to simpler parts.
	Immutability	God does not change
	Eternity	God transcends time
	Immensity	God transcends space
	Infinity	God is beyond measure
	Aseity	God does not need a context or anything else
	Transcendence	God is beyond the realm of human experience
	Immanence	God is intimately involved with his creation

Chart 119

Doctrine of God

The attributes of God	**Omnipotence**	God is perfectly powerful. This means that he can do anything that he purposes to do or anything that is consistent with his nature. Some argue that omnipotence entails the other attributes. God has the maximal set of compossible great-making powers.
	Omniscience	God has perfect knowledge, meaning that he knows anything that can be known that is not in conflict with his nature
	Omnipresence	There is no place from which God is spatially distant
	Omnibenevolence God is perfectly good. God is the source and standard of good. He has at least six different moral attributes.	**Holiness**–God is unique and set apart from all creation. He is also separate from sin and anything unclean.
		Righteousness/justice–God always does right and what ought to be done. He acts in conformity to his law and his nature. God's law reflects the peace and order of his nature. God's own glory is the supreme objective.
		Love–God gives of himself to others
		Mercy–God does not give us the punishment that we deserve
		Grace–God gives us unmerited favor. He gives what we do not and cannot earn.
		Patience–God withholds his judgment, giving people the opportunity to repent
	Necessity	God necessarily exists in any possible world; as such, God has more being than anything else. If we understand goodness and beauty as aspects of being, then God is the personification of goodness and beauty.
Implications The believer can trust God because he is perfectly good. It implies that God's word is trustworthy, and that God will always do what is good and best.	**Theodicy–the problem of pain, evil, and suffering**	Argues that if God has all of these attributes, then why does evil exist? Theodicy did not become a problem until the modern period, with its hermeneutic of doubt. During the premodern period, Augustine and others argued that God allows evil to exist because it serves his purposes.
	Impeccability	Teaches that God cannot sin. There are only two reasons that people sin. Either they lack wisdom/knowledge or they lack power. If God is omnipotent and omniscient he does not lack knowledge or power. Consequently, God cannot sin.
	Moral realism	Moral facts depend upon the existence of God

Chart 120

Doctrine of God/Creeds

Christian ethics requires not just moral action, but belief in the right doctrines concerning who God is. It is only with the right understanding of who God is that one can live according to God's will. God's will is consistent with his nature.

Nicea The council of **Nicea** in 325 AD (revised in **Constantinople** in 381 to include the Holy Spirit) affirmed that God is a Trinity. That is, the Father and the Son are coequal and share one substance.	**Three persons**	**Father**–Coequal and eternal with the Son and the Holy Spirit
		Son–**Jesus Christ,** the God-man, is eternal and coequal with God the Father
		Holy Spirit–The life-giver is eternal and coequal with God the Father. He proceeds from the Father.
	One substance	All three persons share the same substance
	Economic Trinity	The idea that the members of the Trinity have different functions
	Perichoresis	The internal communication that goes on between the members of the Trinity
	Errors	**Modalism**–There are not three separate persons in the Trinity. There is only one person who wears different masks at different times.
		Tri-theism–The three persons are three separate Gods
Chalcedon (451 AD) Declared that Jesus Christ is one person with two natures	**One person**	Jesus Christ, the Son, is the image of God
	Two natures	One nature is fully divine
		One nature is fully human
	Errors	**Arianism**–Suggests that the Son is a created being and is not God
		Subordinationism–Affirms that the Son is not created. It also affirms that the Son is eternal. But it denies that the Son is equal to the Father in his substance and attributes.
		Adoptionism–Suggests that the God the Father adopted Jesus as his son at his baptism. With this adoption, the Father bestowed supernatural powers upon the Son.

Chart 121

God and Time

View	Theologian(s)	Explanation	Comments
Divine timeless eternity	**Augustine, Boethius, Anselm, Paul Helm**	God is outside of time; as such he is both omnipotent and omniscient	Eternity is compatible with a B-theory of time
Eternity as relative timelessness	**Alan Padgett**	God is transcendent. He is the creator of space–time. Eternity is God's time. It is dependent on God's being. Thus God is relatively timeless with respect to our created and measured time.	This view is consistent with both theology and science
Eternity-time simultaneity	**Norman Kretzmann, Eleonore Stump**	There is no common frame of reference for both timeless and temporal beings. God is in eternity while creatures are in time. From God's standpoint, everything is present. From the creature's standpoint, God is always present.	Eternity is timeless, and time is temporal in an A-theory sense
Timelessness and omni-temporality	**John Duns Scotus, William Lane Craig**	God is omni-temporal because he never begins to exist, nor does he cease to exist. God also existed before he created time.	
Unqualified divine temporality	**Nicholas Wolterstorff**	God is a temporal being who is actively involved in the universe	If God is temporal, then his knowledge of the future is limited

Chart 122

Divine Foreknowledge

View	Theologian	Explanation	Problems
Open theism		God has only a limited knowledge of the future. He is not omnipotent. God goes through time in the same way that humans do.	Divine agency and providence are weakened by this view
Simple foreknowledge	**William of Ockham**	God's foreknowledge is not a hard fact. His knowing the future is not causative. This position allows for human freedom without diminishing God's omniscience.	This view is fatalistic. It also places limits on divine agency and providence.
Middle knowledge	**Luis de Molina**	**Middle knowledge** consists of all contingent truths over which God has no control. It leaves room for **counterfactuals of creaturely freedom**. As a result of middle knowledge, God decides which beings to create in which circumstances.	Some argue that counterfactuals of creaturely freedom do not exist
Complete foreknowledge	**John Calvin**	God's knowledge is part of his omnipotence. As such, God's knowledge is causative. God's foreknowledge is coextensive with his foreordination.	Some see this view as fatalistic. It also seems to free creatures of all responsibility.
	Augustine	God has complete foreknowledge, but this in no way affects man's free will. Man alone is responsible for his sin.	How can man's will be completely free if God is omnipotent and omniscient?

Chart 123

Molinism or Middle Knowledge

Luis de Molina attempted to reconcile a libertarian view of freedom with divine providence. Because God's foreknowledge and sovereignty seem to be in conflict with free human action, Molina believed that the two can coexist only if God knows how human beings will act if placed in some situation that is not predetermined.

Natural knowledge–God's pre-volitional knowledge of necessary truths

Middle knowledge–Consists of all contingent truths over which God has no control. It leaves room for **counterfactuals of creaturely freedom**. As a result of middle knowledge, God decides which beings to create in which circumstances.

Counterfactuals of creaturely freedom–The complete set of nondetermining circumstances in which a creature is placed

Free knowledge–God's post-volitional knowledge of contingent truths

God's knowledge	Natural knowledge	Middle knowledge	Free knowledge
Truths known by God are:	Necessary	Contingent	Contingent
	Independent of God's free will	Independent of God's free will	Dependent on God's free will
Human freedom	Does not allow for counterfactuals of creaturely freedom	Allows for counterfactuals of creaturely freedom	Does not allow for counterfactuals of creaturely freedom

Chart 124

Patristic Apologetics

The apologetics of the early church addressed the concerns of converts, philosophers, emperors, and Jews. All of the early apologists were concerned to defend the doctrines of the incarnation and the Trinity. These philosophers believed that Greek philosophy was compatible with their Christian faith.

Apologist	Dates	Books	Description
Athenagoras	2nd century	*Embassy for the Christians*	Argued that Christian morality is superior to paganism
Justin Martyr	100–165	*Apology, Dialogue with Trypho the Jew*	Argued that emperors should not believe false accusations against Christianity. He also attempted to convince Jews of the truth.
Clement of Alexandria	150–214	*Converter, Tutor, Instructor*	Argued that emperors should not believe false accusations against Christianity. He showed how Christ is better than pagan gods.
Origen of Alexandria	184–253	*True Doctrine, Contra Celsum*	He answered false accusations about Christianity that were made by Celsum. He also explained true Christian doctrine.
Latin apologists	**Tertullian** 3rd century	*Apology*	He used Roman juridical principles to defend the faith
	Lactantius 4th century	*Divine Institutes*	He answered accusations against Christianity and taught new converts sound doctrine
Eusebius of Caesarea	263–339	*The Preparation of the Gospel, The Proof of the Gospel*	His argument involved a theology of history: the Christianization of the empire is the goal of history
Athanasius of Alexandria	295–373	*Treatise Against the Pagans, The Incarnation of the Word of God*	He argued against idolatry and polytheism. He also emphasized sound doctrine.
Aurelius Augustine	354–430	*City of God, Confessions*	He argued that Christian morality is superior to paganism and theology of history. Belief comes before understanding.

Chart 125

Augustine's *City of God*

This work is an apologetic that explained to the Romans why Alaric was able to sack Rome. This is arguably the most significant apologetic work of the Patristic period.

Major Division	Minor Division	Book	Explanation
Polemic against paganism **Books 1–10** This part of the book argues that pagan religion is not the cause for the success of any society	**Books 1–5** Man's temporal life	1	Alaric's mercy in victory is due to the power of Christ's name. Rome was sacked as a punishment for its moral degradation.
		2	Pagan society is full of vice
		3	The gods that the Romans worship are impotent
		4	The expansion of the Roman empire was not due to their gods
		5	The one true God is responsible for the rise and fall of nations
	Books 6–10 Life beyond death	6	Pagan gods cannot give either temporal or eternal blessings
		7	Even the higher pagan gods are impotent
		8	Even Plato is indebted to Moses
		9	Angels are only servants of God, and should not be worshiped
		10	The incarnation and the sacrifice of Christ satisfied God's wrath
Theology of history **Books 11–22** Augustine explains the city of God and the city of man	**Books 11–14** An explanation of the origins and problem of sin	11	The two cities resulted from the good and bad angels
		12	Why are angels good or bad?
		13	The problem of original sin
		14	Shame is the punishment for sin
	Books 15–22 The history of the city of God and the city of man (also known as the Devil's city)	15	Augustine begins his history
		16	The progress of the heavenly city
		17	History of Israel until Christ
		18	History to the end of the world
		19	The end of the two cities
		20	The last judgment
		21	The end for the Devil's city
		22	The end for the city of God

Chart 126

Medieval Apologetics

Augustine set the path for all of the medieval apologists. He argued that the understanding of the incarnation and the Trinity are available to all men through reason alone. He also argued that faith precedes understanding. The main threats came from Islam (which reintroduced Aristotle's work) and from defeat in the Crusades.

Apologist	Time period	Book(s)	Views on the Trinity and the incarnation	Emphasis
Anselm of Canterbury	1033–1109	*Proslogium, Monologium, Cur Deus Homo*	These doctrines are available to all men by reason alone	God is a perfect being. Belief comes before understanding.
Peter Abelard	1079–1142	*A Dialogue between a Philosopher, a Jew, and a Christian*	These doctrines are available to all men by reason alone	Reason is a pathway to faith
Thomas Aquinas Dominican order	1225–1274	*Summa Contra Gentiles*	These doctrines are available to all men only by special revelation	Belief comes before understanding. Men have a *sensus divinitatis* which convinces them of the truth of the gospel.
Bonaventure Franciscan order	1221–1274	There is no one work that expresses his ideas on apologetics	These doctrines are available to all men by reason alone	Belief comes before understanding. Faith results from divine illumination.
John Duns Scotus Franciscan order; criticized the ideas of Thomas Aquinas	1266–1308	There is no one work that expresses his ideas on apologetics	These doctrines are available to all men by reason alone	Faith comes before understanding. He also gave 10 reasons for the authority of the Bible.

Chart 127

The Structure of the *Summa Contra Gentiles*

The most important apologetic work of the Middle Ages, Aquinas's *Summa Contra Gentiles*, used Aristotle's work to deal with the threat of Islam. Aquinas thought that this work should "seek to make known that truth which faith professes and reason investigates." After he accomplished this goal in Books 1–3 he attempted to "proceed to make known that truth which surpasses reason" (Book 1, chapter 9, paragraph 3). This second goal he accomplished in Book 4.

Book 1	The focus of this part of this volume is to study the existence of God and his nature	**Part 1** 1. The existence of God 2. Our knowledge of God 3. The divine attributes
		Part 2 1. The intelligence and knowledge of God 2. The will, love, and blessedness of God
Book 2	This book examines God's creation and how it relates to him as the creator	**This book attempts to solve three problems:** 1. How God created 2. How God distinguished one thing from another 3. The nature of the things created and made distinct from each other
Book 3	This book explores the order of creation. There is a special focus on man's relation to God.	**Part 1** God as the end and good of all things
		Part 2 God's general government of all things
		Part 3 Providence and rational creatures
Book 4	This book explores the Trinity and the incarnation. In addition, Aquinas also investigates the end of the world.	This book attempts to make known that truth which surpasses reason, and seeks to enlighten believers on the mystery of our salvation. **Aquinas's threefold knowledge of God is:** 1. The natural light of reason by which one ascends to a knowledge of God 2. Revelation exceeds human intellect and comes from God to bring man divine truth 3. Beatific vision: that by which the human mind will be elevated perfectly to gaze upon the things revealed

Chart 128

Reformation Views of Apologetics

Theologian	Time period	Writings	Apologetics	Emphasis
Martin Luther	1483–1546		Apologetics do not prepare one for faith. Only grace is sufficient to change the hearts and minds of men.	Reason is sufficient only for the natural and temporal world
Philipp Melanchthon	1497–1560	*Loci Communes*	Apologetics are useful for bringing men to the gospel	Reason provides natural evidences in favor of Christianity
John Calvin	1509–1564	*Institutes of the Christian Religion*	Apologetics can be of limited use. Man needs special revelation or he will fall into idolatry.	Belief comes before understanding. Men have a *sensus divinitatis* which convinces them of the truth of the gospel.

Chart 129

Blaise Pascal: *Pensees*

The *Pensees* is a group of scattered sentences and paragraphs that appear to have no order. Filleau De la Chaise explained that Pascal presented the order of his apologetic in a lecture given in 1658. Pascal did not employ any metaphysical arguments for the existence of God. Pascal leaned heavily upon the writings of Augustine to construct his arguments.

Part 1	The situation of man	The typical man of this time is self-satisfied and considers himself to be emancipated from religion. As such, he is free to believe what he wishes and to live as he wishes. Pascal concluded that man is gifted with reason, but that man is also a weak creature. The rational man realizes that he needs God. This kind of man either serves God or seeks to know him.
Part 2	A comparison of religions and philosophies with Christianity	Pascal provided a catalog of all religions and philosophies. He then showed that all of them fail to improve man's situation. Only Christianity tells the truth about man's situation and what will become of him. In this part we find Pascal's wager. He agreed with Augustine that faith must precede understanding.
Part 3	A historical demonstration of the truth of Christianity	Pascal used Scripture to make the case that salvation is to be found only in Jesus Christ. He argued that biblical prophecies are the greatest proofs of who Jesus Christ is.

Pascal's Wager

	God exists	God does not exist
Belief	Heaven and eternal reward	One is a better person for having exercised self-control
Lack of belief	Some temporal pleasures. Hell and eternal punishment.	One is neither better or worse off

Conclusion
The rational person will have belief in God because eternal damnation is costlier than any amount of temporal pleasures

Chart 130

David Hume and Responses to His Arguments

While he is generally thought to be an atheist, Hume was actually more of a deist. He argued that belief in God is not the result of reason, but actually requires faith.

Philosopher	Dates	Writings	Explanation
David Hume A thoroughly consistent **mitigated skeptic**. While he believed in a God, reason told him that he could not know with certainty that God exists.	1711–1776	*Dialogues Concerning Natural Religion*	**Natural theology** Cosmological argument fails because it is based on causation
		A Treatise of Human Nature	**Natural theology** Design argument fails because it is based on induction
		Natural History of Religion	**Revealed theology** Religion is characterized by hypocrisy in the clergy, and superstition in the laity. Revelation is not sufficient to convince a rational man of its authenticity. Belief in God is the result of the fear of unknown causes.
		Enquiry Concerning Human Understanding	**Revealed theology** A rational man does not have sufficient reason to believe in Christianity. There is no proof of miracles.
Thomas Reid As a **Scottish common sense realist**, he disagreed with Hume outright	1710–1796	*An Inquiry into the Human Mind on the Principles of Common Sense*	We do not know or cannot prove that other minds exist, and are rational for believing that they do. In much the same way, we are rational for believing that God exists.
			We know of God's existence because we are designed by God to know that he exists. This kind of knowledge does not need explanation.
Immanuel Kant After reading Hume, he too became a **mitigated skeptic**	1724–1804	*Critique of Pure Reason*	He agreed with Hume that the classical arguments for the existence of God fail because they have a basis in metaphysics and are argued for by induction
			The fact that morality appears to be universal can only be explained by the existence of God

Chart 131

Naturalistic Arguments against Miracles

Baruch Spinoza	*A Political Theological Treatise*	1. Events in Scripture happened in accordance with the laws of nature 2. Moses did not write the Pentateuch, but Ezra the scribe did 3. The resurrection did not happen 4. The prophets did not speak from supernatural revelation 5. One must employ a historical-critical method of interpretation to understand what the Bible is saying
David Hume	*Enquiry Concerning Human Understanding*	1. A miracle is a violation of the laws of nature 2. Experience has established the laws of nature 3. Belief should be apportioned to evidence 4. There is no proof of miracles 5. Nothing that ever happened can be called a miracle
Immanuel Kant	*Critique of Pure Reason*	1. We can only know what sensory experience tells us about the world 2. We cannot know reality itself, so metaphysics is not possible 3. God is in the real world, so we cannot know him by sensory experience 4. We can know of God's existence by means of reason
	Religion within the Bounds of Reason Alone	1. God is unknowable even with the Bible 2. The nature of religion is moral 3. Christianity does not need miracles 4. Jesus Christ is a good moral example
Logical Positivists	The verification principle	If something is not empirically verifiable, then it does not make sense to talk about it
Charles Darwin	*The Descent of Man*	1. Everything in nature is the result of fixed laws 2. It is not logical to believe in miracles 3. The miracles reported in the Bible are the result of superstitious minds 4. Evolution is a naturalistic explanation of all life

Chart 132

Apologetic Methods

Classical apologetics	**Anselm, Thomas Aquinas, William Lane Craig**	This approach to apologetics relies on using the classical arguments for God's existence and for the truth concerning Jesus Christ
Evidentialist apologetics	**Gary Habermas, William Payley**	This approach to apologetics relies upon historical evidence to convince people of the truth concerning Jesus Christ
Cumulative case apologetics	**Paul Feinberg, Basil Mitchell**	This approach to apologetics employs both classical and evidentialist methods to convince one of the truth of the gospel
Presuppositional apologetics	**Cornelius Van Til, John Frame**	This approach to apologetics assumes that man is fallen and his reasoning is darkened. As such, arguments are an insufficient means to bring one to the truth. The only way that people can be brought to the truth is through the simple preaching of the gospel. This approach is also known as fideism.

Chart 133

Classical Apologetics

This approach employs deductive argumentation and evidence to convince people of God's existence. It also relies upon the Holy Spirit to bring them to a knowledge of the truth.

The cosmological argument	**Thomas Aquinas**	1. Everything is either necessary or contingent 2. If something is necessary, then it cannot fail to exist 3. If something is contingent, then at some point it must fail to exist 4. There must be at least one necessary thing 5. God is that necessary being
The ontological argument	**Anselm of Canterbury**	1. God is the most perfect being that can be conceived 2. A perfect being possesses all of the attributes of perfection 3. One of these attributes is existence 4. The idea of God entails his existence
The design argument	**Thomas Aquinas**	Also known as the teleological argument. The orderliness of the universe suggests that it did not come about by accident. It suggests that there is a design and, of course, a designer.
The moral argument	**Athenagoras, Eusebius, Augustine**	Christianity is superior to all false religions because they lead to all kinds of immorality
Theology of history	**Eusebius, Augustine**	History is being used by God to make the truth of the gospel known throughout the world. God is in charge of history and is using everything in history for his purposes.

Chart 134

Thomas Aquinas's Five Proofs for the Existence of God

1. The argument from motion	God is the unmoved mover	There must be something that sets everything else in motion. That something is God.
2. The nature of efficient cause	God is the cause of everything	Everything has a cause. God is the first cause.
3. The argument from possibility and necessity	God is a necessary being	1. Everything is either necessary or contingent 2. If something is necessary, then it cannot fail to exist 3. If something is contingent, then at some point it must fail to exist 4. There must be at least one necessary thing 5. God is that necessary being
4. The argument of gradation	God is the most perfect of all that exists	Everything in this world differs with respect to goodness, truth, and beauty. Before we can know these differences, we must know the standard for them (goodness, truth, and beauty). God is the standard of goodness, truth, and beauty.
5. The governance of the world	God is the designer of the world order	There appears to be a design in the universe because things naturally work so well. God must be the designer of all that exists.

Chart 135

Evidentialist Apologetics

An empirically based approach to apologetics that assumes truth depends upon historical events

Different sorts of evidence	C. H. Dodd	Historical events
	William Payley	External world
	Friedrich Schleiermacher	Present religious experience
Essential elements of evidentialism	Facts	Objective states of affairs which obtain. Private or subjective experience is not sufficient for evidence. Truth must be observable.
	Interpretation	Meaning which grows out of facts
Evidential methodology According to Gary Habermas	Seven tenets	1. The purpose of this method is the development of historical evidences for the Christian faith 2. Historical occurrences are not brute facts that interpret themselves 3. Evidentialism is also used to argue against defeaters 4. One cannot force anyone into the kingdom of God 5. There is some common ground between the believer and the unbeliever. For example: sensory data, scientific theories, and application of inference. 6. The Holy Spirit uses apologetics to convert unbelievers and strengthen the faith of believers 7. Most evidentialists are eclectic in their approach

Chart 136

Cumulative Case Apologetics

An abductive (inference to the best explanation) approach to apologetics. According to Paul Feinberg, it combines both subjective and objective elements of the other approaches to build the strongest possible argument for the truth. It attempts to use the other apologetic methods together so that their weaknesses are minimized.

Tests for truth	**Test of consistency**	A system of belief must not lead to contradiction
	Test of correspondence	Any belief must correspond with reality
	Test of comprehensiveness	The best theory is one that can explain the most
	Test of simplicity	All things being equal, the best theory is the simplest one
	Test of fruitfulness	The best theory is the one that has the fewest negative consequences
The Holy Spirit	**Internal witness**	The Holy Spirit convicts or convinces unbelievers
		The Holy Spirit appeals to the conscience of unbelievers
		The Holy Spirit works on the unbeliever's innate knowledge of God
		The Holy Spirit also works on believers to give them a sense of certainty about what they believe
	External witness	Theistic arguments
		Religious experience
		Moral law
		The Bible

Chart 137

Epistemology Associated with Apologetic Approaches

All of these approaches to apologetics employ internalist epistemologies, meaning that knowledge equals justified true belief. One must also know how he knows what he knows.

Apologetic Method	Evidence	Justification	Evaluation
Classical apologetics	Arguments for the existence of God are sufficient to provide enough evidence for Christian faith	Foundationalism	These arguments cannot bring anyone to faith but they can cause one to seriously consider the faith. The Holy Spirit must still act to convert one from an unbeliever to a believer.
Evidentialism	Historical facts provide sufficient evidence to convince one of the truth of Christianity	Foundationalism	The Holy Spirit must still act upon a person before they can come to faith. But the Holy Spirit can and does use cumulative case apologetics to initially bring the hearer to faith.
Cumulative case apologetics	The weight of evidence from a number of different approaches provides sufficient evidence for belief	Foundationalism	This apologetic method provides knowledge but not faith. The Holy Spirit must still act for one to gain faith.
Fideisim (presuppositionalism)	There is no sufficient evidence that one human being can give another	Foundationalism or coherentism	Only preaching the Word of God in accordance with the Holy Spirit is capable of producing faith. Apologetic methods are never sufficient and are a waste of time.

Chart 138

Augustinian Virtue Ethics

Augustine assumed metaphysical but not epistemological realism		
Meta-ethical presuppositions	**Metaphysics of morals**	**Moral realism**–Moral facts exist independent of the observer. Moral facts are found and not made.
		The good–God is the greatest and highest good
		Predestination–After Pelagius, Augustine held to a strong view of election and moral culpability
	Moral epistemology	Augustine was not clear on how one knows morality, but Scripture reading is essential. Aquinas explained that the conscience is composed of a moral faculty (*synderesis*) plus reasoning (the virtue of prudence).
	Moral psychology The believer can do acts of supererogation. The believer can have the character of the man of superhuman virtue.	**Motivation internalism**–Recognition of moral facts does provide motivation for moral action
		Moral development–Before salvation, does not matter. After salvation, one goes through the process of sanctification.
		Mental health–Before salvation, one does not function properly. Sin causes a kind of insanity. Happiness (*eudaimonia*–the happiness that comes from self-effort) is fleeting. After salvation one can achieve true happiness (*makarious*–the happiness that comes from God).
Theological virtues Created in the believer by the Holy Spirit giving him the power and knowledge to live righteously	**Love** Greek: *agape* Latin: *caritas*	The love of God and the love of man for God's sake. This is the primary virtue that unifies all of the other virtues, whether theological, moral, or intellectual. Its opposite is *cupiditas* (Latin: self-love).
	Faith	Grows out of love and gives one spiritual knowledge
	Hope	Grows out of love and causes man to look at eternity
Cardinal virtues	Augustine viewed all of the cardinal virtues as different manifestations of love (*caritas*)	
Eternal law	This is all of God's laws by which he governs the universe. It existed before time began. Some argue that it is God himself.	
Temporal law	These are man-made laws that should reflect aspects of the eternal law	

Chart 139

Thomas Aquinas's (and Bonaventure's) Virtue Ethics

Thomas Aquinas and Bonaventure assumed both metaphysical and epistemological realism

Meta-ethical presuppositions	**Metaphysics of morals**	**Moral realism**–Moral facts exist independent of the observer. Moral facts are found and not made.
		The good–God is the greatest and highest good
	Moral epistemology	*Synderesis*–The natural law
		Conscientia–Practical reason
	Moral psychology	**Motivation internalism**–Recognition of moral facts does provide motivation for moral action
		Moral development–Before salvation, does not matter. After salvation, one goes through the process of sanctification.
		Mental health–Before salvation, one does not function properly. Sin causes a kind of insanity. Happiness (*eudaimonia*–the happiness that comes from self-effort) is fleeting. After salvation one can achieve true happiness (*makarious*–the happiness that comes from God).
Theological virtues	**Love**	The love of God and the love of man for God's sake. This is the primary virtue that unifies all of the other virtues, whether theological, moral, or intellectual. Its opposite is *cupiditas* (Latin: self-love).
	Faith	Grows out of love and gives one spiritual knowledge
	Hope	Grows out of love and causes man to look at eternity
Cardinal virtues	**Justice**	Equity and fairness
	Wisdom	Practical reason
	Courage	Strength to do what is right
	Temperance	Self-control
Laws	**Eternal law**	This is all of God's laws by which he governs the universe. It existed before time began. Some argue that it is God himself.
	Divine law	The Old and the New Testament
	Natural law	General revelation makes known to all the morality of the Ten Commandments
	Civil law	Natural law should serve as the foundation for civil law. This law is man-made and should encourage virtue.

Chart 140

Divine Command Theory (Theological Voluntarism)

Contemporary divine command theorists include Philip Quinn and Robert Merrihew Adams

John Duns Scotus	Argued that goodness is based upon God's will and his nature, and that God's will is consistent with his nature. Both natural law and virtue ethics are compatible with this version of divine command theory.
William of Ockham	Wanted to emphasize the freedom of God. He asserted that goodness is based only upon God's will. This version of divine command theory is compatible only with deontological ethical theories. As such, this version of divine command theory is vulnerable to Plato's **Euthyphro dilemma**.
The Euthyphro dilemma	Two parts: 1. If something is good because God declares it so, then goodness is arbitrary 2. If, on the other hand, God approves of something because it is good, then goodness is something apart from God

Divine Command Meta-ethics

Metaphysics of morals	**The good**	Moral facts are based upon God's will. To be or do good is to act in accordance with the will of God. Natural law is in accordance with God's will. Virtue ethics can be consistent with divine command theory.
Moral epistemology	**The noetic effects of sin**	Man is so constructed by God that moral knowledge is inherent. Because of sin, moral knowledge is confused. Consequently, moral knowledge results from hearing the Word of God.
Moral psychology	**Internalism**	Moral knowledge provides motivation for moral action
	Mental health	Moral action results in *eudaimonia*

Chart 141

Graded Absolutism (Hierarchicalism)

Norman Geisler holds this moral theory, expressed in his work *Christian Ethics: Options and Issues*. Geisler asserts Augustine and Charles Hodge held to this moral theory as well. This approach to deontology does not involve metaphysical nominalism.

Meta-ethical presuppositions	**Metaphysics of morals**	**Moral realism**–Moral facts exist independent of the observer
		The good–Depends on God's will
		Free will–Moral agents have free will
	Moral epistemology	**Cognitivism**–Moral judgments express beliefs
	Moral psychology	**Motivational internalism**–Recognition of moral facts or obligations provides motivation for moral action
		Cognitivism–Moral motivation comes from within the moral agent
Other pressupositions	According to Geisler, "God is one in nature, but he has many moral attributes. Each absolute moral law is traceable to one of God's unchangeable moral attributes."	
	Christian ethics are deontological	
	Ethical conflicts are resolved by use of a hierarchy of laws. Avoid the greater evil by doing the lesser.	
	Graded absolutism recognizes moral absolutes	
	Graded absolutism should not be confused with utilitarianism	
	Graded absolutism should not be confused with situational ethics	
	Graded absolutism recognizes **exemptions** but not **exceptions** to absolute moral laws: <ul><li>Geisler argues that "**exceptions** violate the universality and absoluteness of a moral law"</li><li>An **exemption** only eliminates the individual's culpability of a lower law while still recognizing absolute moral laws</li></ul>	
Geisler's hierarchy	**1.** Love for God over love for man **2.** Obey God over government **3.** Mercy over veracity	

Chart 142

PART 5
HISTORY OF PHILOSOPHY

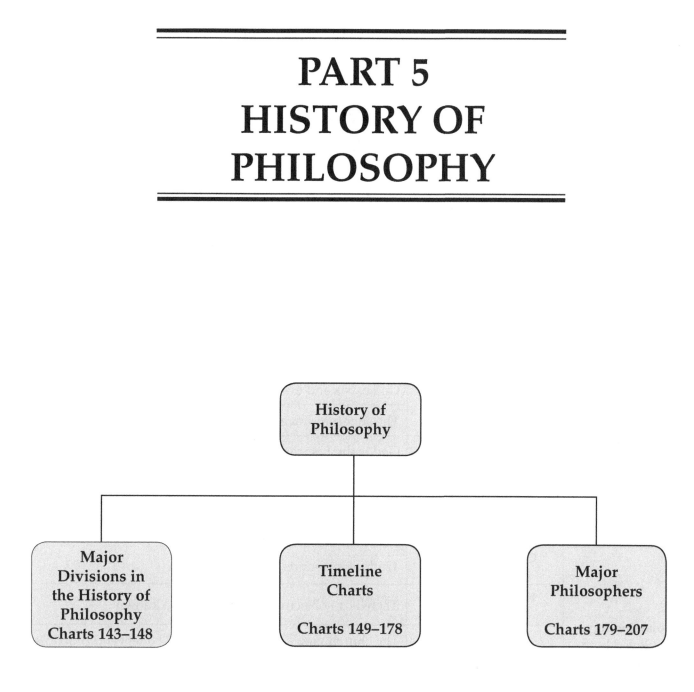

The History of Philosophy

The first section of Part 5 provides an explanation of the major divisions within the history of philosophy. More specifically, it provides an explanation of premodernity, modernity, and postmodernity.

The second section provides historical timeline charts so that one can see which philosopher influenced others. These charts allow one to see the history of ideas visually.

The last section provides an overview of the major philosophers and their ideas.

Premodernity

Recorded History–1600

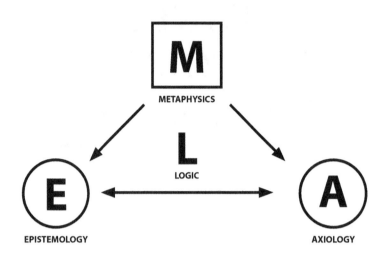

Premodernity Christianity is most compatible with this worldview		
Metaphysics (is the first philosophy)	**Theology**	God exists and everything else is contingent upon him
		The supernatural exists and does not conflict with science
	Cosmology	God is the first cause and the creator of everything
	Ontology	Man exists as part of the community, thus the community has precedence over the individual
		Realism–Things exist independent of the observer
Epistemology Employed both empiricism and rationalism	**Correspondence theory of truth**	Truth corresponds to reality
	Epistemological realism	There is an objective truth that can be known
	Community	The church views corporately shared beliefs and practices to be important. Creeds and traditions are to be adhered to, and protected for the good of the church.
	Hermeneutic of trust	The content of the Bible is inerrant, sufficient, and authoritative
	Teleological	Epistemology is dependent upon metaphysics
Axiology	**Realism**	Values are real and objective
	Teleological	Axiology is dependent upon metaphysics
	Community	The rights of the individual are subordinate to the needs of the community

Chart 143

Modernity

1600–1950

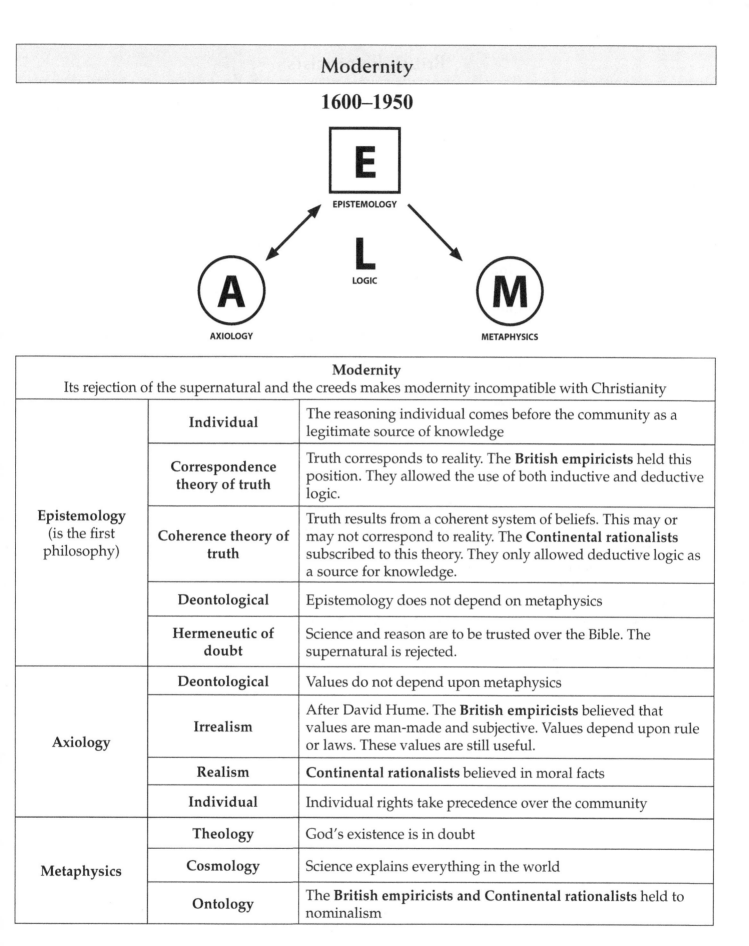

Modernity		
Its rejection of the supernatural and the creeds makes modernity incompatible with Christianity		
Epistemology (is the first philosophy)	Individual	The reasoning individual comes before the community as a legitimate source of knowledge
	Correspondence theory of truth	Truth corresponds to reality. The **British empiricists** held this position. They allowed the use of both inductive and deductive logic.
	Coherence theory of truth	Truth results from a coherent system of beliefs. This may or may not correspond to reality. The **Continental rationalists** subscribed to this theory. They only allowed deductive logic as a source for knowledge.
	Deontological	Epistemology does not depend on metaphysics
	Hermeneutic of doubt	Science and reason are to be trusted over the Bible. The supernatural is rejected.
Axiology	Deontological	Values do not depend upon metaphysics
	Irrealism	After David Hume. The **British empiricists** believed that values are man-made and subjective. Values depend upon rule or laws. These values are still useful.
	Realism	**Continental rationalists** believed in moral facts
	Individual	Individual rights take precedence over the community
Metaphysics	Theology	God's existence is in doubt
	Cosmology	Science explains everything in the world
	Ontology	The **British empiricists and Continental rationalists** held to nominalism

Chart 144

British Empiricists

Logic	Deduction	The empiricists allowed for the use of deduction. David Hume argued that knowledge derived from deduction was trivial.
	Induction	The empiricists allowed for the use of induction. David Hume explained that induction cannot guarantee knowledge.
Epistemology	Truth	Correspondence theory of truth
	Innate ideas	The British empiricists rejected the possibility of innate ideas
Metaphysics	God	Some thought that belief in God was essential (Berkeley, Reid). Many did not believe in God.
	Cosmology	Cosmology can be known empirically
	Ontology	They were nominalists because of skepticism about substance
Axiology	Value	Ethics and aesthetics are seen as part of the same thing
	Reason	Moral/aesthetic knowledge does not depend upon reason. It comes from a moral/aesthetic sense or from the emotions.

Analytic Philosophers

- Descended from the British empiricists and began in 1903 with G. E. Moore
- Emphasized Hume's fork
- Rejected idealism and subjectivism
- Believed that philosophical problems are largely linguistic problems
- Emphasized rigorous use of logic
- Emphasized precision of language
- Aimed at breaking down complex concepts into their simpler constituents

Chart 145

The Continental Rationalists

Logic	Deduction	The Continental rationalists allowed for the use of deduction because it can provide certainty
	Induction	They rejected the use of induction because it cannot provide certainty
Epistemology	Cartesian certainty	Cartesian certainty is absolute certainty of knowledge. This is achieved via **methodological doubt**, which rejects any knowledge of which one is not certain.
	Innate ideas	They accepted innate ideas
	Truth	They began with a correspondence theory of truth but moved to a coherence theory of truth
Metaphysics	Cartesianism	**Metaphysical dualism**–Everything is either mind or body
	Ontology	With the exception of Baruch Spinoza, they were nominalists. After Kant, many were also idealists.
Axiology	Value	Ethics and aesthetics are two separate disciplines
	Deontology	Axiology is separated from metaphysics

Continental Philosophy

- Began at the end of the Enlightenment (the Age of Reason), after Kant
- Began with Johann Gottlieb Fichte
- Emphasized Romanticism (the belief that knowledge results from intuition and feelings)
- Emphasized idealism and subjectivism
- Resulted in existentialism
- Resulted in phenomenology
- Phenomenology/existentialism was followed by structuralism

Chart 146

Postmodernity

1950–Present

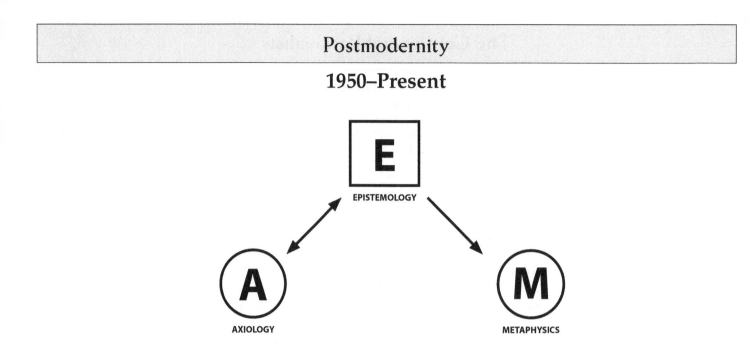

Postmodernists reduce epistemology and axiology to hermeneutics. They reduce metaphysics to ontology.

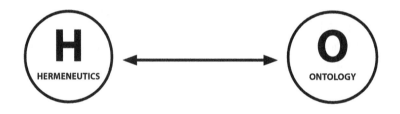

Postmodernists believe that there is no objective truth or knowledge. They are convinced that there are only interpretations (hermeneutics). Postmodernists also believe that truth and knowledge are determined by power. Postmodernity results from combining existentialism, phenomenology, pragmatism, and structuralism/post-structuralism.

Chart 147

Postmodernity

Because it rejects logic, objective truth, and morality, postmodernity is not compatible with Christianity

Epistemology Is still the first philosophy, but reason and science cannot deliver knowledge	**Irrealism**	There is no objective truth to be known
	Community	The power of the community determines knowledge
	Theories of truth	Pragmatic theory of truth
		Phenomenological theory of truth
		Structuralist theory of truth
	Hermeneutic of suspicion	The author is dead and has no rights over the text. Meaning is determined by the power of the community.
Axiology	**Community**	The power of the community determines beauty and morality
	Nihilism	There is no objective morality or beauty. There is only what is of use to the community.
Metaphysics	**Ontology**	Idealism and nominalism characterize the ontology of the postmodern philosophers
	Theology	Accepts the possibility of the supernatural. Also accepts the possibility of a plurality of gods.

Cultural Postmodernity

- It is important to realize that just as there is a philosophical postmodernity, there is also a cultural postmodernity.
- Cultural postmodernity arrived at about the same time as philosophical postmodernity (1950s).
- Cultural postmodernity is a Western phenomenon in which people argue that truth is relative because so many different cultures and religions coexist within the same country.
- Like philosophical postmodernity, cultural postmodernity emphasizes the importance of one's community to determine truth, morality, and beauty.
- Another aspect of cultural postmodernity is that culture has changed from orality in the premodern worldview to literacy in the modern worldview to visual orientation in the postmodern worldview. This resulted from poor reading skills and short attention spans. Television is at least partially to blame for both of these trends. Television caused the visual focus of contemporary Western culture.

Chart 148

Historical Overview

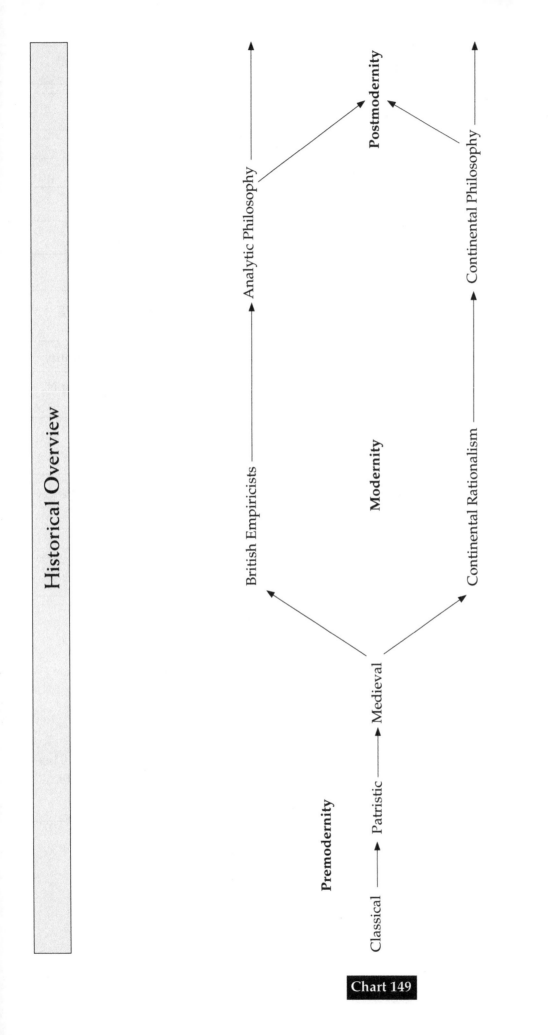

Premodernity

Classical ——▶ Patristic ——▶ Medieval

Modernity

British Empiricists ——▶ Analytic Philosophy

Continental Rationalism ——▶ Continental Philosophy

Postmodernity

Chart 149

Pre-Socratic Philosophy

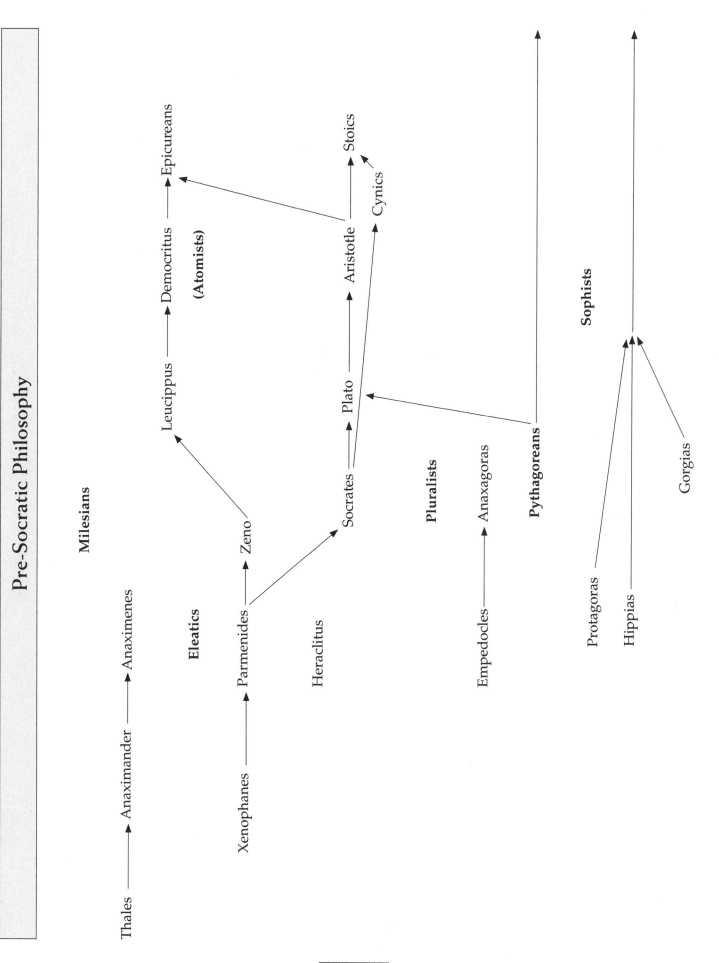

Chart 150

Classical Period 470 BC–1 BC

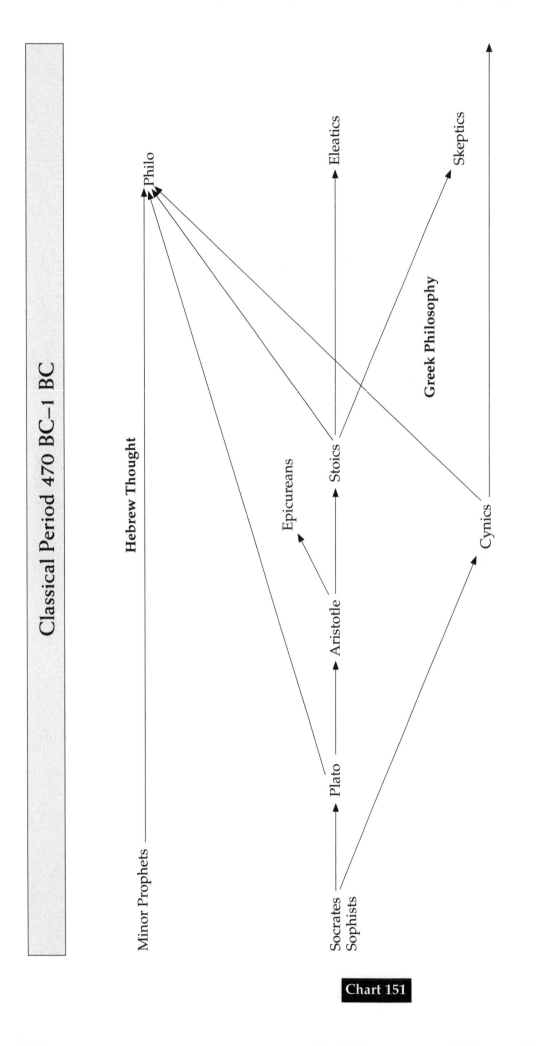

Hebrew Thought

Minor Prophets

Philo

Eleatics

Skeptics

Greek Philosophy

Stoics

Epicureans

Cynics

Socrates
Sophists

Plato

Aristotle

Chart 151

The Patristic Period 100–400 AD

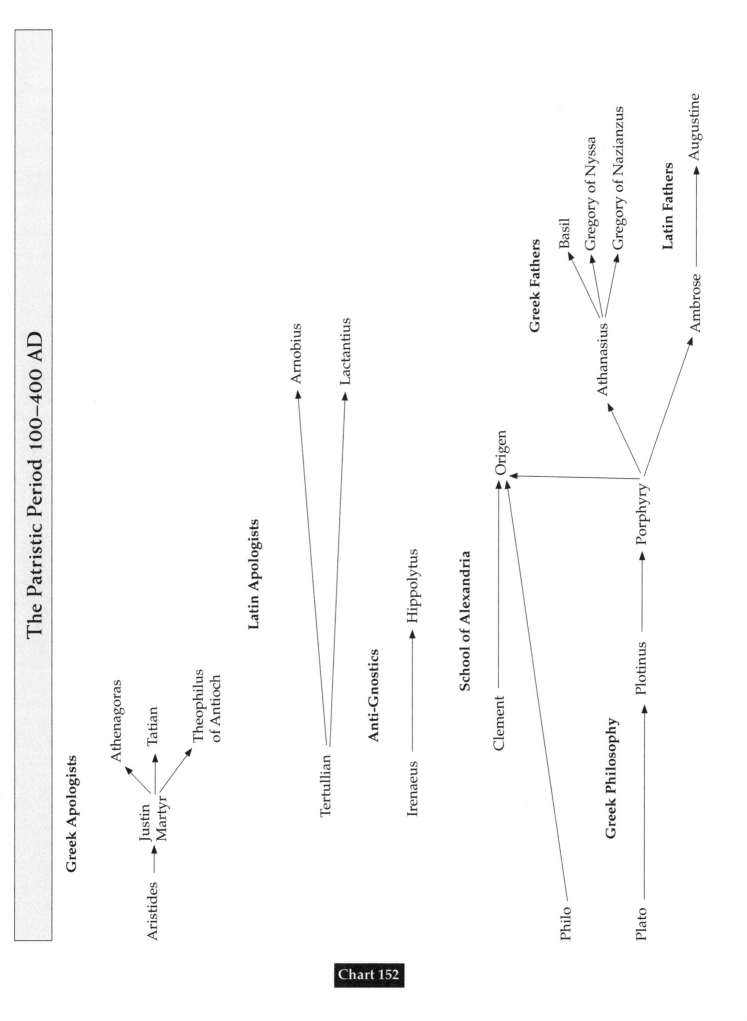

Greek Apologists

Aristides → Justin Martyr → Athenagoras

Justin Martyr → Tatian

Justin Martyr → Theophilus of Antioch

Latin Apologists

Tertullian → Arnobius

Tertullian → Lactantius

Anti-Gnostics

Irenaeus → Hippolytus

School of Alexandria

Clement → Origen

Philo → Origen

Greek Philosophy

Plato → Plotinus → Porphyry

Greek Fathers

Athanasius → Basil

Athanasius → Gregory of Nyssa

Athanasius → Gregory of Nazianzus

Porphyry → Origen

Porphyry → Athanasius

Latin Fathers

Ambrose → Augustine

Porphyry → Ambrose

Chart 152

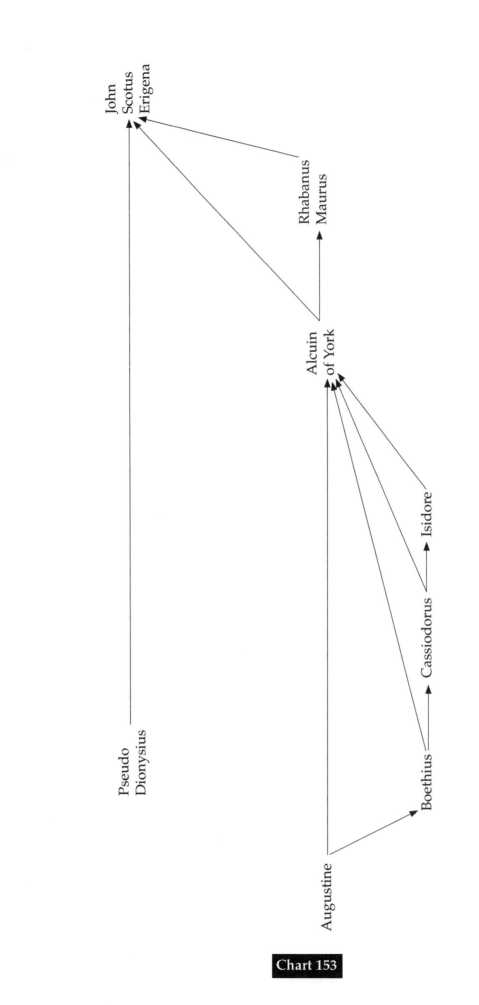

5th–9th Centuries

Pseudo
Dionysius

John
Scotus
Erigena

Rhabanus
Maurus

Alcuin
of York

Isidore

Cassiodorus

Boethius

Augustine

Chart 153

10th–12th Centuries (Medieval Philosophy)

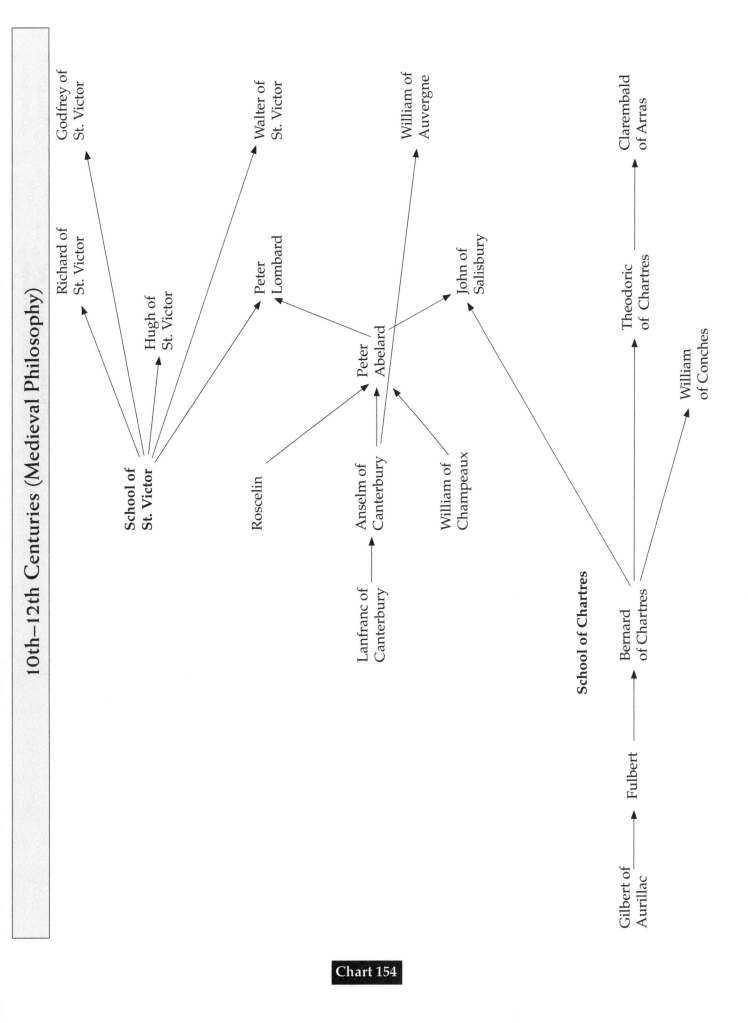

Godfrey of
St. Victor

Richard of
St. Victor

Walter of
St. Victor

William of
Auvergne

Clarembald
of Arras

Hugh of
St. Victor

Peter
Lombard

Theodoric
of Chartres

**School of
St. Victor**

Peter
Abelard

John of
Salisbury

William
of Conches

Roscelin

Anselm of
Canterbury

William of
Champeaux

Lanfranc of
Canterbury

School of Chartres

Bernard
of Chartres

Gilbert of
Aurillac

Fulbert

Chart 154

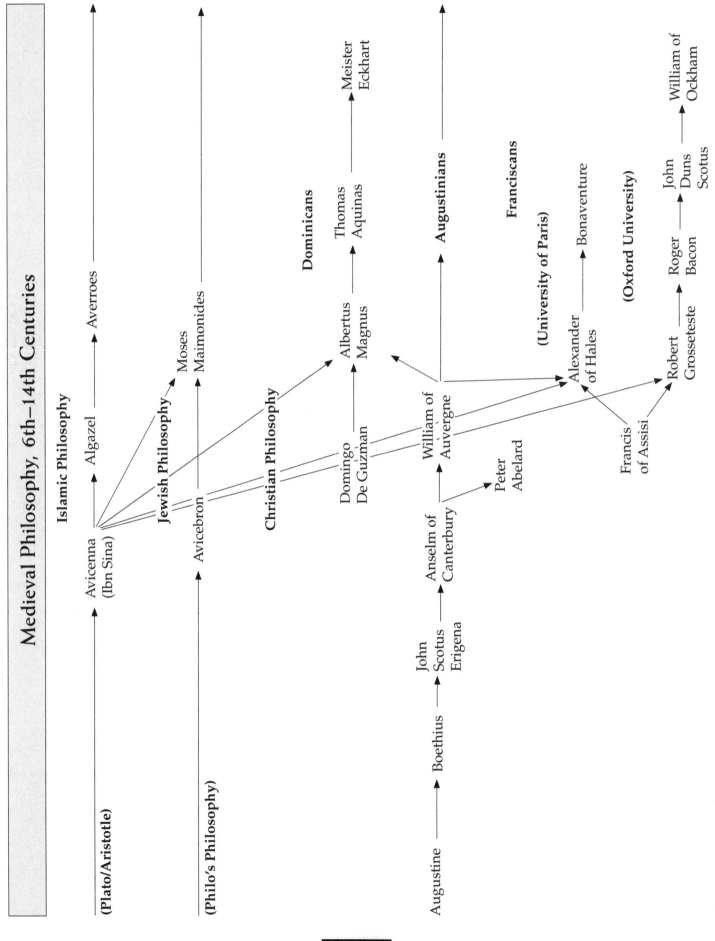

Medieval Philosophy, 6th–14th Centuries

Islamic Philosophy

Avicenna (Ibn Sina) → Algazel → Averroes →

(Plato/Aristotle) →

Jewish Philosophy

Avicebron → Moses Maimonides →

(Philo's Philosophy) →

Christian Philosophy

Dominicans

Domingo De Guzman → Albertus Magnus → Thomas Aquinas → Meister Eckhart →

William of Auvergne

Augustinians →

Franciscans

(University of Paris)

Alexander of Hales → Bonaventure

(Oxford University)

Robert Grosseteste → Roger Bacon → John Duns Scotus → William of Ockham

Francis of Assisi

Peter Abelard

Augustine → Boethius → John Scotus Erigena → Anselm of Canterbury

Chart 155

15th–16th Century, The Salamanca School

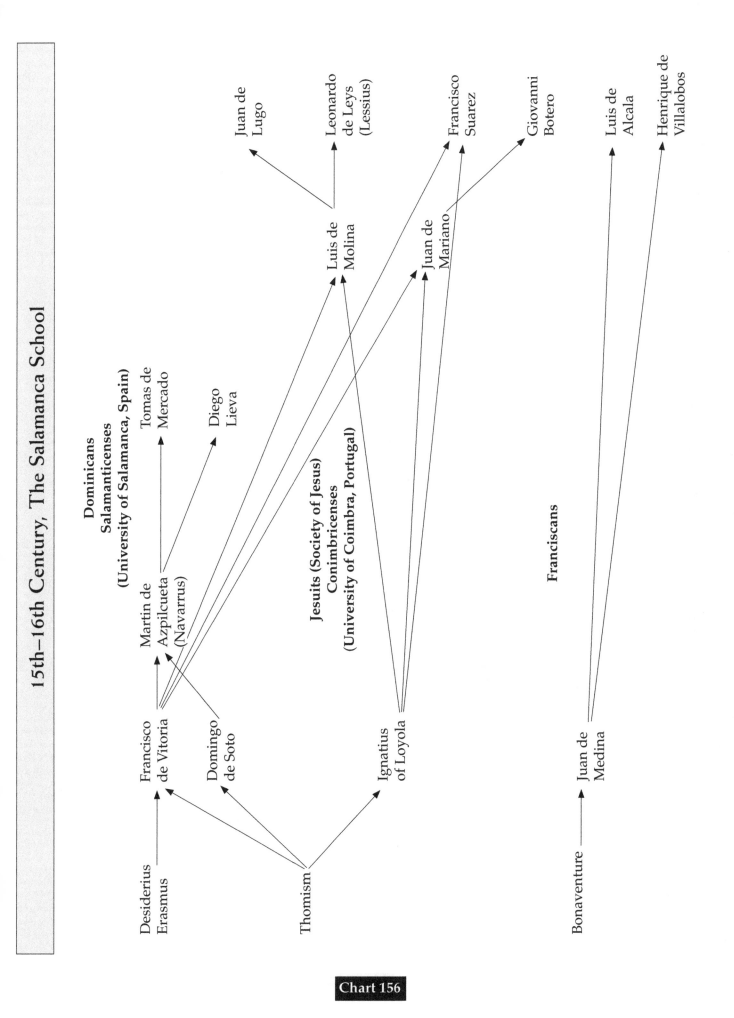

Chart 156

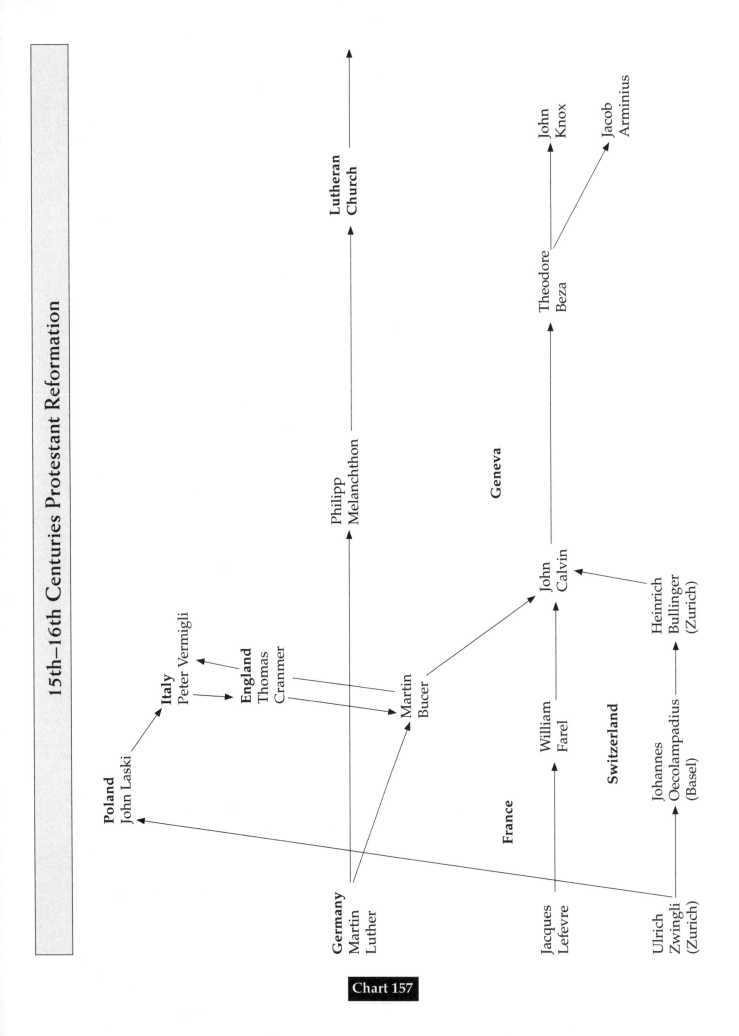

15th–16th Centuries Protestant Reformation

Poland
John Laski

Italy
Peter Vermigli

England
Thomas Cranmer

Martin Bucer

John Calvin

Philipp Melanchthon

Geneva

Theodore Beza

John Knox

Jacob Arminius

Lutheran Church

William Farel

Heinrich Bullinger (Zurich)

France

Switzerland

Jacques Lefevre

Johannes Oecolampadius (Basel)

Germany
Martin Luther

Ulrich Zwingli (Zurich)

Chart 157

17th–19th Century European Philosophy

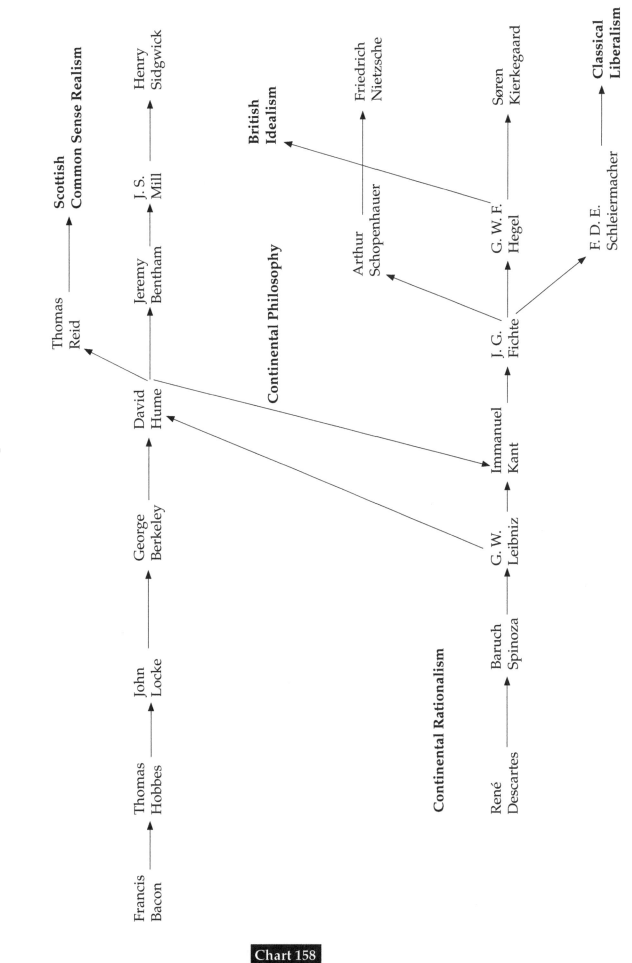

British Empiricists

Francis Bacon → Thomas Hobbes → John Locke → George Berkeley → David Hume → Thomas Reid → Jeremy Bentham → J. S. Mill → Henry Sidgwick

Scottish Common Sense Realism

Continental Rationalism

René Descartes → Baruch Spinoza → G. W. Leibniz → Immanuel Kant → J. G. Fichte → G. W. F. Hegel → Søren Kierkegaard

Continental Philosophy

Arthur Schopenhauer → Friedrich Nietzsche

British Idealism

F. D. E. Schleiermacher → **Classical Liberalism**

Chart 158

17th–18th Century European Philosophy

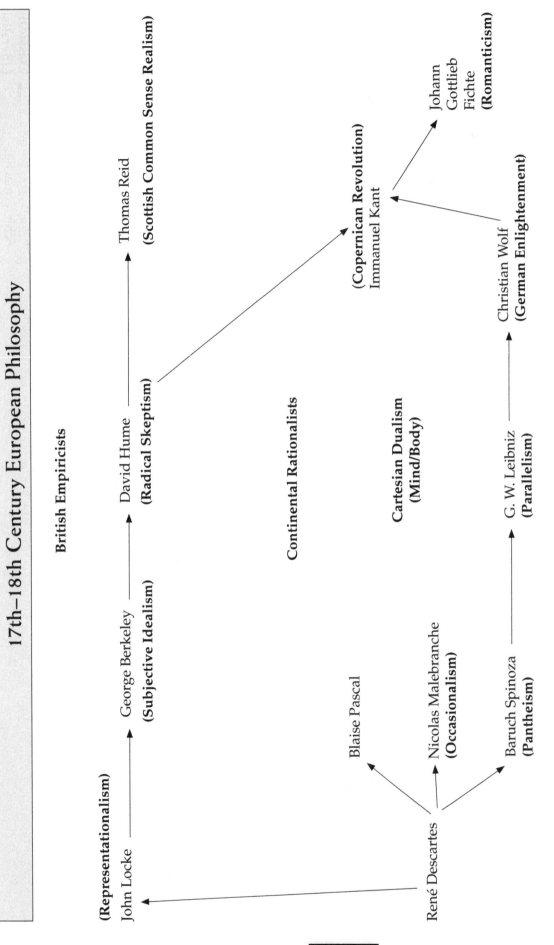

British Empiricists

(Representationalism)
John Locke →

George Berkeley
(Subjective Idealism)

David Hume
(Radical Skepticism)

Thomas Reid
(Scottish Common Sense Realism)

Continental Rationalists

**Cartesian Dualism
(Mind/Body)**

Blaise Pascal

Nicolas Malebranche
(Occasionalism)

Baruch Spinoza
(Pantheism)

G. W. Leibniz
(Parallelism)

René Descartes

Christian Wolf
(German Enlightenment)

(Copernican Revolution)
Immanuel Kant

Johann
Gottlieb
Fichte
(Romanticism)

Chart 159

19th–Century Continental Philosophy

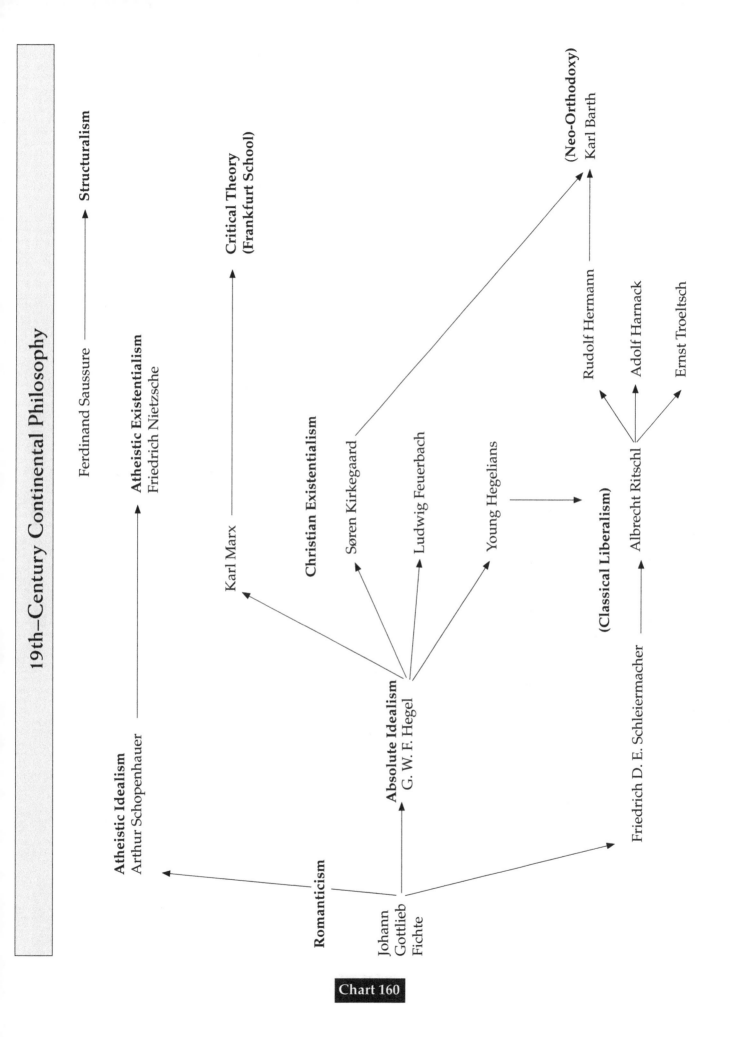

Structuralism

Ferdinand Saussure

Atheistic Existentialism
Friedrich Nietzsche

**Critical Theory
(Frankfurt School)**

Atheistic Idealism
Arthur Schopenhauer

Karl Marx

Christian Existentialism

Søren Kirkegaard

Ludwig Feuerbach

Young Hegelians

Absolute Idealism
G. W. F. Hegel

(Neo-Orthodoxy)
Karl Barth

Rudolf Hermann

Adolf Harnack

Ernst Troeltsch

(Classical Liberalism)

Albrecht Ritschl

Friedrich D. E. Schleiermacher

Romanticism

Johann
Gottlieb
Fichte

Chart 160

Post-Humean British Empiricism

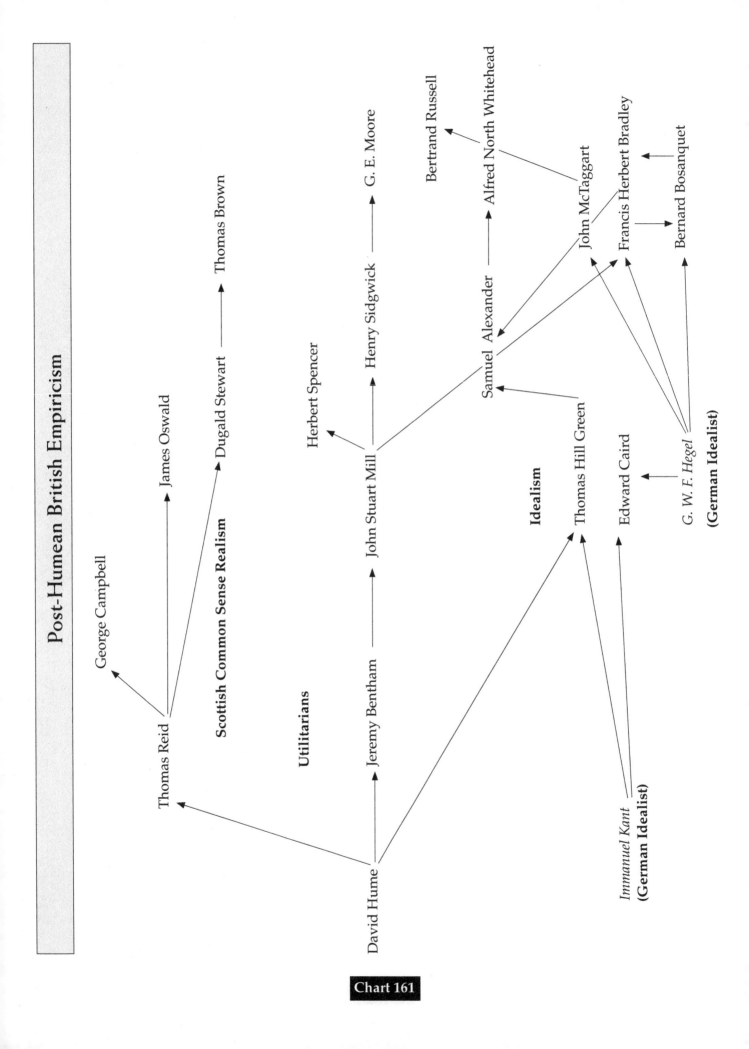

George Campbell

James Oswald

Thomas Brown

Scottish Common Sense Realism

Dugald Stewart

Thomas Reid

Herbert Spencer

G. E. Moore

Henry Sidgwick

Utilitarians

John Stuart Mill

Jeremy Bentham

Bertrand Russell

Alfred North Whitehead

John McTaggart

Francis Herbert Bradley

Bernard Bosanquet

Samuel Alexander

Idealism

Thomas Hill Green

Edward Caird

G. W. F. Hegel
(German Idealist)

Immanuel Kant
(German Idealist)

David Hume

Chart 161

Franz Brentano and 20th-Century European Philosophy

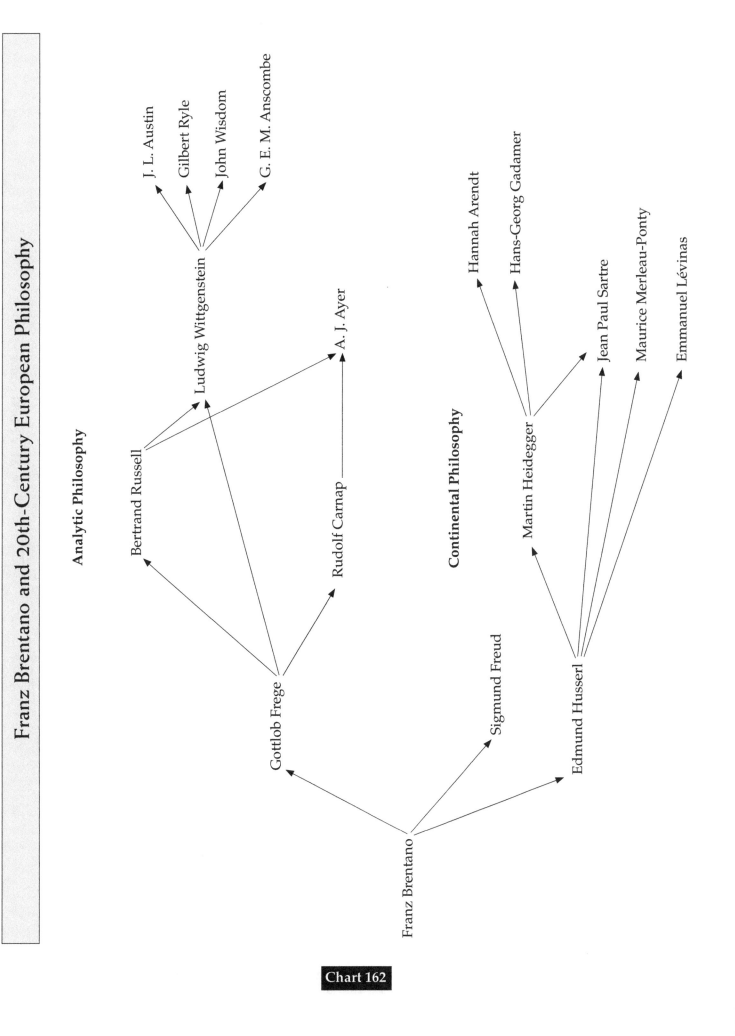

Analytic Philosophy

J. L. Austin

Gilbert Ryle

John Wisdom

G. E. M. Anscombe

Ludwig Wittgenstein

A. J. Ayer

Bertrand Russell

Rudolf Carnap

Gottlob Frege

Continental Philosophy

Hannah Arendt

Hans-Georg Gadamer

Jean Paul Sartre

Maurice Merleau-Ponty

Emmanuel Lévinas

Martin Heidegger

Sigmund Freud

Edmund Husserl

Franz Brentano

Chart 162

20th-Century Continental Philosophy

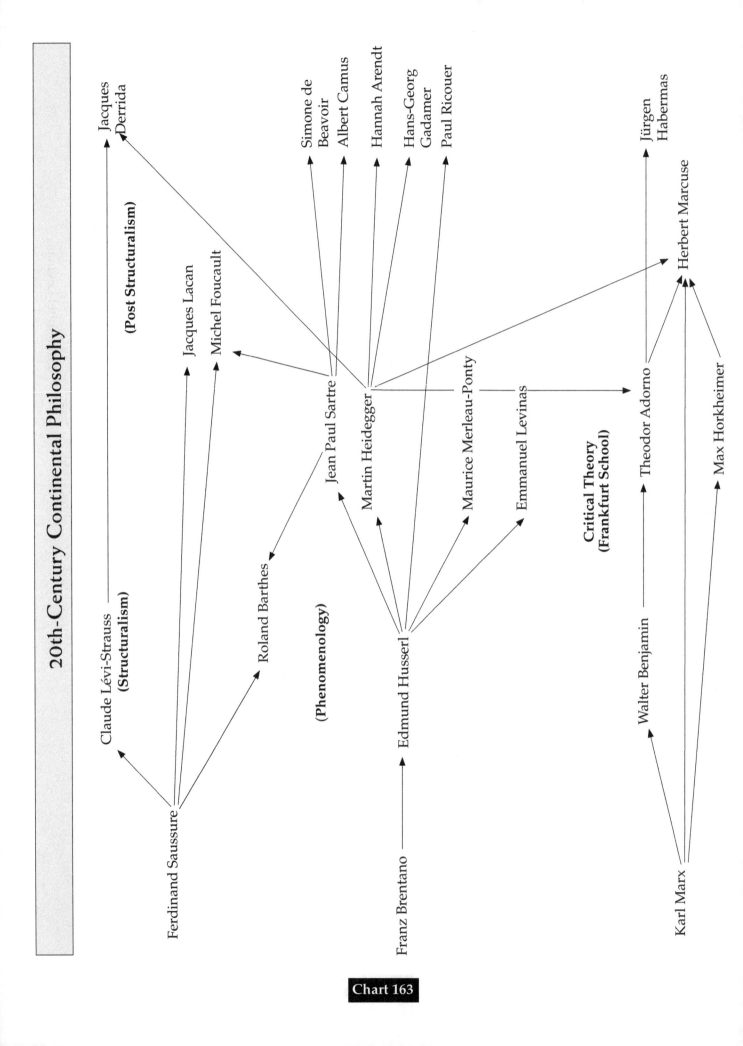

(Post Structuralism)

Jacques Derrida

Claude Lévi-Strauss
(Structuralism)

Jacques Lacan

Michel Foucault

Simone de Beavoir

Albert Camus

Hannah Arendt

Hans-Georg Gadamer

Paul Ricouer

Jürgen Habermas

Herbert Marcuse

Jean Paul Sartre

Martin Heidegger

Maurice Merleau-Ponty

Emmanuel Levinas

Theodor Adorno

Max Horkheimer

Roland Barthes

(Phenomenology)

Critical Theory
(Frankfurt School)

Ferdinand Saussure

Edmund Husserl

Franz Brentano

Walter Benjamin

Karl Marx

Chart 163

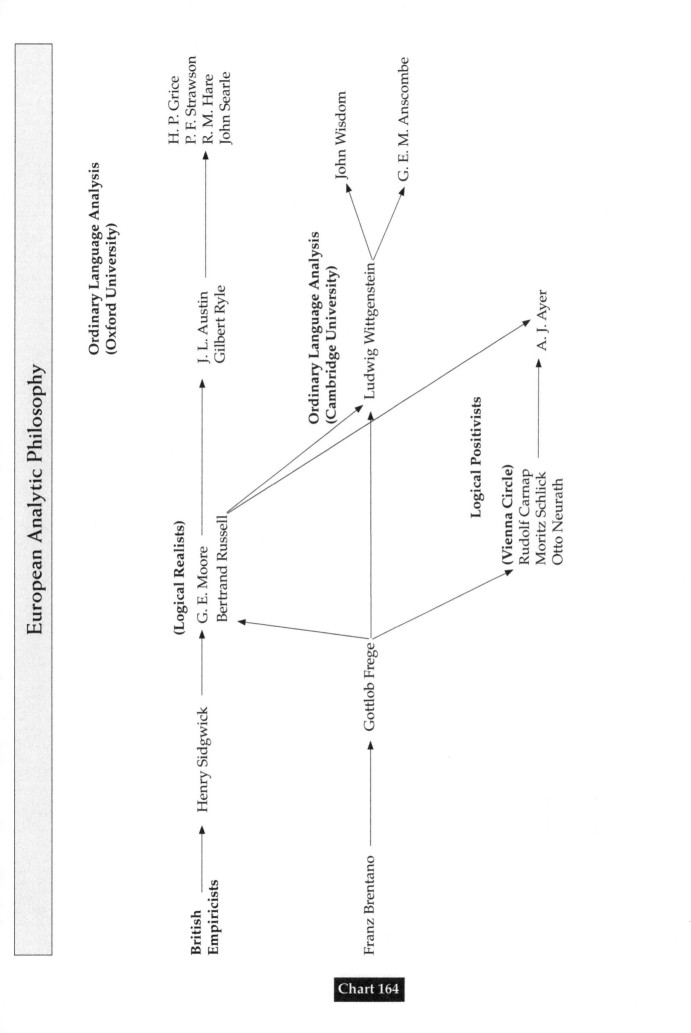

European Analytic Philosophy

**Ordinary Language Analysis
(Oxford University)**

H. P. Grice
P. F. Strawson
R. M. Hare
John Searle

J. L. Austin
Gilbert Ryle

(Logical Realists)

G. E. Moore
Bertrand Russell

**British
Empiricists**

Henry Sidgwick

**Ordinary Language Analysis
(Cambridge University)**

John Wisdom

G. E. M. Anscombe

Ludwig Wittgenstein

Logical Positivists

(Vienna Circle)
Rudolf Carnap
Moritz Schlick
Otto Neurath

A. J. Ayer

Gottlob Frege

Franz Brentano

Chart 164

Early American Philosophy

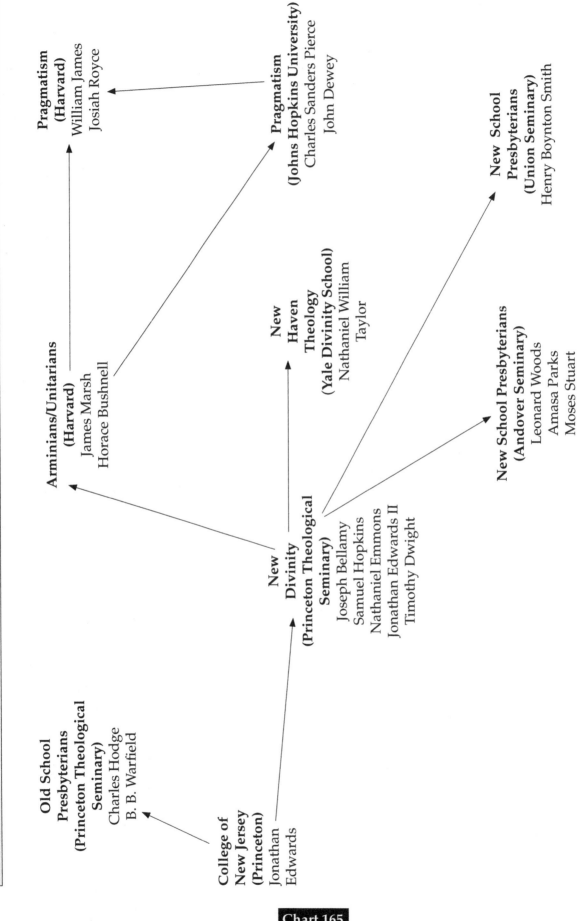

Pragmatism (Harvard)
William James
Josiah Royce

Pragmatism (Johns Hopkins University)
Charles Sanders Pierce
John Dewey

New School Presbyterians (Union Seminary)
Henry Boynton Smith

Arminians/Unitarians (Harvard)
James Marsh
Horace Bushnell

New Haven Theology (Yale Divinity School)
Nathaniel William Taylor

New School Presbyterians (Andover Seminary)
Leonard Woods
Amasa Parks
Moses Stuart

New Divinity (Princeton Theological Seminary)
Joseph Bellamy
Samuel Hopkins
Nathaniel Emmons
Jonathan Edwards II
Timothy Dwight

Old School Presbyterians (Princeton Theological Seminary)
Charles Hodge
B. B. Warfield

College of New Jersey (Princeton)
Jonathan Edwards

Chart 165

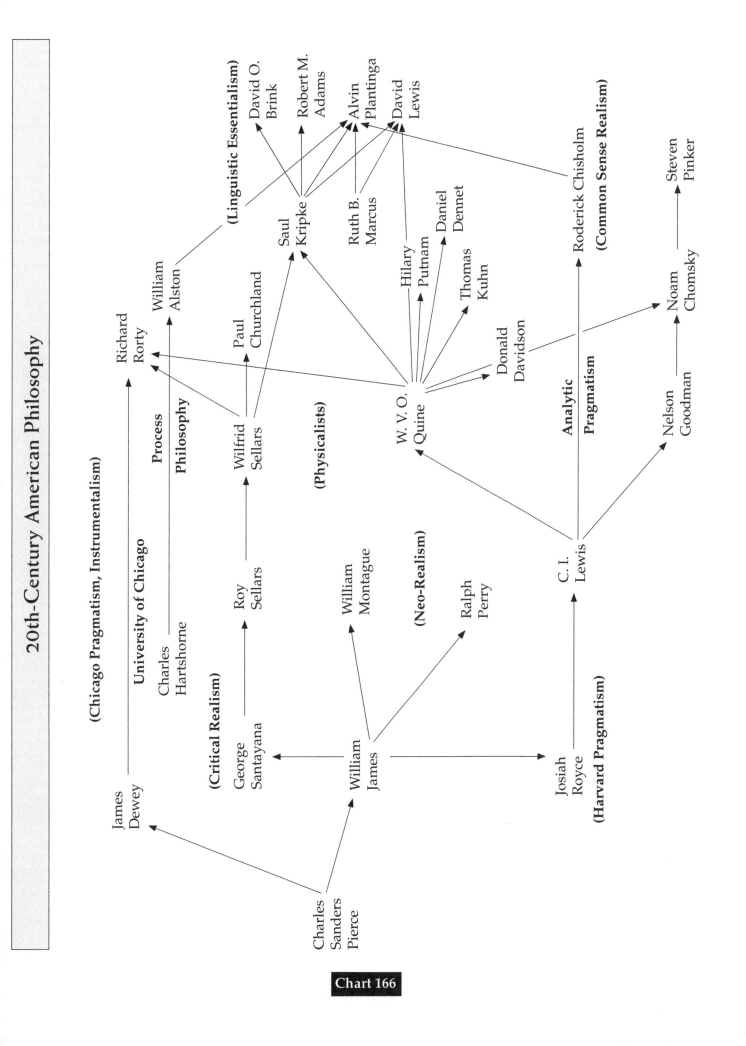

20th-Century American Philosophy

Chart 166

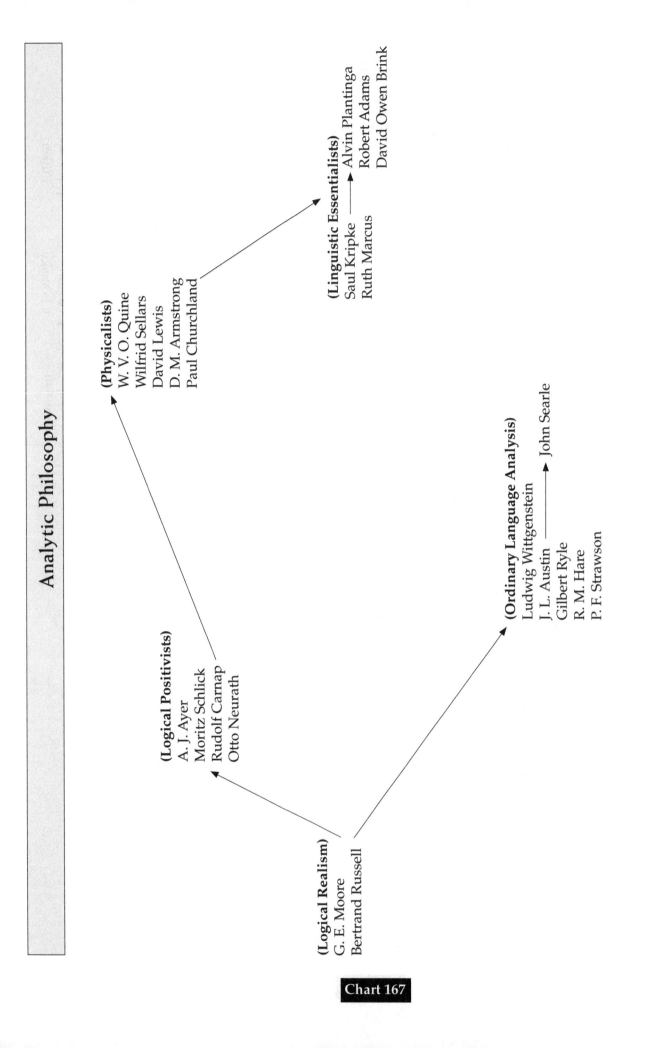

Analytic Philosophy

(Physicalists)
W. V. O. Quine
Wilfrid Sellars
David Lewis
D. M. Armstrong
Paul Churchland

(Linguistic Essentialists)
Saul Kripke ⟶ Alvin Plantinga
Ruth Marcus   Robert Adams
           David Owen Brink

(Logical Positivists)
A. J. Ayer
Moritz Schlick
Rudolf Carnap
Otto Neurath

(Ordinary Language Analysis)
Ludwig Wittgenstein
J. L. Austin ⟶ John Searle
Gilbert Ryle
R. M. Hare
P. F. Strawson

(Logical Realism)
G. E. Moore
Bertrand Russell

Chart 167

Karl Barth and 20th-Century Theology

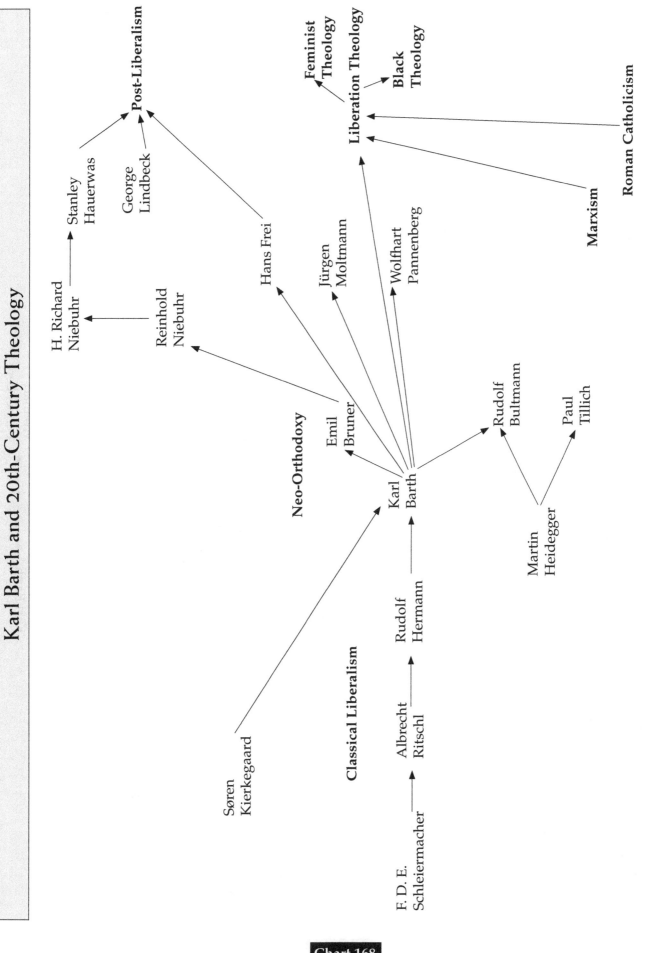

Chart 168

20th-Century Evangelical Theology

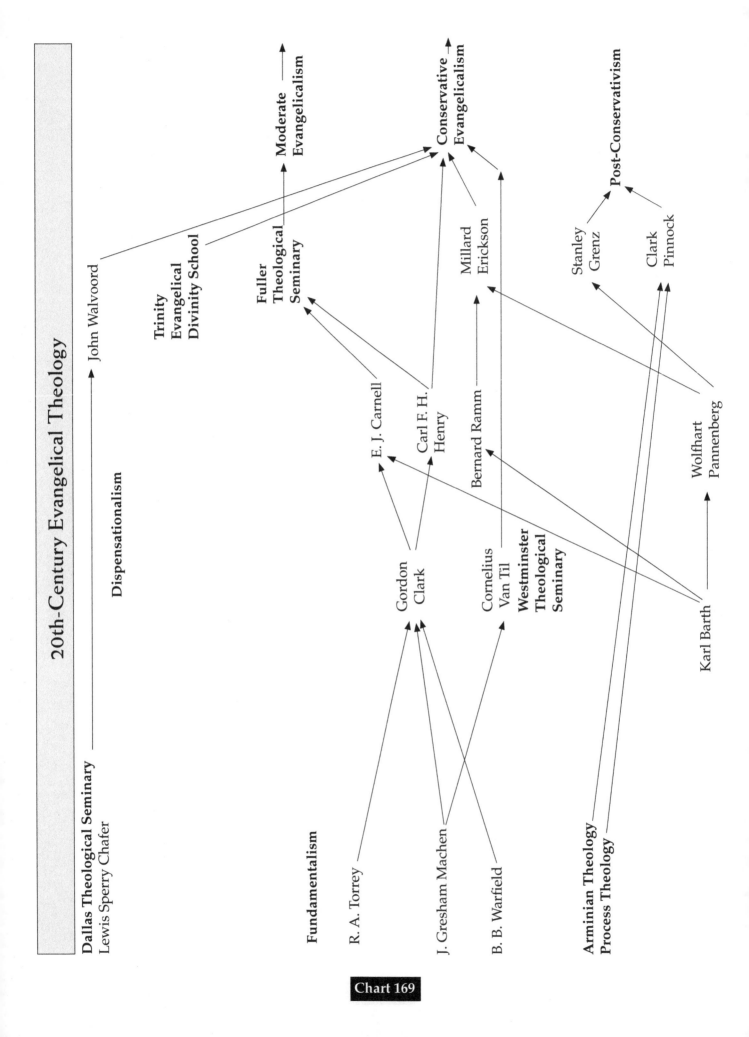

Chart 169

20th-Century British Philosophy of Religion

The Metaphysicals, Oxford University

Nolloth Chair, Oriel College

C. C. J.
Webb
→
L. W.
Grensted
→
I. T.
Ramsey
→
Basil
Mitchell
→
Richard
Swinburne

Trinity College
Austin Farrer

Christ Church and King's College
Eric Mascall
John Macquarrie

Edinburgh University
Thomas F. Torrance

Cambridge University

Donald
Mackinnon
→
Nicolas
Lash

Chart 170

Process Theology

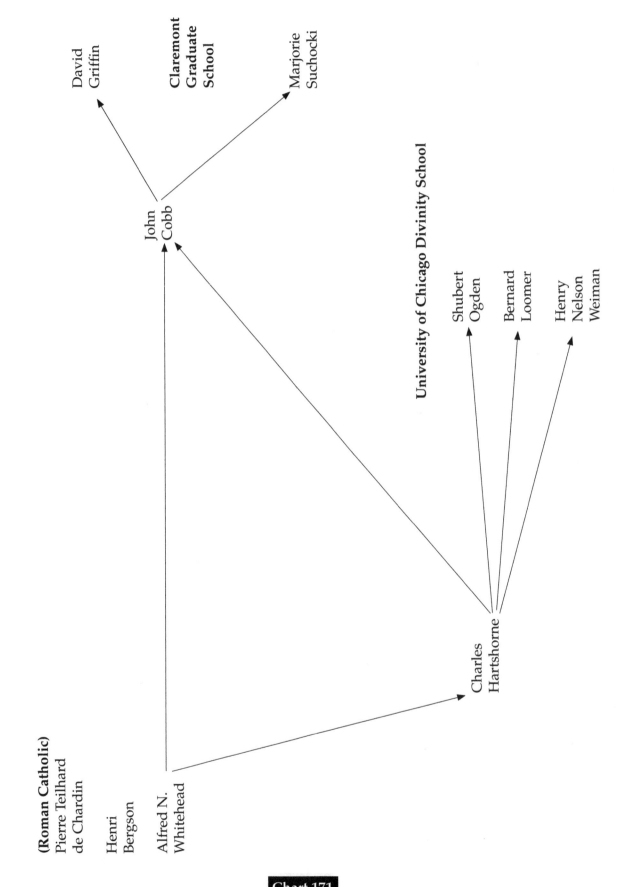

(Roman Catholic)
Pierre Teilhard
de Chardin

Henri
Bergson

Alfred N.
Whitehead

Charles
Hartshorne

John
Cobb

David
Griffin

**Claremont
Graduate
School**

Marjorie
Suchocki

University of Chicago Divinity School

Shubert
Ogden

Bernard
Loomer

Henry
Nelson
Weiman

Chart 171

20th-Century Thomistic Philosophy of Religion

Neo-Thomism

Leo XIII
*Aeterni
Patris*

Désiré-
Joseph
Mercier

Frederic
Copleston

→ Brian
Davies

Jacques
Maritain

→ Ralph
McInerny

Etienne
Gilson

Alasdair
MacIntyre

→ Mark
Murphy

G. E. M. Anscombe
Peter Geach

Analytic Thomism

Anthony Kenny
(Cambridge University)

Austin
Farrer

The Metaphysicals
(Oxford University)

Eric
Mascall

**Transcendental
Thomism**

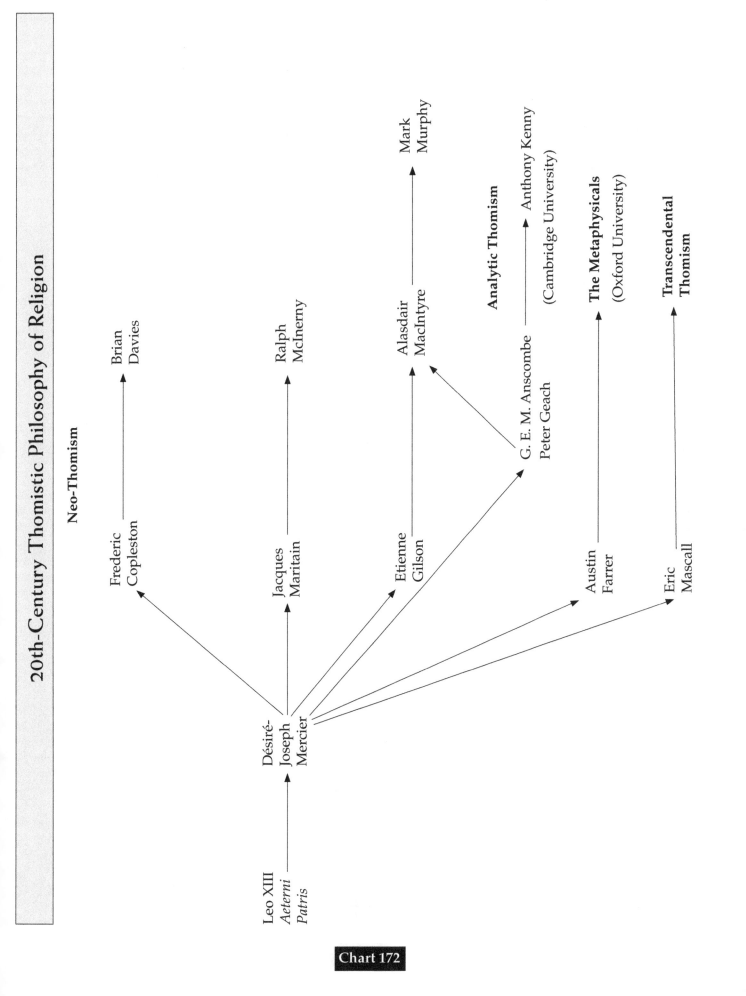

Chart 172

Political Philosophy (Economics)

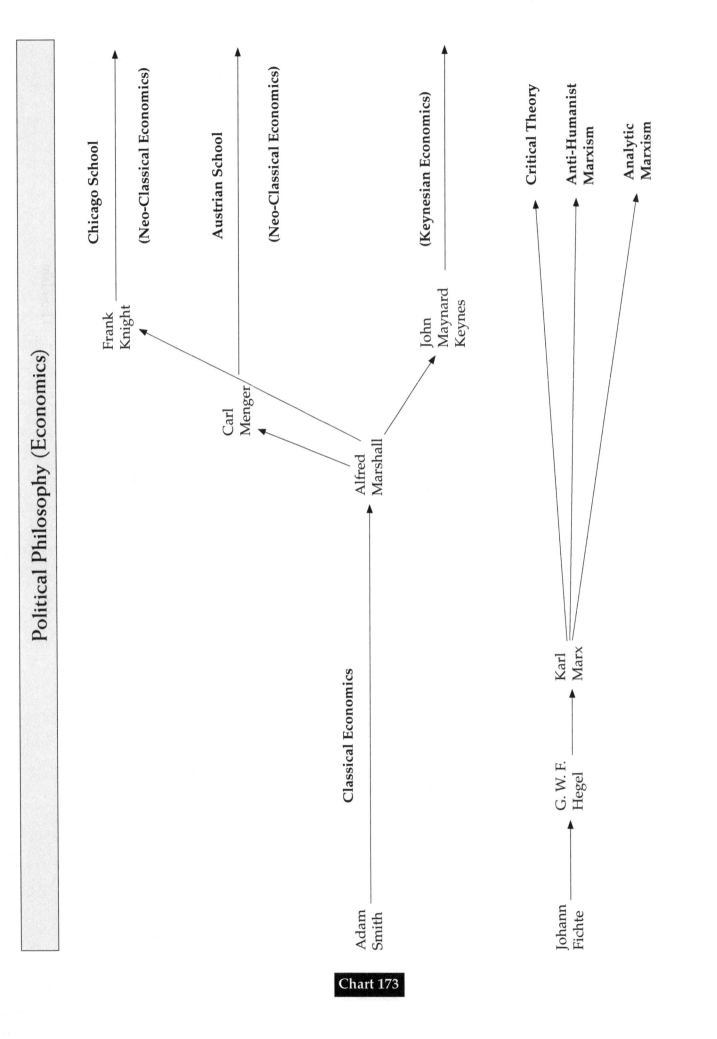

Chicago School

(Neo-Classical Economics)

Austrian School

(Neo-Classical Economics)

(Keynesian Economics)

Critical Theory

Anti-Humanist
Marxism

Analytic
Marxism

Frank
Knight

Carl
Menger

John
Maynard
Keynes

Alfred
Marshall

Classical Economics

Adam
Smith

Karl
Marx

G. W. F.
Hegel

Johann
Fichte

Chart 173

Political Philosophy (Free Market Economics)

(Chicago School)

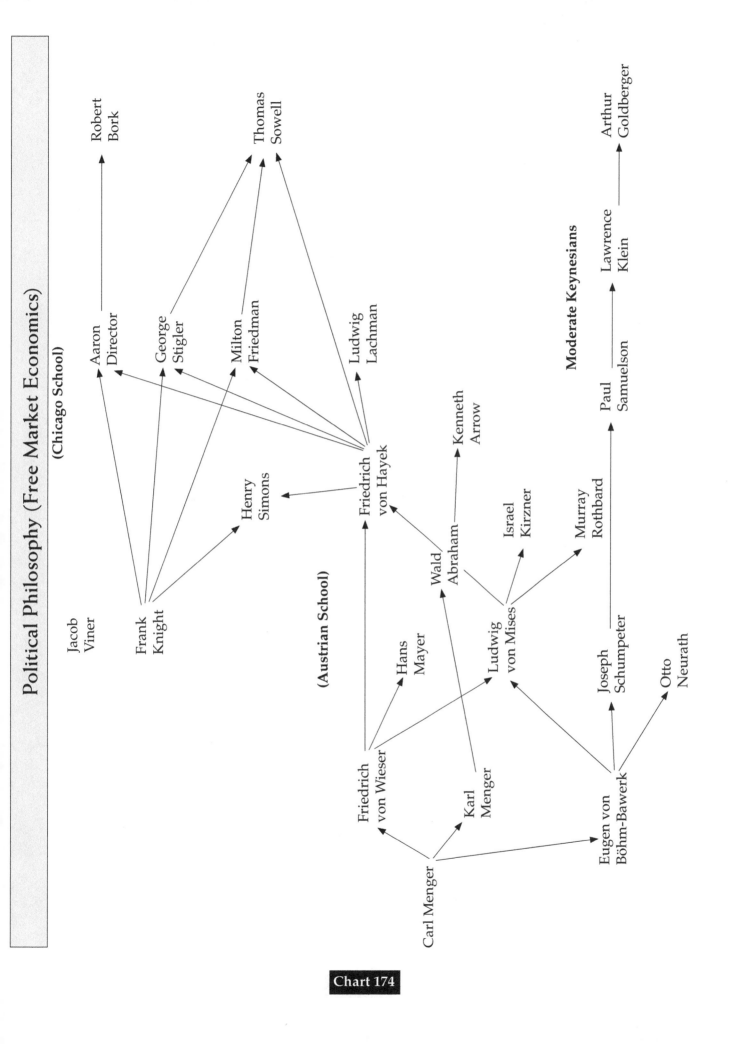

Jacob Viner

Robert Bork

Aaron Director

George Stigler

Milton Friedman

Thomas Sowell

Ludwig Lachman

Henry Simons

Frank Knight

Friedrich von Hayek

(Austrian School)

Hans Mayer

Wald Abraham

Kenneth Arrow

Israel Kirzner

Murray Rothbard

Friedrich von Wieser

Ludwig von Mises

Moderate Keynesians

Lawrence Klein

Arthur Goldberger

Paul Samuelson

Joseph Schumpeter

Otto Neurath

Karl Menger

Eugen von Böhm-Bawerk

Carl Menger

Chart 174

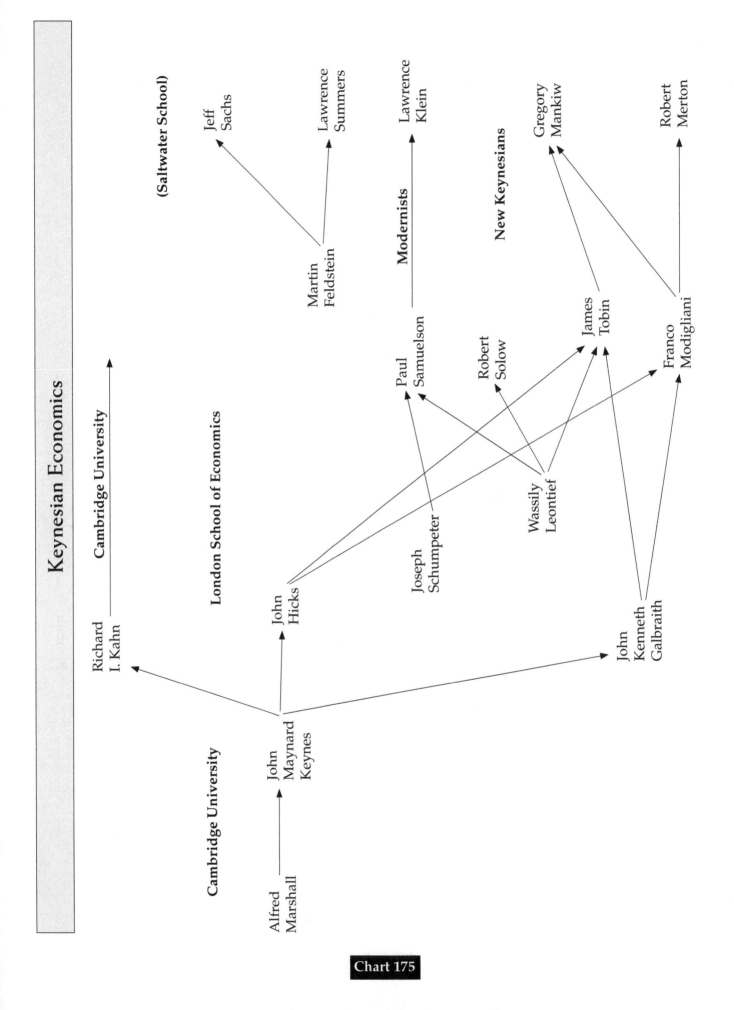

Keynesian Economics

Cambridge University

(Saltwater School)

Jeff Sachs

Lawrence Summers

Martin Feldstein

Modernists

Lawrence Klein

Gregory Mankiw

New Keynesians

Robert Merton

Paul Samuelson

Robert Solow

James Tobin

Franco Modigliani

Richard I. Kahn

London School of Economics

John Hicks

Joseph Schumpeter

Wassily Leontief

John Kenneth Galbraith

Cambridge University

Alfred Marshall

John Maynard Keynes

Chart 175

Classical Liberalism

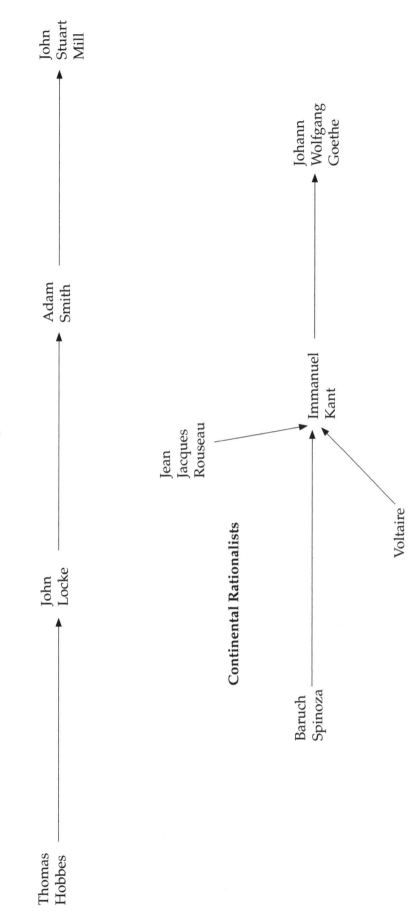

British Empiricists

Thomas
Hobbes

John
Locke

Adam
Smith

John
Stuart
Mill

Continental Rationalists

Baruch
Spinoza

Jean
Jacques
Rouseau

Voltaire

Immanuel
Kant

Johann
Wolfgang
Goethe

Chart 176

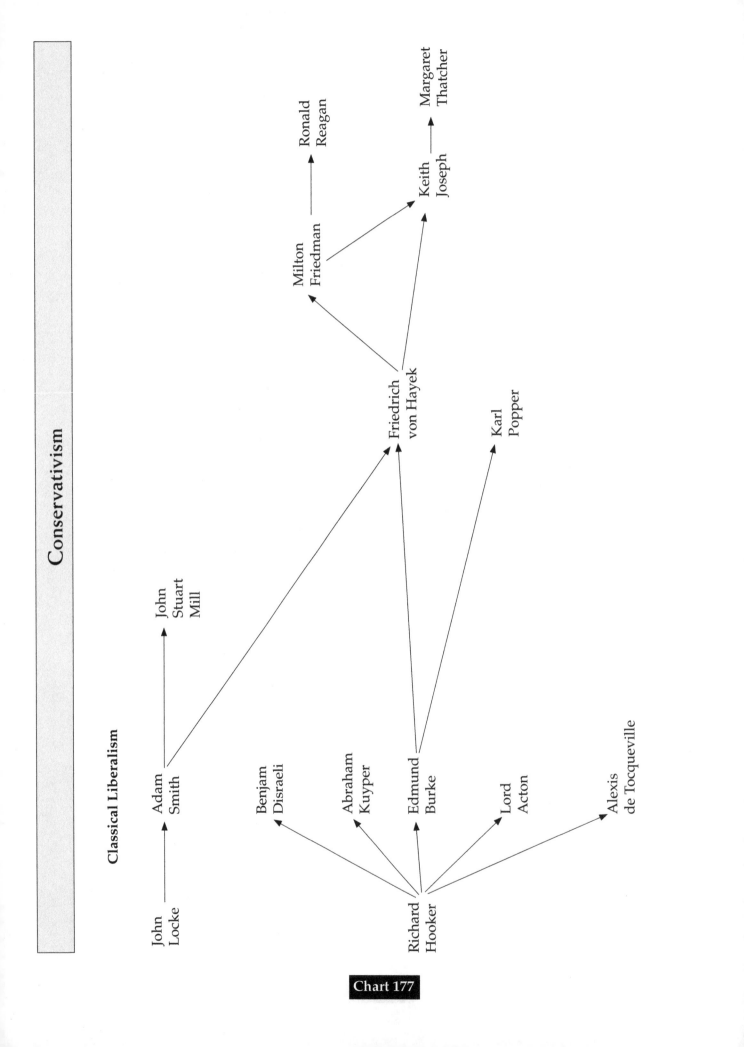

Conservativism

Classical Liberalism

John
Locke → Adam
Smith → John
Stuart
Mill

Benjam
Disraeli

Abraham
Kuyper

Edmund
Burke → Friedrich
von Hayek → Milton
Friedman → Ronald
Reagan

Karl
Popper → Keith
Joseph → Margaret
Thatcher

Lord
Acton

Richard
Hooker

Alexis
de Tocqueville

Chart 177

Neo-Conservativism

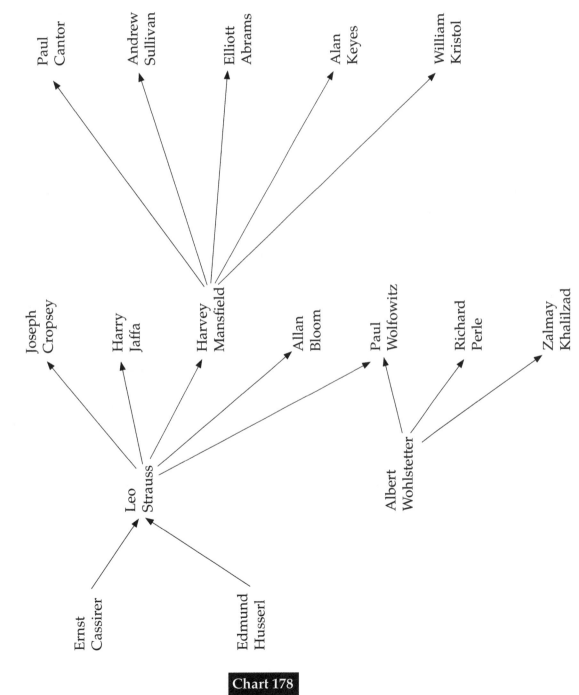

Chart 178

Premodern Philosophers

Pre-Socratics

Group	Date	Location	Description
Milesians Includes: Thales, Anaximander, and Anaxemenes	585–500 BC	This group came from Miletus	These men were monists, believing that everything is made of only one element
Eleatics Includes: Xenophanes, Parmenides, and Zeno		This group came from Elea, Italy	These men were also monists
Pluralists Includes: Empedocles and Anaxagoras	500–428 BC	Anaxagoras came from Athens. Empedocles came from Acragas, Italy.	These men believed that there exist at least two or more fundamental elements on which everything is based
Pythagoreans Includes: Pythagoras and Philolaus	570–494 BC	These men came from southern Italy	These men believed that everything is based on mathematics
Sophists Includes: Protagoras, Hippias, and Gorgias		This group was located in Athens, Greece	These men were skilled in the use of rhetoric and were often hired as tutors for the young men of Athens. Sophists were known for being unscrupulous. Because they were contemporaries of Socrates, he was confused as being one of them.
Atomists Includes: Leucippus and Democritus	440–370 BC	This group came from Abdera, Thrace	These men believed that everything is composed of atoms which move about randomly. They both emphasized the importance of virtue ethics and had elaborate views regarding political theory.

Chart 179

Premodern Philosophers

Plato				
Biography	**Metaphysics**	**Epistemology**	**Axiology**	**Theology**
Name: Plato **Date:** 427–347 BC **Location:** Athens, Greece **Student of:** Socrates **Teacher of:** Aristotle	**Metaphysical realism:** Plato had a two-world ontology: the world of the forms and the world of concrete particulars. Plato believed that the world of the forms is more real than the world of concrete particulars. Plato also believed that the world of the forms contains more forms than are instantiated in this world of concrete particulars. **Theory of truth:** Plato held to a correspondence theory of truth. **Book:** *The Republic*	**Epistemic theory:** It is not entirely clear what theory of knowledge Plato held to. It is commonly held that Plato argued that knowledge is justified true belief. This idea is problematic. It appears that Plato believed that only philosophers can have true knowledge (others can have only true belief) because only philosophers can know the world of the forms. Everyone else can perceive only concrete particulars. Some argue that Plato was a foundationalist, while others argue that he was a coherentist. **Books:** *The Republic, Theatetus*	**Value theory:** Intrinsic value is based on being. He listed the good, the beautiful, and the true as those things having intrinsic value. **Ethical theory:** Plato took a teleological approach to ethics, focusing on character developed through the use of virtues. Plato had five primary virtues that benefit the moral agent as well as society. These are: justice, courage, temperance, piety, and wisdom. Virtue is equated with knowledge. Proper functioning results in character and gains happiness (*eudaimonia*). **Books:** *The Republic, The Hippias, Euthyphro*	Plato did not subscribe to the theology of the traditional Greek gods. While it is not entirely clear, it appears that he believed in one supreme god who constructed the world. This supreme being created the world because he was inspired by the forms of goodness, truth, and beauty. **Books:** *The Republic, Timaeus*

Chart 180

Plato's Philosophy

The starting point of Plato's philosophy is his metaphysics			
Metaphysics (Ontology)		**Epistemology**	
Abstract universals (the intelligible world) These exist in another world without space or time	**The good**		**Knowledge** (*scientia*) Reached via reason
	Higher forms Truth, beauty, and justice	**Dialectic** Pure reason	
	Lower forms Mathematics, geometry, class concepts	**Understanding** Makes use of hypotheses and images	
Concrete particulars (the sensible world) These exist in this world of space and time	**Particular objects** Actual things	**Belief** Based on reliable perception	**Opinion** (*opinio*) Reached via sensory experience
	Images Perception of things	**Conjecture** Based on unreliable perception	

Example of Plato's Metaphysics

Abstract universals The world of the forms	**Higher forms**	**The good**	This is the highest of the forms	This is what is the most real of all things
		The form of beauty	An objective, unchanging, eternal thing	It is merely real
	Lower forms	**The concept of beauty**	Ideas of beauty accessible to human reason	This is less real than the form of beauty because it can be misperceived
Concrete particulars The world that we experience	**Particular objects**	**Individual beautiful things**	Anything that instantiates the property (or form) of beauty	This is less real than the concept of beauty because it is a copy of what is real
	Images	**Imitations of beautiful things**	Includes things like art and representations of reality, like photographs, recordings, etc.	This is the least real of all things because it is a copy of a copy

Chart 181

Premodern Philosophers

Aristotle				
Biography	**Metaphysics**	**Epistemology**	**Axiology**	**Theology**
Name: Aristotle **Date:** 384–322 BC **Location:** Athens, Greece **Student of:** Plato **Teacher of:** Alexander the Great	**Metaphysical moderate realism:** Aristotle had a one-world ontology. Universals or "forms" exist in the world of concrete particulars. Consequently, the only universals or forms that exist are those that are instantiated in concrete particulars. **Truth:** Aristotle held to a correspondence theory of truth. **Book:** *Metaphysics*	**Epistemic theory:** Aristotle was a reliabilist who employed intellectual virtues. Aristotle took a teleological approach to epistemology. He believed that knowledge resulted from properly functional cognitive faculties. These faculties are regulated by intellectual virtues, such as prudence, philosophic wisdom, art, scientific knowledge, and intuitive reason. **Books:** *Nicomachean Ethics,* *De Anima*	**Ethical theory:** Aristotle took a teleological approach to ethics. He equated ethical living with functioning properly. To function properly one must act in accordance with one's nature. For the human being there are four primary or "cardinal" virtues. These are: justice, wisdom, courage, and temperance. Proper functioning results in character and happiness (*eudaimonia*). **Books:** *Nicomachean Ethics,* *Eudomean Ethics,* *Magna Moralis,* *The Politics,* *Economics,* *Poetics*	Aristotle rejected the traditional Greek view of god/s. He argued that the prime mover (God) puts all else into motion and sets everything into order. God is immaterial and eternal. Everything is attracted to him because he is both good and beautiful. God thinks of himself because there is nothing greater. **Book:** *Metaphysics*

Chart 182

Aristotle's Philosophy

Metaphysics (*Meta la Phusis*–After the physics)				
Ontology The study of being or existence. It is concerned with the nature of a thing.	**Abstract universals** exist in the **concrete particulars**. Consequently, there are no forms that are not exemplified in this reality. Everything that exists is a combination of a form and a substance together.			
	Cosmology	**Time**–When a thing exists		
		Space–Where a thing exists		
		Causation–The reason that a thing exists. There are four types of causes:	**Formal**–The shape or "blueprint" to which an entity conforms	
			Material–The physical "stuff" of which an entity is made	
			Efficient–Forces or activities that produce an entity	
			Final–The purpose for which an entity exists	
Theology	The **Prime Mover** orders all of creation. He is eternal, immutable, and immaterial. He is also happy because he thinks of himself. Motion results from attraction to him because he is both beautiful and good.			

Ethics	Epistemology
Ethics Ethics are based upon a thing's ontology. They are teleological. The goal is character.	**Epistemology** Epistemology is based upon ontology, it is teleological. The goal is truth.
Goodness has intrinsic value. The emotions are attuned to virtuous behavior. *Eudaimonia* (well-being) results from virtuous behavior.	Truth has intrinsic value. The emotions are attuned to virtuous thinking. *Eudaimonia* (well-being) results from virtuous thinking.
Goodness depends upon the nature of the actor. Man is both a rational and a social creature. **Natural law** applies to all men because of their common nature. Virtue is in accordance with this **natural law**.	Knowledge depends upon the nature of the knower. Man has both reason and sensory input as sources of knowledge.
Because the will is involved, virtue is necessary to regulate behavior. Virtue leads to **proper functioning, in accordance with nature, and to good character**.	Because the will is involved, virtue is necessary to regulate knowledge acquisition. Virtue leads to **proper functioning, and to good character**.

Moral or cardinal virtues		Intellectual virtues	
Moral or cardinal virtues	**Justice**–Since man is a social creature, he needs an extra helping of this virtue. It ensures that men will get what is due to them.	**Intellectual virtues**	**Scientific thinking**
			Skill–*Techne,* intuitive reason
	Courage		**Artistic thinking**
	Temperance–Self-control		**Philosophic wisdom**–*Sophia*

Phronesis	(Greek: practical wisdom or reason)–This is both a moral and an intellectual virtue. It is said to be a special virtue because it is essential in right action and right thinking.

Chart 183

Aristotelian (Classical) Virtue Ethics

Aristotle's ethical theory can be found in his *Nichomachean Ethics*, *Eudomean Ethics*, *Magna Moralia*, and *The Politics*. He assumes metaphysical and epistemological realism. Civil law should be based upon natural law.

Meta-ethical presuppositions	**Metaphysics of morals**	**Moral realism**–Moral facts exist independent of the observer. Moral facts are found and not made.
		Free will–Man is free to act as he chooses
	Moral epistemology	**Cognitivism**–Moral knowledge results from the use of the virtue prudence (Greek: *phronesis*)
	Moral psychology	**Motivational internalism**–Recognition of moral facts does provide motivation for moral action
		Cognitive moral development–One begins life as an egoist but as he matures becomes more altruistic
		Mental health–One cannot be happy without being virtuous
Cardinal virtues These virtues are based upon natural law (human nature) and are required for everyone. One's employment and position will require some of these more than others.	**Justice**	Because man is a social creature, this is the most important virtue. It ensures that everyone gets what is due to them.
	Prudence (practical wisdom)	This is a special virtue because it is both an intellectual virtue and a moral virtue
	Courage	This is an ability to overcome fear. It allows one to do what must be done even in difficult circumstances.
	Temperance (self-control)	This is an ability to delay gratification because to succumb to one's desire may be detrimental to his well-being
Types of character Aristotle believed that men act viciously only when they lack knowledge (training) or power	**Superhuman virtue**	Does the right thing because he desires to do what is right
	The continent man	He does the right thing, even when he does not desire to do so
	The virtuous man	This man is governed by prudence and temperance
	The vicious man	This man lacks prudence and temperance
	The incontinent man	This man does wrong because he is ruled by his passions
	The brutish man	This man does wrong and is unrepentant over his actions

Chart 184

Premodern Philosophers

Stoics & Epicureans

Biography	Metaphysics	Epistemology	Axiology	Theology
Stoics **Date:** 300 BC and after **Founded by** Zeno. Stoics came largely from the ruling class **Influenced by:** Heraclitas, Aristotle	There are two principles in reality. The active principle is immanent reason (logos) or God. The passive principle is matter devoid of properties. Fire is the substance of all things. The logos (God) is the active fire and the source of all other elements. God orders all things for the best. Everything is predetermined. The Stoics did not believe in free will.		Everything has an order which is perceivable through reason. Hence the Stoics subscribed to natural law. To act in accordance with natural law is to be virtuous. To act contrary to it is to be vicious. We must control our desires if we are to be successful. The Stoics were very individualistic.	The logos is the agent of creation and the principle of reality. The logos created everything and set everything in order. Many Stoics were polytheists. The Stoics also participated in divination and employed oracles when possible because they believed that everything is predetermined and interconnected. Even evil had a purpose in their system of belief.
Epicureans **Date:** 300 BC and after **Founded by:** Epicurus of Samos. The Epicureans came largely from the lower classes. **Influenced by:** Democritus, Aristotle	They believed that everything was composed of atoms that are constantly moving about in a random manner. The Epicureans rejected fate and emphasized the idea that human beings have free will.		Like Aristotle and the Stoics, the Epicureans held to virtue theory. Unlike the Stoics, the Epicureans were focused on the community.	The gods do not interfere with the concerns of men, so we should not worship them. The Epicureans denied immortality and believed that in death there is no sensation or consciousness.

Chart 185

Premodern Philosophers

Skeptics & Middle Platonists				
Biography	Metaphysics	Epistemology	Axiology	Theology
Skeptics **Date:** 360 BC and after **Founded by:** Antiochus of Ascalon, Pyrrho of Elis. Later revived by Aenesidemus of Knossos. **Influenced by:** Plato, Parmenides	The Skeptics were metaphysical nominalists. They also argued against the idea of causation because cause is essentially relative.	They believed that one cannot know anything. Pyrrho of Elis believed that one cannot know that he cannot know anything. Sensory experience is not to be trusted. We can only know appearances. The Skeptics subscribed to relativism. They believed that nothing can be rendered certain through itself or anything else.	The Skeptics believed that we should satisfy our natural instincts. At the same time, law and tradition are important and should be followed. While the truth is unattainable, we should continue to seek after it.	The Skeptics subscribed to antimonies in theology: for example, God's finiteness and his infinity
Middle Platonists **Date:** 130 BC–200 AD **Names:** Eudorus of Alexandria, Plutarch of Chaeronea, Albinus **Influenced by:** Plato, Aristotle, Stoics, Neo-Pythagoreans	The Middle Platonists were metaphysical realists		Their ethics were similar to Aristotle's and that of the Stoics	All Middle Platonists emphasized divine transcendence. Eudorus of Alexandria argued that the godhead is a threefold One. Plutarch of Chaeronea argued that God is not responsible for evil. Many held to the existence of angels and demons.

Chart 186

Premodern Philosophers

Plotinus

Biography	Metaphysics	Epistemology	Axiology	Theology
Name: Plotinus He started the movement known as Neo-Platonism **Date:** 205–270 AD **Location:** Alexandria, Egypt **Student of:** Ammonius Saccus **Teacher of:** Porphyry He popularized Neo-Platonism	**Metaphysical realism** **Plotinus's emanations:** **1st principle** is the "One" or God. This is the supreme cause of all being. **2nd principle** is the "intellect" or the "mind," which is the locus of the eternal forms. The "mind" is a causal instrument of the "One." **3rd principle** is the "soul," which accounts for the rest of the human life apart from the "mind." The "soul" is the causal instrument of the "One" and the "mind." **Truth:** Correspondence theory of truth **Book:** *Enneads*	The forms are real, but are not sensible. To the degree that one seeks after the eternal forms, he has knowledge.	**Ethics:** The eternal forms are intrinsically valuable. To the degree that one seeks after these eternal forms, he is good. To the degree that one does not seek after the eternal forms, he is in darkness or bad. **Aesthetics:** The universe is beautiful because it emanates from the "One." The "One" is the great beauty and the greatest good. "Soul" recognizes beauty because it participates in this form. The perception of beauty requires training and exercise. Beauty involves the proportion of the parts to the whole.	Plotinus took a mystical approach to theology. He emphasized that a person should contemplate the "One" (God) via the eternal forms. Plotinus described the "One" as the first of all principles. He thought that men should seek union with the "One." Union with the "One" may result in the destruction of the individual.

Chart 187

Plotinian Metaphysics

Plotinus (205–270 AD) defined himself as a Platonist. Many defined his thought as middle Platonism. These ideas were conveyed in *The Enneads* which were edited by Porphyry. In the first *Ennead* Plotinus explains beauty. In the fifth *Ennead* Plotinus's ideas served as the basis for much Christian theology/philosophy.

The ONE		This is the simple, one-all unity. The **ONE** is beyond being and beyond knowing. The **ONE** is transcendent and eternal. The **ONE** is the supreme cause of all being. Many in the early church equated the **ONE** with God.	**Immaterial**
Emanations Plotinus explained that emanations and the ONE are analogous to the sun and the rays which proceed from it. Even though the rays of the sun carry light and heat from the sun, the sun is not diminished.	**The intellectual principle** Also known as the Nous (divine mind) or the Logos	This is the one-many unity of multiplicity. The **intellectual principle** is a self-gathered duality. It is the knower and the known. The intellectual principle is also eternal and actual. It also contains the world of the forms. The intellectual principle exists entirely focused on the **ONE** (the state of repose or contemplation).	
	The all soul	**Celestial soul**—Exists entirely focused on the intellectual principle (the state of repose or contemplation). It contains the eternal forms. The **celestial soul** is also the one and the many. It is the unity and the multiplicity.	
		Generative soul—This part of the **all soul** exists in a state of activity and is responsible for the material universe	
	Material universe	This is the many-multiplicity. It involves what is temporal and potential. The **material universe** is the final emanation.	**Sensible world of bodies**

Porphyry
Porphyry edited the works of Plotinus. He believed that matter (including the body) is evil. It is difficult to separate Porphyry's ideas from Plotinus's. Porphyry played an important part in the development of middle Platonism. Augustine, like many other Christians, was heavily influenced by the work of Porphyry and Plotinus.

Chart 188

Premodern Philosophers

Augustine

Biography	Metaphysics	Epistemology	Axiology	Theology
Name: Augustine **Date:** 354–430 AD **Location:** Thagaste, Algeria; Carthage, Rome, and Milan **Student of:** Bishop Ambrose of Milan	Augustine was a metaphysical realist. Universals exist in the mind of God. He held to a correspondence theory of truth.	Like all middle Platonists, Augustine believed that what is apparent to the senses is only a shadow of the real world **Religious epistemology:** We can know the truth through the reading of Scripture guided by the Holy Spirit. When the believer interprets the Scriptures with the theological virtues of faith, hope, and love, and with the creeds, he comes to a knowledge of the truth. **Book:** *On Teaching Christian Doctrine*	In many respects Augustine's ethics are similar to the Stoics. He held to a kind of virtue ethics. But he also believed that man is not capable of being righteous on his own, because man is a sinful and fallen creature. For this reason, man needs Jesus Christ. Rather than depending upon natural virtues, the believer employs the theological virtues. These theological virtues are: faith, hope, and love. The theological virtues are special gifts of the Holy Spirit that help the believer to live in a way that glorifies God.	Perhaps the greatest theologian since biblical times. Augustine emphasized the creeds. Thus, he held a Trinitarian view of the Godhead. He also held that Jesus Christ is one person with two natures. One nature is wholly God and the other is wholly man. Equally important is the saving work of Jesus Christ. The Scripture played an important part of his theology. **Books:** *The Trinity, The Confessions, The City of God, Against the Pelagians, The Enchiridion.* He also wrote many other books.

Chart 189

Augustine's Philosophy

Augustine believed that all being and knowledge comes from God			
Metaphysics (Ontology)		**Epistemology**	
Abstract universals The mind of God	**God** Truth itself, ultimate reality	**Beatific vision** (requires faith)	**Divine illumination** (this kind of knowledge is the most reliable)
	Eternal truth The true, the real, universals	*Sapientia* Divine wisdom (requires faith)	
Concrete particulars This world	**Objects** Temporal truths, material things	*Scientia* Belief and understanding together (requires faith)	**Knowledge** Sensory knowledge (this kind of knowledge is less reliable)
	Representations Temporal truths like history and empirical science	**Authority** (*Opinio*) No firsthand knowledge	

Chart 190

Augustine's Hierarchy of Thought

In *De Vera Religione* (*On True Religion*) Augustine equated goodness and beauty with being

Ultimate reality (Truth)	**Worship of God (The Creator)** **God** is eternal. As a necessary being, God is the most real of all things. God is the most beautiful and is the highest good. **Fallen man** can know some things about God through general revelation, but he cannot come to a full knowledge of who God is. God is above man's sensory perception so our knowledge of him is limited. **The believer** should love God above all else. God can only be fully revealed in his Word. Those who desire to know God must read his Word, praise him, and pray to him.
True	**Thinking of Creation (The Real World)** All of **creation** reflects the nature of its **Creator**. As such, this world and everything in it is contingent. Everything that **God** created is good, but it is not eternal like God. **Fallen man's** sensory perception appreciates creation and is pointed to the Creator. Unfortunately, fallen man often confuses creation with the Creator. Fallen man loves what is true rather than what is truth. **The believer** also perceives the creation but he remembers that it is only temporal and should not be loved more than the Creator
Falsehood	**Vice** **Vice** results from an improper love of **creation** **Fallen man** participates in creation by satisfying his lusts, such as: eating, drinking, and sexual intercourse. He uses his mind for that which is not fruitful because his view of creation is corrupt and he worships idols. **The believer** should avoid this state of mind
Ultimate unreality (Fantasy)	**Fantasy (Amusement)** **Fantasy** is the least real of all things, because it is based upon imagination. This is the worst state of affairs. **Fallen man** spends most of his free time thinking on fantasy. His view of **creation** is corrupt and he cannot free himself from these views. Consequently, fallen man cannot be happy. **The believer** should spend little or no time thinking of fantasy

Chart 191

Premodern Philosophers

	Boethius & John Scotus Erigena			
Biography	**Metaphysics**	**Epistemology**	**Axiology**	**Theology**
Name: Boethius **Date:** 480–524 AD **Location:** Italy, Alexandria, Athens **Influenced by:** Aristotle, Augustine	Boethius was a metaphysical realist (universals exist in the mind of God). He held to a correspondence theory of truth. Boethius separated dogmatic theology from natural theology **Book:** *The Consolation of Philosophy*			He emphasized that both the divine and the human natures of Jesus Christ are distinct and real. He compared God with time by saying that God is like a man on a mountaintop who can see the beginning and the end of a road simultaneously. **Books:** *The Trinity*, *Opuscula*
Name: John Scotus Erigena **Date:** 810–877 AD **Location:** France **Influenced by:** Gregory of Nyssa, Pseudo-Dionysius	John Scotus was a metaphysical realist (universals exist in the mind of God). He held to a correspondence theory of truth. **Book:** *The Divisions of Nature*			God should not be called truth or wisdom or essence, but rather super-truth, super-wisdom, and super-essence because God has nothing in common with creatures. In other words, God is more than human truth, wisdom, or essence. **Book:** *The Divisions of Nature*

Chart 192

Premodern Philosophers

Anselm of Canterbury & Peter Abelard

Biography	Metaphysics	Epistemology	Axiology	Theology
Name: Anselm of Canterbury **Date:** 1033–1109 AD **Location:** Italy, England **Taught by:** Lanfranc **Influenced by:** Augustine	Anselm was a metaphysical realist who subscribed to a correspondence theory of truth (universals exist in the mind of God)			Anselm is noted for his perfect being theology. He argued that God is the most perfect being, and exists necessarily. Anselm made important contributions in natural theology by his arguments for God's existence. **Books:** *Cur Deus Homo? Monologium, Proslogium*
Name: Peter Abelard **Date:** 1079–1142 AD **Location:** France **Influenced by:** William of Champeaux, Boethius	Abelard was a metaphysical conceptualist, believing that universals exist in our minds. He held to a correspondence theory of truth. He was one of the first philosophers to employ modal logic. **Book:** *Logica*		Abelard's ethics serve as a guide to Christian doctrine. He believed that ethics is the "end and fulfillment of all other disciplines." His ethics involve virtue, love, and merit. **Books:** *Ethics; Dialogue Between a Philosopher, a Jew and a Christian*	God is the highest good and always does what is best. Abelard emphasized divine necessity. **Books:** *Theologia Christiana, Theologia Scholarium*

Chart 193

Premodern Philosophers

Thomas Aquinas

Biography	Metaphysics	Epistemology	Axiology	Theology
Name: Thomas Aquinas **Date:** 1224–1274 AD **Location:** Paris and Rome **Taught by:** Albert the Great **Influenced by:** Aristotle, Augustine	Aquinas followed Aristotle in that he was a moderate metaphysical realist. He believed that universals must be instantiated in concrete particulars. He held to a correspondence theory of truth. **Book:** *Commentary on Aristotle's Metaphysics*	Aquinas argued that knowledge results from the proper functioning of our cognitive faculties aimed at truth. Our reasoning is regulated by intellectual virtues. **Books:** *Commentary on Aristotle's De Anima, Commentary on Aristotle's Nicomachean Ethics*	Aquinas argued for the use of moral and theological virtues. He emphasized Aristotle's cardinal virtues: justice, courage, wisdom, and temperance. He also emphasized Augustine's theological virtues: faith, hope, and love. Aquinas also placed great importance on laws, such as : eternal law, divine law, natural law, and temporal law. Divine law and natural law are part of God's eternal law. Temporal laws are made by men. **Books:** *Summa Theologia, Commentary on Aristotle's Nicomachean Ethics*	Aquinas appropriated Aristotle's prime mover for understanding the Christian concept of God **Book:** *Summa Theologia*

Chart 194

Thomas Aquinas's Philosophy

Metaphysics				
	Abstract universals exist in the concrete particulars. Consequently, there are no forms that are not exemplified in this reality. Everything that exists is a combination of a form and a substance together.			
Ontology The study of being or existence. It is concerned with the nature of a thing.	**Cosmology**	**Time**–When a thing exists		
		Space–Where a thing exists		
		Causation–The reason that a thing exists. There are four types of causes:	**Formal**–The shape or "blueprint" to which an entity conforms	
			Material–The physical "stuff" of which an entity is made	
			Efficient–Forces or activities that produce an entity	
			Final–The purpose for which an entity exists	
Theology	**God** (Yahweh) is the cause of creation and orders all of it in accordance with his will and nature. He is eternal, immutable, and immaterial. He is also happy because he thinks of himself. Everything is in motion because of attraction to him because he is both beautiful and good. The **eternal law** comes from God and includes both the **natural law** and the **divine law** (the Old and New Testaments). Creation is affected by the degrading influences of sin and must be redeemed by **Jesus Christ** to restore the perfection of the created order.			

Ethics	Epistemology
Ethics are based upon a thing's ontology. They are teleological. The goal is character.	Epistemology is based upon ontology, it is teleological. The goal is truth and character.
Goodness has intrinsic value. The emotions are attuned to virtuous behavior. *Felicitas* (Latin: happiness from self-effort, well-being) results from virtuous behavior.	Truth has intrinsic value. The emotions are attuned to virtuous thinking. *Felicitas* (Latin: happiness from self-effort) results from truth via virtuous thinking.
Goodness depends upon the nature of the actor. Man is both a rational and a social creature. **Natural law** applies to all men because of their common nature. Virtue is in accordance with the **natural law**. This law is also an aspect of the **eternal law**.	Knowledge depends upon the nature of the knower. Man has both reason and sensory input as sources of knowledge. Knowledge of God comes from reason and the *sensus divinitatis*. Knowledge of God is damaged by the noetic effects of sin.
Because the will is involved, virtue is necessary to regulate behavior. Virtue leads to **proper functioning**, in accordance with nature, and to good character.	Because the will is involved, virtue is necessary to regulate knowledge acquisition. Virtue leads to **proper functioning**, and to good character.
Moral (cardinal) virtues–Regulate man's behavior. Man still does wrong because sin causes a lack of knowledge and power.	**Intellectual virtues**–Regulates man's thinking. Man fails to think rightly because of the noetic effects of sin.

Prudentia (Latin: practical wisdom or reason)–It unites the natural (moral and intellectual) virtues. This virtue is affected by the noetic effect of sin.	
Theological virtues Gifts of the Holy Spirit given to every believer	**Love** (*Agape*, Greek; *Caritas*, Latin)–The love of God and the love of man for God's sake. The other theological virtues, **faith** and **hope**, grow out of **love**. **Love** unites all of the virtues.
	Beatitudo (Greek, *Makarios*)–Happiness that comes from God; results from acting in accordance with the theological virtues

Chart 195

Premodern Philosophers

John Duns Scotus & William of Ockham

Biography	Metaphysics	Epistemology	Axiology	Theology
Name: John Duns Scotus **Date:** 1265–1308 AD **Location:** Paris, France; Oxford, England **Taught by:** Gonsalvus of Spain **Influenced by:** Augustine, Aristotle	Moderate metaphysical realist. **Three types of universals:** **1. Physical universal**–The specific nature existing in individual objects **2. Metaphysical universal**–The common nature, not as it exists in some concrete particular **3. Logical universal**–The universal in the strict sense **Correspondence theory of truth**	Knowledge is based on sensory experience. **Two kinds of knowledge:** **Intuitive knowledge** concerns that which is present and existent. **Abstract knowledge** deals with that which is neither existent or present. Man has no intuitive knowledge of God. **Books:** *Quodlibet*, *De Anima*	Scotus subscribed to virtue ethics. He also held to divine command theory. In his version, God's will is not separated from his nature. Consequently, natural law is consistent with the will of God.	God is not an object of metaphysical science. Theology is a science, but it is not subordinate to metaphysics. Theology is instead a practical science. Scotus used Anselm's ontological argument as proof of God's existence. **Books:** *Opus Oxoniense*, *De Primo Principia*
Name: William of Ockham **Date:** 1290-1349 AD **Location:** England **Influenced by:** Aristotle, John Duns Scotus	Metaphysical nominalist. Universals are nothing more than a term or a concept in the mind. God is the primary subject of metaphysics. Ockham held to a correspondence theory of truth **Books:** *Quodlibet*, *Commentary on the Sentences*	Ockham emphasized intuitive or sensory knowledge. He believed that God could cause us to intuit something that did not exist.	Ockham subscribed to a version of divine command theory in which God's will is separated from his nature. Ockham developed this system because he did not want to limit God's power or freedom in any way.	Ockham emphasized divine omnipotence and liberty. He did not believe that God's existence cannot be proved through reason alone.

Chart 196

Premodern Philosophers

Luis de Molina & Francisco Suarez				
Biography	Metaphysics	Epistemology	Axiology	Theology
Name: Luis de Molina **Date:** 1535–1600 **Location:** Salamanca, Spain **Influenced by:** Augustine, Aquinas, Francisco de Vitoria	Metaphysical realist		He contributed to economic theory as a member of the **Salamanca school**. Many assert that this is the first scientific school of economics. He argued that a free market always assigns a just price for a given good. **Books:** *La Teoria del Justo Prico, De Justitia et Jure*	A defender of divine providence and libertarian free will, Molina developed the idea of middle knowledge **Book:** *Concordia*
Name: Francisco Suarez **Date:** 1548–1617 **Location:** Spain **Influenced by:** Augustine, Aquinas	Metaphysical realist	Knowledge of "the good" and "the right" results from a prior knowledge of what is natural for man	A natural law theorist who argued that international law should be based upon the natural law **Book:** *On Law and God the Lawgiver*	**Books:** *De Defensione Fidei, De Deo Incarnatio*

Chart 197

Modern Philosophers/Continental Rationalists

	René Descartes			
Biography	**Epistemology**	**Axiology**	**Metaphysics**	**Theology**
Name: René Descartes **Date:** 1596–1650 **Location:** France **Influenced by:** Isaac Beeckman	He started the modern period with a hermeneutic of doubt. By using the method of doubt, he hoped to attain absolute certainty of knowledge (Cartesian certainty). Descartes believed that knowledge results primarily from reason. He also believed that the senses are not the most reliable source of knowledge. He concluded that the individual has priority over the community. **Book:** *Meditations on First Philosophy*	Descartes was not an innovator in ethics. He believed that ethical principles could be understood by reason alone. At the same time, he seemed to subscribe to the virtue theory of ethics. His moral psychology was largely based upon the passions and the interaction between mind and body. **Book:** *Passions of the Soul*	**Cartesianism**–There are two types of matter. There is mind (or spirit) and there is body (or matter). Science has authority with the body (or matter). The church has authority over the spirit. The mind and the body are joined via the pineal gland. **Books:** *Discourse on Methods, Meditations on First Philosophy*	Descartes used another version of Anselm's ontological argument for God's existence. Descartes believed that reason was the most important thing needed to get to God, even more important than prayer or reading the Bible.

Chart 198

Modern Philosophers/Continental Rationalists

Blaise Pascal & Nicolas Malebranche				
Biography	Epistemology	Axiology	Metaphysics	Theology
Name: Blaise Pascal **Date:** 1623–1662 **Location:** France **Influenced by:** Augustine	Pascal argued that knowledge comes from both reason and the heart. Pascal's view of reason is not as high as Descarte's. Pascal emphasized the importance of the heart for the knowledge of God.	Christian ethics result from supernatural charity. Pascal's approach to ethics was somewhat Augustinian. Moral knowledge comes from the heart. **Book:** *Lettres provinciales*	Pascal was not a Cartesian. But he was a mathematician and scientist of the first order. He rejected the idea that metaphysics can be subsumed under mathematical methods. He also rejected metaphysical arguments for God's existence.	Pascal differentiated between the god of the philosophers and the God of Abraham, Isaac, and Jacob. He emphasized the importance of special revelation. **Book:** *Memorial, Lettres provinciales, Pensées*
Name: Nicolas Malebranche **Date:** 1638–1715 **Location:** France **Influenced by:** Plato, Augustine, Descartes	"To be a faithful Christian, one must believe blindly, but to be a philosopher one must see evidently." While certainty of knowledge is attainable, we should not always wait for it. The will causes deception and not the senses. **Books:** *De la recherché de la verite, Eclaircissements sur la recherché de la verite'*	Christian ethics represent the only true morality. All other systems are insufficient. **Book:** *Traite de morale*	Malebranche was a Cartesian with a theocentric metaphysic. His position is known as occasionalism. The mind and the body are separate. God is the source of all causation bodily and otherwise. **Books:** *Traite de la nature et de la grace, Entretiens sur la metaphysique*	Malebranche subscribed to the theology of Augustine and the church fathers **Book:** *Meditationes Chretiennes*

Chart 199

Modern Philosophers/Continental Rationalists

Baruch Spinoza

Biography	Epistemology	Axiology	Metaphysics	Theology
Name: Baruch Spinoza **Date:** 1632–1677 **Location:** Holland **Influenced by:** Plato, the Stoics, Descartes	Spinoza held a high view of reason. **Four levels of perception:** 1. Hearsay 2. Perception via vague or confused experience 3. Perception via inadequate inference of the essence of one thing from another 4. Perception of a thing through its essence or proximate cause **Three types of knowledge** 1. **Opinion**–The level of imagination 2. **Scientific knowledge**–The level of reason 3. **Intuitive knowledge**–Arises from scientific knowledge and is accompanied by *eudaimonia* **Book:** *Treatise on the Correction of the Understanding*	Spinoza held a view that was very similar to the Stoics. To seek God was the *summum bonum*. To act in accordance with virtue is to act in accordance with reason and the natural law. Spinoza believed that the source of all political problems was theology. More specifically, he identified the problem as being one of hermeneutics. In response, he developed the historical-critical method of biblical interpretation. **Books:** *Ethics Demonstrated According to the Geometrical Order, Theological Political Treatise*	Spinoza argued that philosophical arguments should begin with ontology and should proceed from there to ethics and epistemology. He was not a Cartesian because he did not subscribe to mind/body dualism. Instead he believed that there is only one substance in existence. This substance is a divine substance, which is identified as God or nature. In other words, Spinoza held to panentheism. **Book:** *Principles of Philosophy*	Spinoza was a Jew, but he subscribed to panentheism. He did so because he thought that a personal, transcendent God was not reasonable. Some of these ideas may have come from his reading of the Cabala. He also thought that philosophical truth cannot be found in the Bible. **Books:** *Short Treatise on God, Man and His Well-being*

Chart 200

Modern Philosophers/Continental Rationalists

	Gottfried Wilhem Leibniz			
Biography	**Epistemology**	**Axiology**	**Metaphysics**	**Theology**
Name: Gottfried Wilhelm Leibniz **Date:** 1646–1716 **Location:** Germany and France **Influenced by:** René Descartes, Baruch Spinoza	Men can know truths of reason because they are necessary. Men can also know truths of fact. Men cannot know with certainty contingent truths. Leibniz was responsible for creating the analytic/synthetic distinction of propositions **Book:** *Monadology*	**Three types of evil** **1. Metaphysical–** Imperfection involved with finite being **2.** Physical **3.** Moral Evil is the privation of the good. God does not will moral evil, he only permits it because this will allow a greater good. **Book:** *Essays in Theodicy*	**Principle of internal harmony–**God actualizes only those substances that will necessarily harmonize with each other to the greatest extent possible **Monads–**Leibnizian substances which are simple units of psychic force. These are not material substances. Each monad is a mirror of the entire universe. Human beings are nothing more than a grouping of monads under the influence of a dominant monad. Human beings are free agents. **Books:** *Discourse on Metaphysics, The New System of Nature and of the Interaction of Substances, Monadology*	God is both rational and good. Only God knows contingent truths. God created this world because this world is the best of all possible worlds. The argument that God exists is analytic and this type of knowledge is *a priori* **Books:** *The Principles of Nature and Grace, Essays in Theodicy*

Chart 201

Modern Philosophers/Continental Rationalists

Immanuel Kant

Biography	Epistemology	Axiology	Metaphysics	Theology
Name: Immanuel Kant **Date:** 1724–1804 **Location:** Koenigsburg, Prussia **Influenced by:** Christian Volf	Kant emphasized the importance of reason. He attempted to combine rationalism with empiricism. Kant's **Copernican revolution** completed the priority of epistemology by moving from the **Cartesian mind/body dualism** to the **phenomenal/noumenal dualism**. Kant argued that all we can know is the phenomenal (the world of sensory experience). We cannot know the noumenal (or the thing in itself). Kant also argued for a new category of knowledge, the *synthetic a priori.* **Book:** *Critique of Pure Reason*	Kant took a deontological approach to morality because he argued that virtue and happiness cannot be united in this life. For this reason, Kant believed in a post-mortem judgment. God will judge men's deeds in the next life. **Books:** *Groundwork for a Metaphysics of Morals, Critique of Practical Reason, Metaphysics of Morals, Critique of Judgment*	Kant believed in the existence of God and in the immortality of the human soul. Kant also thought that human beings have free will. Kant was a mitigated skeptic, believing that the noumenal world is unknowable. **Book:** *Groundwork for Any Future Metaphysics*	Kant believed in the existence of God, but his beliefs were not consistent with either the Nicean or Chalcedonian creeds. He believed that the Bible is a good and useful book, but he also believed that reason could provide the same information. Kant also believed that the church was important because it served as a moral community. Kant had a system of works righteousness. His views are inconsistent with Christianity. **Book:** *Religion Within the Bounds of Reason Alone*

Chart 202

Modern Philosophers/British Empiricists

John Locke

Biography	Epistemology	Axiology	Metaphysics	Theology
Name: John Locke **Date:** 1632–1704 **Location:** England **Influenced by:** René Descartes	Locke held an internalist epistemology which involved a classical foundationalist approach to knowledge. Locke developed the **represent-ationalist theory of knowledge**. In other words, the mind is like a photograph that accurately represents the world. Locke thought that we come into the world with our minds as blank slates. Our experiences write knowledge upon our minds. **Book:** *An Essay Concerning Human Understanding*	All men have natural rights based upon natural law. These include the rights to life, liberty, and property. Moral good and evil is only the conformity or disagreement of our voluntary actions to some law. **Three types of laws:** **1. Divine law**–Laws given by God through general or special revelation to regulate our behavior **2. Civil law**–Laws made by the commonwealth are engaged to protect the lives, liberty, and possessions of those who live according to its laws **3. Law of opinion or reputation**–Virtue is associated with praise as vice is with shame	Locke was a metaphysical nominalist who held a **Cartesian** view of substances. A substance is the bearer of properties. **Three properties of a substance:** **1. Primary properties**–Involve the inherent qualities of an external object. These include things like size, number, extension, and solidity. **2. Secondary properties**–Involve powers to create sensations **3. Tertiary properties**–Involve the powers to alter the primary qualities of other objects	Locke was a devout Christian who held an orthodox view of the faith

Chart 203

Modern Philosophers/British Empiricists

George Berkeley

Biography	Epistemology	Axiology	Metaphysics	Theology
Name: George Berkeley **Date:** 1685–1753 **Location:** Cloyne, Ireland **Influenced by:** John Locke	He agreed with Locke that we come into the world with our minds as blank slates. He believed that all knowledge results from sensory experience. **Book:** *Principles of Human Knowledge*	Berkeley hoped to make an ethical theory that worked in accordance with a mathematical method. He thought that pleasure was the *summum bonum*. By this he does not mean gratification of sensual appetite. Reason can perceive a natural moral law. Moral law suggests that we should seek our true interest according to reason. The first principle over our action is self-love. **Books:** *Alciphron, Passive Obedience*	Berkeley was a metaphysical nominalist who was also a **subjective idealist**. He said that "to be is to be perceived." He did not believe in material substances. **Primary properties** have no existence apart from our minds. Primary properties are dependent upon secondary properties. **Secondary properties** are also mind dependent. Berkeley believed that only God's mind and our minds exist. God is the source of all causation and the source of our sensory experiences. **Book:** *Three Dialogues between Hylas and Philonus*	Berkeley was the Anglican bishop of Cloyne. He was a devout Christian who developed his theories to defend the existence of God and his providential activity. Berkeley believed that theories involving material substances led one to atheism because belief in matter is the real skeptic position. **Book:** *Des Motu*

Chart 204

Modern Philosophers/British Empiricists

David Hume

Biography	Epistemology	Axiology	Metaphysics	Theology
Name: David Hume **Dates:** 1711–1776 **Location:** Scotland **Influenced by:** John Locke, George Berkeley, Adam Smith **Taught by:** Francis Hutcheson	All knowledge results from sensory experience. Perceptions are contents of the mind which fall into two categories: **impressions** and **ideas**. **Impressions** include sensations, passions, and emotions. **Ideas** result from thinking and reasoning about **impressions**. **Deductive** reason can provide little knowledge. **Inductive** knowledge is used to fill in gaps between what we experience, based upon probability. As such, inductive reason cannot provide certainty either. **Book:** *A Treatise of Human Nature*	Hume did not believe in moral or aesthetic facts. He believed that morality, as well as our concept of beauty, was created by men. Since reason is a slave of the passions, morality is subjective. He was a sentimentalist. He believed that the passions served as a moral and aesthetic sense. Both ethics and aesthetics are learned. Hume held to utilitarianism. **Books:** *Essays Moral and Political,* *An Enquiry Concerning the Principles of Morals,* *Political Discourse*	Hume was a metaphysical nominalist One can know that one thing follows another, but one cannot know that one thing causes another. What we can know about causation is only the result of our sensory experience aided by inductive reason. We cannot know that everything has a cause.	Hume was not an atheist, but he was a deist He did not believe in miracles because miracles are a suspension of the laws that God created **Book:** *Dialogues Concerning Natural Religion*

Chart 205

Modern Philosophers/British Empiricists

Thomas Reid

Biography	Epistemology	Axiology	Metaphysics	Theology
Name: Thomas Reid **Date:** 1710–1796 **Location:** Scotland **Influenced by:** John Locke, George Berkeley, David Hume, René Descartes, Nicolas Malebranche, Joseph Butler **Taught by:** Francis Hutcheson	Common sense realist, holding to a realist theory of perception, in which the object is present to the mind as a representation, sense datum, or idea. An **idea** is a mental entity that exists as long as the mind is aware of it. How a sensation and a perception differ: **Sensation** does not involve an object apart from the act of sensing. It is an act of the mind. **Perception:** **1.** The notion of an object perceived **2.** Belief of the object's present existence **3.** Belief not based on reasoning **Books:** *An Inquiry into the Human Mind on the Principles of Common Sense,* *Essays on the Intellectual Powers of Man*	Reid had a systematic theory of moral freedom based on the idea of a human being as a free and morally responsible agent. Moral responsibility includes having the power to act contrary to the way that one has chosen to act. Reid believed in the existence of moral facts. Moral facts are known by intuition. Reid held to a deontological moral theory divided into general and particular principles. Beauty is equated with virtuous activity because aesthetic properties supervene on moral ones. **Book:** *Essays on the Active Powers of Man*	Metaphysical nominalist, who held to a correspondence theory of truth Regarding the nature of substances, Reid agreed that there are primary and secondary properties. He was not in full agreement with Locke as to the nature of properties. Primary properties provide the senses with a "direct and distinct notion." Secondary properties provide the senses with only a relative and obscure notion. They inform us only that they are qualities that affect us in a certain manner, that is, produce in us a certain sensation. They do not reveal what their true natures are.	Reid was a Christian philosopher who subscribed to orthodoxy. He believed that there are five arguments for the existence of God. These are: **1.** The cosmological argument **2.** The design argument **3.** The argument that the world cannot be eternal **4.** The argument from miracles, and **5.** The argument that all men everywhere know that God exists.

Chart 206

Modern Philosophers/British Empiricists

John Stuart Mill

Biography	Epistemology	Axiology	Metaphysics	Theology
Name: John Stuart Mill **Date:** 1806–1873 **Location:** London, England **Taught by:** James Mill **Influenced by:** Jeremy Bentham, August Comte **Book:** *Autobiography*	Mill subscribed to some kind of foundationalism He was an empiricist who emphasized the importance of inductive logic. He did so by reducing deductive reason to inductive reason. He allowed intuition as a source of knowledge. By intuition he meant consciousness and immediate awareness of our sensations and feelings. He rejected the idea of *a priori* knowledge. Mill valued the scientific method and divided science into the study of the material world and the study of human nature **Book:** *System of Logic*	Mill held to the utilitarian system of Bentham and his father, James Mill. Mill differed from them in that he did not equate happiness with pleasure. Mill believed instead that *eudaimonia* is what should be emphasized rather than mere pleasure. **Books:** *Essays on Some Unsettled Questions of Political Economy, On Liberty, Considerations on Representative Government, Utilitarianism*	Mill thought that the "laws of nature" exist. By laws of nature he meant the uniformities in nature. The purpose of science is to find these laws. Mill was a metaphysical nominalist. Because he identified his position with Berkeley (not believing in the existence of matter), one might draw the conclusion that Mill was some sort of idealist or phenomenalist. He thought that the mind is nothing more than a series of feelings. He appears to have subscribed to solipsism as well. He thought that the study of causality should be limited to experience	Mill did not agree with his father that "religion is the greatest enemy of morality" He rejected the ontological argument for the existence of God but he accepted the argument from design because it was scientific. Mill was a rational skeptic concerning God's existence rather than an agnostic. Still he believed that the probability of God's existence was low. Mill allowed that if God exists, he might be omnipotent and good **Book:** *Essays in Religion*

Chart 207

Index
By Chart Number

Abduction, 1, 82, 137
Abelard, Peter, 127, 154, 155, 193
Abraham, Wald, 174
Abrams, Elliott, 178
Absolute idealism, 8, 160
Absolutism, 55
    graded, 47, 142
Abstract knowledge, 196
Abstract references, 9
Abstract universals, 181, 183, 190, 195
Absurdity of life, 93
Accessibility relation, 80
Act consequentialism, 43
Act non-consequentialism, 43
Acton, Lord, 177
Actualist possible worlds, 13
Actual worlds, 12, 34
Act utilitarianism, 50
Adams, Robert, 65, 70, 103, 141, 166, 167
Ad hominem attacks, 3
Ad ignorantiam beliefs, 3
Adoptionism, 121
Adorno, Theodor, 64, 100, 163
Advancement of Learning (Bacon), 85
Aenesidemus of Knossos, 186
Aesthetics, 19, 187, 205, 206
    axiology of, 55
    intrinsic value and, 26
    meta-, 54
    realism, 20
Aeterni Patris, 103, 106, 172
Affluent Society, The (Galbraith), 62
After Virtue (MacIntyre), 46
Against Method (Feyerabend), 87
Against the Pelagians (Augustine), 189
Agent based ethics, 44
Agent neutral value, 27
Akrasia, 45
Alaric, 126
Albinus, 186
Alciphron (Berkeley), 204
Alcuin of York, 153
Alethia, 95
Alexander, Samuel, 161
Alexander of Hales, 155
Algazel, 155
Allegory, 114–116
Alston, William, 103, 108, 166
Althusser, Louis, 64
Altruism, 42
Ambiguity, semantic, 3
Ambrose, 152, 189
American philosophy
    early, 165
    20th century, 166
American pragmatism, 71
Analogical language, 111

Analyticity, 73
Analytic Marxism, 64, 173
Analytic philosophy, 162, 164, 167
    history of, 65–71, 149
    language in, 72–81
    of the mind, 88–91
    science in, 82–87
Analytic pragmatism, 166
Anaxagoras, 150, 179
Anaximander, 150, 179
Anaximenes, 150, 179
Anderson, Elizabeth, 27
Andover Seminary, 165
Andronicus of Rhodes, 5
Angst, 93
Anomalous monism, 91
Anscombe, G. E. M., 43, 47, 106, 107, 162, 164, 172
Anselm of Canterbury, 110, 119, 122, 127, 133, 134, 154, 155
Anti-gnostics, 152
Antiochus of Ascalon, 186
Anti-realism, 20
    scientific, 82, 83, 86
Antisymmetry, 16
Anxiety, 93
Apologetics
    classical, 133, 134, 138, 149, 151
    cumulative case, 133, 137, 138
    epistemology associated with, 138
    evidentialist, 133, 136, 138
    Greek, 152
    Latin, 125, 152
    medieval, 127, 149
    methods, 133
    naturalistic arguments against miracles and, 132
    patristic, 125, 126, 149
    Pensees and, 130
    presuppositional, 133, 138
    reformation views of, 129
    responses to David Hume, 131
Apology (Martyr), 125
Apology (Tertullian), 125
a posteriori knowledge, 30, 32–34
Apostolic exegesis, 115
Appraisers, art, 55
a priori knowledge, 30, 32–34
Aquinas, Thomas, 59, 103, 106, 110, 155, 197
    apologetics, 127, 128, 133, 134
    axiology, 194
    epistemology, 194, 195
    ethics, 194, 195
    metaphysics, 194, 195
    ontology, 195

    proofs for the existence of God, 135
    religious language according to, 111
    theology, 194, 195
    virtue ethics, 140
Aquinas (Geach), 107
Aquinas's Moral Theory (Stump), 107
Aquinas (Stump), 107
Aquinas's Theory of Natural Law (Lisska), 107
Arbitrariness, 98
Architecture, 55
Arendt, Hannah, 96, 162, 163
Arguments
    for anti-realism, 86
    against causation, 31
    against David Hume, 131
    against equivocal language, 111
    against induction, 31
    against materialism, 91
    against miracles, 132
    for realism, 84
    slippery slope, 3
    straw man, 3
    study of, 1
    against univocal language, 111
    against verification principle, 113
Arianism, 121
Aristides, 152
Aristocracies, 56
Aristotelian Chain of Causes, 17
Aristotelian realism, 7, 10, 13
Aristotelian substance, 11
Aristotelian virtue ethics, 44
Aristotle, 150, 151, 182–186, 192, 194, 196
    axiology, 182
    economics and, 58
    epistemology and, 30, 182
    ethics and, 45, 46, 184
    Islam and, 127, 128, 155
    logic and, 5
    metaphysics and, 24, 28, 182, 183
    naïve simile theory, 81
    theology and, 182
    on types of government, 56
Arminian theology, 165, 169
Arminius, Jacob, 157
Armstrong, D. M., 13, 65, 167
Arnobius, 152
Arrow, Kenneth, 174
Art, nature of, 55
Aseity of God, 119
Assertions, 83
Athanasius of Alexandria, 125, 152
Atheism, 63, 69, 93, 94, 101
    existentialism, 160
    idealism, 160
Athenagoras, 125, 134, 152

"A" theory of time, 17, 18
Atomism in mereology, 15, 16
Atomists, 150, 179
Augustine, 46, 134, 142, 152, 153, 155, 192–194, 196, 197, 199
  axiology, 189
  City of God, 125, 126
  on divine foreknowledge, 123
  epistemology, 189, 190
  on God and time, 122
  hermeneutics, 116
  hierarchy of thought, 191
  metaphysics, 189, 190
  theology, 189
  virtue ethics, 139
Augustinian virtue ethics, 44
Austin, J. L., 65, 68, 75–77, 162, 164, 167
Austrian School of economics, 173, 174
Authenticity, 93
Authority, biblical, 115–117
Autobiography (Mill), 207
Autonomy, 48
Averroes, 155
Avicebron, 155
Avicenna, 155
Axiology, 19, 24, 143
  of aesthetics, 55
  Aristotle on, 182
  Augustine on, 189
  Baruch Spinoza on, 200
  Blaise Pascal on, 199
  British empiricists and, 145
  Continental rationalists and, 146
  David Hume on, 205
  epicurean, 185
  G. W. Leibniz on, 201
  George Berkeley on, 204
  Immanuel Kant on, 202
  John Duns Scotus on, 196
  John Locke on, 203
  John Stuart Mill on, 207
  linguistic essentialism and, 70
  logical positivism and, 67
  logical realism and, 66
  Luis de Molina on, 197
  middle platonist, 186
  Nicolas Malebranche on, 199
  ordinary language analysis, 68
  Peter Abelard on, 193
  Plato on, 180
  Plotinus on, 187
  postmodernity and, 148
  post positivists and physicalists and, 69
  René Descartes on, 198
  science and, 82
  skeptics, 186
  stoic, 185
  Thomas Aquinas on, 194
  Thomas Reid on, 206
  William of Ockham on, 196
Axiom, 2
Ayer, Alfred Jules, 40, 41, 65, 67, 75, 110, 113, 162, 164, 167

Bacon, Francis, 85, 158
Bacon, Roger, 155
Balibar, Etienne, 64
Bandwagon appeal, 3
Bare particulars, 5, 10
Barth, Karl, 93, 103, 160, 168, 169
Barthes, Roland, 98, 99, 118, 163

Basic nominalism, 14
Basil, 152
Bauer, Bruno, 94
Bauer, Edgar, 94
Bayes theory, 83
Beatific vision, 190
Beatitudo, 195
Beauty, 54, 84, 205, 206
Beeckman, Isaac, 198
Begging the question, 3
Behaviorism, 91
Being and Nothingness (Sartre), 96
Being and Time (Heidegger), 95, 96
Belief
  ethics of, 29, 36, 37, 38
  justified true, 35
  preceding understanding, 129, 130
  value of, 37
Bellamy, Joseph, 165
Belnap, Nuel, 23
Benevolent monarchies, 56
Benjamin, Walter, 100, 163
Bentham, Jeremy, 50, 158, 161, 207
Bergson, Henri, 105, 171
Berkeley, George
  philosophers influenced by, 205, 206
  philosophy of, 6, 8, 11, 30, 87, 90, 158, 159, 204
Bernard of Chartres, 154
Beza, Theodore, 157
Biblical hermeneutics, 114
  modern, 117
  premodern, 116
  premodern Old Testament, 115
Biblical interpretation, postmodern, 118
Binary product in mereology, 15
Binary sum in mereology, 15
Black box, the brain as a, 91
Blackburn, Simon, 41
Black theology, 118, 168
Bloch, Ernst, 100
Bloom, Allan, 178
Boethius, Anicius, 122, 153, 155, 193
Bonaventure, 127, 140, 155, 156
Bonum progressionis, principle of, 25
Bonum variationis, principle of, 25
Books as sets of proposition, 12
Borderline violations, 77
Bork, Robert, 174
Bosanquet, Bernard, 161
Boserup, Esther, 97
Botero, Giovanni, 156
Bradley, Francis Herbert, 161
Brentano, Franz, 24, 96, 162–164
Brentano and Intrinsic Value (Chisholm), 24
Brink, 167
Brink, David, 65, 70, 166
British empiricists, 144, 145, 149, 158, 159, 164, 176, 203–207
  post-Humean, 161
British philosophy of religion, 104, 170
Brown, Thomas, 161
Brunner, Emil, 93, 168
"B" theory of time, 17, 18
Bucer, Martin, 157
Bullinger, Heinrich, 157
Bultmann, Rudolf, 93, 96, 168
Bundle theory, 11, 13
Burke, Edmund, 177
Bushnell, Horace, 165
Business law, 57
Butler, Joseph, 206

Caird, Edward, 161
Calculus of happiness, 50
Calvin, John, 123, 129, 157
Cambridge Companion to Aquinas, The (Stump), 107
Cambridge University, 104, 107, 164, 170, 172, 175
Camp, Joseph, 23
Campbell, George, 161
Camus, Albert, 93, 163
Cantor, Paul, 178
Capitalism, 58
Capitalism and Freedom (Friedman), 61
Carnap, Rudolf, 65, 67, 113, 162, 164, 167
Carnell, E. J., 169
Cartesian certainty, 146, 203
Cartesian dualism, 88, 90, 146, 159, 198, 202
Cassiodorus, 153
Cassirer, Ernst, 178
Causal-historical theory, 74
Causation, 17, 31, 87, 183
  God as, 135
  mental, 90
  Thomas Aquinas on, 195
Certainty, Cartesian, 146
Chafer, Lewis Sperry, 169
Chain of causes, Aristotelian, 17
Chalcedon, 116, 121, 202
Character, components of, 45, 184
Chicago pragmatism, 166
Chicago School of economics, 58, 61, 173, 174
Chisholm, Roderick, 24, 32, 166
Choice, 93
Chomsky, Noam, 166
Christian ethics, 139–142
Christian Ethics (Geisler), 142
Christian existentialism, 93, 160
Christian philosophy, 155
Christian theology and philosophy. See Religion, philosophy of
Churchland, Paul, 65, 166, 167
City of God (Augustine), 125, 126, 189
Civil law, 140, 184, 203
Clarembald of Arras, 154
Claremont Graduate School, 171
Clark, Gordon, 169
Classical apologetics, 133, 134, 138
Classical disciplines
  epistemology in, 29–38
  ethics in, 39–55
  logic in, 1–4
  metaphysics in, 5–28
  political philosophy in, 56–64
Classical economics, 173
Classical extensional mereology, 15
Classical liberalism, 56, 158, 160, 168, 176, 177
Classical philosophy, 149, 151
Classic foundationalism, 36
Class nominalism, 10
Class struggles, 63, 101
Clement of Alexandria, 125, 152
Closure mereology, 16
Cobb, John, 103, 105, 171
Code of Canon Law, 106
Code of rules, 51
Cognitive moral development, 184
Cognitive science, 88
Cognitivism
  Aristotle on, 184

deontology and, 48, 49
  graded absolutism and, 142
  linguistic virtue ethics and, 46
  moral development and, 45
  moral epistemology and, 39, 41
  moral psychology and, 42
Cohen, Jonathan, 77
Coherence theory of truth, 20, 22, 114, 117, 144
Coherentism, 35, 41, 138
  linear, 36
  wholistic, 36
Combinatorial realism, 13
Commentaries by Thomas Aquinas, 194
Common sense realism, 30, 32, 131, 158, 159, 161, 166
Communicable attributes of God, 119
Communist Manifesto (Marx), 63
Communitarians, 56
Community
  epistemology, 143
  postmodernity and, 148
Compatibilism, 40
Complement in mereology, 15
Complete foreknowledge, 123
Complex truth, 71
Compositionality principle, 79
Compossibility, 12
Comprehensiveness, test of, 137
Computer, the brain as a, 91
Comte, August, 207
Conception and modal illusion, 34
Concept nominalism, 10
Conceptualism, 7
Concordia (de Molina), 197
Concrete particulars, 181, 190, 195
Conditionality, principle of, 25
Cone, James, 118
Confessions (Augustine), 125, 189
Conjectures and Refutations (Popper), 85
Consciousness and the mind, 89, 91, 95
Consequentialism, 27, 29, 43
  virtue, 37, 50
Conservatism, 56, 177
  neo-, 178
Conservative evangelicalism, 169
Considerations on Representative Government (Mill), 207
Consistency, test of, 137
Consolation of Philosophy, The (Boethius), 192
Constantinople, 116, 121
Constitutional law, 57
Constitutive rules, 77
Constructive empiricism, 86, 87
Contemporary realism, 30
Context, extensional and intentional, 79
Contextualism, 76
Continental philosophy, 149, 158, 160, 162, 163
  critical theory in, 64, 100, 101
  existentialism/phenomenology in, 93–97
  philosophy of religion and, 112
  romanticism in, 55, 92
  structuralism in, 98, 99
Continental rationalists, 144, 146, 149, 158, 159, 176, 198–202
Contingency
  modal epistemology and, 34
  state, 5, 12
  truth, 21
Contra Celsum (Origen), 125

Contractarianism, 52
Contractualism, 53
Contradictories, law of, 4
Contraries, law of, 4
Conventional implicature, 76, 78
Conversational maxims, 76, 78
Cooperative principles, 76, 78
Copernican revolution, 159, 202
Copleston, Frederic, 106, 172
Correspondence, test of, 137
Correspondence theory of truth, 22, 66, 70, 143, 196
  hermeneutics and, 114–116
Cosmology, 5, 143–145, 183
  Thomas Aquinas on, 195
  time and, 17, 195
Counterfactuals of creaturely freedom, 124
Courage, 46, 140, 184
Craig, William, 103, 122, 133
Cranmer, Thomas, 157
Creeds, 116, 121, 202
Criminal law, 57
Critical idealism, 8
Critical realism, 166
Critical theory, 64, 100, 101, 160, 163, 173
Criticism, biblical, 117
Critique of Interventionism (von Mises), 61
Critique of Judgment (Kant), 202
Critique of Practical Reason (Kant), 202
Critique of Pure Reason (Kant), 131, 132, 202
Cropsey, Joseph, 178
Crusades, the, 127
Cultural postmodernity, 148
Cultural relativism, 55
Cumulative case apologetics, 133, 137, 138
Cupiditas, 139–140
Cur Deus Homo (Anselm), 127, 193
Cynics, 150, 151

Dallas Theological Seminary, 169
Dance, 55
Darwin, Charles, 132
Dasein, 95, 102
Das Kapital (Marx), 63
Davidson, Donald, 69, 75, 79, 81, 91, 166
Davies, Brian, 107, 172
De Alcala, Luis, 156
De Anima (Aristotle), 28
De Azpilcueta, Martin, 59, 156
De Beauvoir, Simone, 93, 97, 163
De Chardin, Pierre Teilhard, 105, 171
Deconstruction, 118
De Defensione Fidei (Suarez), 197
De Deo Incarnatio (Suarez), 197
De dicto modality, 12
De Doctrina Christiana (Augustine), 116
Deduction, 1, 205
  British empiricists and, 145, 205
  Continental rationalists and, 146
Definite descriptions, 74
Deflationary theories of truth, 21, 23, 35
De Grammatico (Anselm of Canterbury), 110
De Guzman, Domingo, 155
De Indis et de Ivre Belli Relectione (de Vitoria), 59
De Iustitia et Iure (de Molina), 59
De Iustitia et Iure (de Soto), 59
De Justitia (de Vitoria), 59, 197
De la Chaise, Filleau, 130
De la recherché de la verite (Malebranche), 199
Deleuze, Gilles, 99
De Leys, Leonardo, 59, 156
De Lugo, Juan, 59, 156

De Mariano, Juan, 59, 156
De Medina, Juan, 156
De Mercado, Tomas, 59, 156
Democracy, 56
Democritus, 150, 179, 185
De Molina, Luis, 59, 123, 124, 156, 197
Denison University, 107
Dennet, Daniel, 166
Deontic logic, 1
Deontology, 29, 37, 43
  Continental rationalists and, 146
  intuitionism, 49
  Kantian, 48
  non-consequentialist, 47
De Primo Principia (Scotus), 196
De re modality, 12
Derrida, Jacques, 96, 99, 118, 163
Descartes, René, 36, 88, 90, 158, 159, 198, 199, 203, 206
Descent of Man, The (Darwin), 132
Description theory, 74
Designators, rigid, 80
Desires and character, 45
Des Motu (Berkeley), 204
De Soto, Domingo, 59, 156
De Tocqueville, Alexis, 177
Determinism/free will, 39, 40
Development, moral, 39, 42
  cognitive, 184
  internalist, 45
  salvation and, 139, 140
De Vera Religione (Augustine), 191
De Veritate (Anselm of Canterbury), 110
De Villalobos, Henrique, 156
De Vitoria, Francisco, 59, 156, 197
Dewey, John, 71, 165, 166
Dialogue between a Philosopher, a Jew, and a Christian (Abelard), 127, 193
Dialogues Concerning Natural Religion (Hume), 131, 205
Dialogue with Trypho the Jew (Martyr), 125
Difference in mereology, 15
Dilemmas, false, 3
Dilthey, Wilhelm, 102
Director, Aaron, 174
Direct reference theory, 74, 80
Discourse on Metaphysics (Leibniz), 201
Discourse on Methods (Descartes), 198
Disjointness in mereology, 15
Dispensationalism, 169
Disquotational theory of truth, 23, 69
Disraeli, Benjamin, 177
Distributive justice, 57
Disvalue, 24
Divine command theory, 47, 141
Divine foreknowledge, 123, 124
Divine illumination, 190
Divine Institutes (Lactantius), 125
Divine law, 140, 203
Divine transcendence, 111, 186
Divisions of Nature, The (Erigena), 192
Doctrine of God, 120, 121
Doctrine of the mean, 44
Doctrines, metaphysical, 14
Dodd, C. H., 136
Dominicans, 59, 127, 155, 156
Doubt, hermeneutic of, 117, 120, 144
Dualism, 198
  Cartesian, 88, 90, 146, 159
  epistemological, 30
Dwight, Timothy, 165

Eckhart, Meister, 110, 155
Eclaircissements sur la recherché de la verité (Malebranche), 199
Economics
    Adam Smith on, 60
    classical, 173
    defined, 56
    ethics and, 58
    feminist philosophy, 97
    free market, 60, 61, 174
    Keynesian, 58, 62, 173–175
    law and, 57
    Salamanca school of, 59
    socialist/Marxist, 58, 63, 64, 173
    theories, 58
    types of, 58
Economics and the Public Purpose (Galbraith), 62
Edinburgh University, 104, 170
Educated observers, 55
Edwards, Jonathan, 165
Edwards, Jonathan, II, 165
Ego and superego, 101
Egoism, 42
Einstein, Albert, 17
Eleatics, 150, 151, 179
Eliminativism, 9, 40, 88, 91
Elster, Jon, 64
Embassy for the Christians (Athenagoras), 125
Emmons, Nathaniel, 165
Emotivism, 40, 41, 67
Empedocles, 150, 179
Empirical naturalism, 71
Empiricism, 29, 30, 144, 145
    British, 144, 145, 149, 158, 159, 164, 176, 203–207
    constructive, 86, 87
    hard, 41
    naturalistic, 71
    post-Humean British, 161
    view of language, 111
Enchiridion, The (Augustine), 189
Endurantism, 18
Engels, Friedrich, 94
Enneads (Plotinus), 187, 188
Enquiry Concerning the Principles of Morals (Hume), 205
Entretiens sur la metaphysique (Malebranche), 199
Epicureans, 150, 151, 185
Epicurus of Samos, 185
Epiphenomenalism, 90
Epistemic logic, 1
Epistemic realism, 20
Epistemological dualism, 30
Epistemological particularism, 66
Epistemological realism, 143
Epistemology, 19
    aesthetic, 54
    Alvin Plantinga on, 109
    Aristotle on, 30, 182, 183
    associated with apologetic approaches, 138
    Augustine on, 189, 190
    Baruch Spinoza on, 200
    Blaise Pascal on, 199
    British empiricists and, 145
    common sense realism in, 30, 32
    community, 143
    Continental rationalists and, 146
    David Hume on, 30, 31, 205
    externalist theories of knowledge and, 38
    feminist philosophy, 97

G. W. Leibniz on, 201
George Berkeley on, 204
Immanuel Kant on, 33, 202
intrinsic value and, 26
John Duns Scotus on, 196
John Locke on, 203
John Stuart Mill on, 207
linguistic essentialism and, 70
logical positivism and, 67
logical realism and, 66
Luis de Molina on, 197
meta-, 29
modal, 34
moral, 39, 41, 46, 49, 51, 139–141, 184
naturalized, 35, 38, 41, 69
Nicolas Malebranche on, 199
ordinary language analysis, 68
perception metaphysics of, 30
Plato on, 180, 181
Plotinus on, 187
postmodernity and, 148
post positivists and physicalists and, 69
René Descartes on, 198
science and, 82, 84, 86
skeptics, 186
theories of knowledge, 35, 36
Thomas Aquinas on, 194, 195
Thomas Reid on, 32, 206
virtue, 35, 37, 41
William of Ockham on, 196
Equality, 48
Equivocal language, 111
Erasmus, Desiderius, 156
Erigena, John Scotus, 153, 155
Escape, art as, 55
Essay Concerning Human Understanding, An (Locke), 203
Essays in Religion (Mill), 207
Essays in Theodicy (Leibniz), 201
Essays Moral and Political (Hume), 205
Essays on Some Unsettled Questions of Political Economy (Mill), 207
Essays on the Active Powers of Man (Reid), 206
Essays on the Intellectual Powers of Man (Reid), 206
Essence of things, 6
Essentialism, 12, 13, 40
    linguistic, 65, 70, 167
    theological, 103, 119
Eternalism, 17
Eternal law, 195
Eternity of God, 119, 122, 191
Ethical altruism, 42
Ethical and Religious Thought in Analytic Philosophy of Language (Smith), 65
Ethical egoism, 42
Ethical nominalism, 40
Ethics, 19
    act utilitarianism and, 50
    aesthetics and, 54
    Aristotle on, 183
    of belief, 29, 36–38
    Christian, 139–142
    economics and, 58
    feminist philosophy, 97
    internalist moral development and, 45
    linguistic virtue, 44, 46
    meta-, 39, 141
    metaphysics of, 40
    moral epistemology and, 41
    moral psychology and, 42

non-consequentialist deontology and, 47
normative, 43
Plotinus on, 187
rule utilitarianism and, 51
situational, 43
social contract theory and, 52
Thomas Aquinas on, 195
Virtue, 43, 44, 46, 139, 140, 184
.See also Deontology
Ethics (Abelard), 193
Ethics Demonstrated According to the Geometrical Order (Spinoza), 200
Eudaimonia, 141, 207
Eudomean Ethics (Aristotle), 182, 184
Eudorus of Alexandria, 186
Eusebius of Caesarea, 125, 134
Euthyphro dilemma, the, 141
Evaluation, 24
Evangelical theology, 169
Events, 5
Evidentialist apologetics, 133, 136, 138
Evil, 109, 185, 188, 201
Evolution, 83
Excluded middle, law of the, 4
Existence
    judgment, 24
    principle of, 25
Existentialism
    atheistic, 160
    Christian, 93, 160
    Continental rationalists and, 146
    Edmund Husserl's phenomenology and, 95
    non-consequentialist deontology and, 47
    philosophers, 94
    types of, 93
Explanation, 1, 50
Expressionism, 55
Expressive theory of value, 27
Expressivism, norm, 41
Extensional semantics, 79
Externalism, 35
    moral, 42, 50, 51, 52
    virtue epistemology and, 37
Extreme coherentism, 36
Extreme foundationalism, 36
Extreme nominalism, 7, 10, 13, 30
Extreme realism, 10, 30
Extrinsic value, 26

Facts, 5
    evidentialism and, 136
    moral, 40
    value dichotomy, 28
Factualism, 14
Fair exchange, 58
Faith, 46, 116, 139, 140, 195
    reason and, 127, 129
Fallacies, logical, 2
    formal, 2
    informal, 2, 3
Fallen man, 191
False dilemmas, 3
Falsification, 83–85
Fantasy, 191
Farel, William, 157
Farrer, Austin, 104, 106, 170, 172
Federal Reserve Board, 61
Feeling and romanticism, 92
Feinberg, Paul, 133, 137
Feldstein, Martin, 175
Felicitas, 195

Feminist philosophy, 97
Feminist theology, 118, 168
Feuerbach, Ludwig, 94, 160
Feyerabend, Paul, 85, 87
Fichte, Johann Gottlieb, 8, 92, 146,
    158–160, 173
Fideisim, 138
Fidelity, 49
Field, Hartry, 38
Figurative simile theory, 81
Film, 55
Fiorenza, Elisabeth Schüssler, 97
Fogelin, R., 81
Foreknowledge, divine, 123
Formal logical fallacies, 2
Form criticism of the Bible, 117
Foucault, Michel, 23, 98, 99, 118, 163
Foundationalism, 32, 35, 41, 66, 138
    classic, 36
    extreme, 36
    moderate, 36
Frame, John, 133
Franciscans, 127, 155, 156
Francis of Assisi, 155
Frankfurt School, 64, 100, 160, 163
Freedom, 40, 206
Free knowledge, 124
Free market economics, 60, 61, 174
Free to Choose (Friedman), 61
Free trade, 60
Free will/determinism
    Alvin Plantinga on, 109
    Aristotle on, 184
    ethics and, 39, 46, 48–52
    existentialism and, 93
    God's foreknowledge and, 123, 124
    graded absolutism and, 142
Frege, Gottlob, 74, 76, 162, 164
Frei, Hans, 168
Freud, Sigmund, 101, 162
Freudianism, 101
Friedman, Milton, 58, 61, 174, 177
Fruitfulness, test of, 137
Fulbert, 154
Fuller Theological Seminary, 169
Functionalism, 88, 91
    proper, 35, 38, 41
Fundamentalism, 169
Fusion principles in mereology, 16

Gadamer, Hans Georg, 96, 102, 162, 163
Galbraith, John Kenneth, 62, 175
Games, language, 68, 75, 110
Garry, Ann, 97
Geach, Peter, 106, 107, 172
Geisler, Norman, 47, 142
General sum and product in mereology, 15,
    16
*General Theory of Employment, Interest, and
    Money, The* (Keynes), 58, 62
Genuine possible worlds, 13
German Enlightenment, 159
Gettier, Edmund, 35
Gettier problem, 35
Gibbard, Allan, 41
Gilbert of Aurillac, 154
Gilligan, Carol, 97
Gilson, Etienne, 103, 106, 172
God
    British empiricists and, 145
    communicable attributes of, 119

divine foreknowledge of, 123, 124
    doctrine of, 120, 121
    as eternal, 119, 122, 191
    grace of, 129
    incommunicable attributes of, 119
    judgment by, 202
    miracles and, 132
    perfect being theology and, 119
    proofs for the existence of, 134, 135
    time and, 122
    as truth, 190, 192
    will of, 47, 141, 196
God, Freedom, and Evil (Plantinga), 109
Godfrey of St. Victor, 154
Goethe, Johann Wolfgang, 176
Goldberger, Arthur, 174
Gonsalvus of Spain, 196
Goodman, Nelson, 166
Goods and character, 45
Good will, 49
Gorgias, 150, 179
Government, types of, 56
Grace of God, 129
Gradation and God as perfect, 135
Graded absolutism, 47, 142
Grammar, 73
Gratitude, 49
Greatest happiness principle, 50
Greco, John, 37
Greek apologists, 152
Greek fathers, 152
Greek philosophy, 151, 152
Green, Thomas Hill, 161
Gregory of Nazianzus, 152
Gregory of Nyssa, 152, 192
Grensted, L. W., 104, 170
Grenz, Stanley, 169
Grice, H. P., 75, 76, 78, 164
Griffin, David, 171
Grosseteste, Robert, 155
Grotius, Hugo, 59
Ground mereology, 16
Groundwork for a Metaphysics of Morals
    (Kant), 48, 202
Grover, Dorothy, 23
Guide for the Perplexed (Maimonides), 110
Guilt and moral constraint, 101
Gutiérrez, Gustavo, 118

Habermas, Gary, 133, 136
Habermas, Jürgen, 64, 100, 163
Hacceities, 12, 13
Haldane, John, 107
Happiness, 51
Hard empiricism, 41
Hare, Richard, 40, 65, 68, 164, 167
Harnack, Adolf, 160
Hartshorne, Charles, 103, 105, 166, 171
Harvard University, 165, 166
Hauerwas, Stanley, 46, 168
Health
    mental, 39, 139–141, 184
    moral, 42
Heaven, 130
Hebrew thought, 151
Hedonic calculus, 50
Hedonism, 27
Hegel, G. W. F., 8, 92, 94, 99, 158, 160,
    161, 173
Heidegger, Martin, 23, 93, 95, 96, 99, 102,
    112, 162, 163, 168

Hell, 130
Helm, Paul, 122
Henry, Carl F. H., 169
Heraclitus, 150, 185
Hermann, Rudolf, 160, 168
Hermeneutics, 73, 95, 102
    biblical, 114
    of doubt, 117, 120, 144
    feminist philosophy, 97
    modern biblical, 117
    premodern biblical, 116
    premodern Old Testament, 115
    of suspicion, 118, 148
    of trust, 143
Hess, Moses, 94
Hicks, John, 175
Hierarchicalism. *See* Graded absolutism
Higher criticism of the Bible, 117
Hindess, Barry, 64
Hippias, 150, 179
Hippolytus, 152
Hirst, Paul, 64
Historical-critical methodologies, 114, 117
Historical-grammatical interpretation, 114,
    116
Historicizing, 115
History of philosophy
    major divisions in, 143–148
    major philosophers and, 179–207
    timeline charts, 144–178
Hobbes, Thomas, 52, 158, 176
Hodge, Charles, 142, 165
Holy Spirit, the, 116, 121, 136–138, 195
Homo economicus, 58
Hooker, Richard, 177
Hope, 46, 116, 139, 140, 195
Hopkins, Samuel, 165
Horkheimer, Max, 64, 100, 163
Horwich, Paul, 23
Hugh of St. Victor, 154
Human Action (von Mises), 61
Human Condition, The (Arendt), 96
Humanism, Marxist, 64
Hume, David, 110, 144, 145, 158, 159,
    161, 205, 206
    arguments against miracles, 132
    axiology, 205
    epistemology, 30, 31, 205
    ethics, 47, 50
    metaphysics, 11, 28, 205
    responses to, 131
    scientific anti-realism, 87
    skepticism, 67
    theology, 205
    verification principle and, 113
Husserl, Edmund, 95, 96, 162, 163, 178
Hutcheson, Francis, 50, 205, 206
Hybrid welfarism, 42
Hypotheses
    contrary to fact, 3
    scientific method, 83, 84
Hypothetical imperative, 48

Idealism, 7, 161
    absolute, 8, 160
    atheistic, 160
    British, 145, 158
    Cartesian dualism and, 90
    Continental rationalists and, 146
    realism and, 20
    subjective, 6, 8, 30, 204

Ideas, 205
Identity
    of indiscernables, 9
    personal, 88, 89
    theory, 91
Idolatry, 125, 129
Ignatius of Loyola, 156
Illocution, 77
Illumination, divine, 190
Illusion, modal, 34
Imitation, art as, 55
Immanence of God, 119
Immensity of God, 119
Immutability of God, 119
Impeccability of God, 120
Imperatives, hypothetical, 48
Implicature, 76, 78
Impressions, 205
In a Different Voice (Gilligan), 97
Incarnation of the Word of God, The (Athanasius), 125
Incommensurability, 85
Incommunicable attributes of God, 119
Indeterminancy of translation, 69
Indexical theory of actuality, 13
Indiscernability of identicals, 9
Induction, 1, 31, 87, 205
    British empiricists and, 145, 205
    Continental rationalists and, 146
Inerrancy, biblical, 115–117
Inference, 2
Infinity of God, 119
Informal logical fallacies, 2, 3
Innate ideas, 73
    British empiricists and, 145
    Continental rationalists and, 146
Inquiry Concerning Human Understanding, An (Hume), 31, 131, 132
Inquiry into the Human Mind on the Principles of Common Sense (Reid), 131, 206
Inquiry into the Nature and Causes of the Wealth of Nations, An (Smith), 60
Instantiation, principle of, 9
Institutes of the Christian Religion (Calvin), 129
Instrumentalism, 86, 166
    pragmatic, 71
Instrumental value, 24, 26
    of knowledge, 29
Intentionality
    intrinsic value and, 26
    language and, 73
    the mind and, 89, 91
    phenomenology and, 95
Intentional semantics, 75, 79
Internal harmony, principle of, 201
Internalism, 35, 36
    moral, 42, 48, 49, 53, 139–141, 184
    virtue epistemology and, 37
Internalist moral development, 45
International law, 57
Interpretation
    evidentialism and, 136
    postmodern biblical, 118
Intrinsic value, 24, 26
    of knowledge, 29
Intrinsic Value (Lemos), 24
Introduction to Value Theory (Rescher), 24
Intuition
    aesthetics and, 54
    knowledge and, 196
    romanticism and, 92

Intuitionism, 29, 30
    Rossian, 47, 49
Irenaeus, 152
Irrealism
    aesthetic, 54
    epistemic, 29, 40
    moral, 46, 50, 51
    postmodernity and, 148
Isidore, 153
Islam, 127, 128, 155

Jaffa, Harry, 178
James, William, 71, 165, 166
Jaspers, Karl, 96
Jesuits, 59, 156
Jesus Christ, 121, 192
    salvation through, 130
Jewish philosophy, 155
John of Salisbury, 154
Johns Hopkins University, 165
John XXIII, Pope, 106
Joseph, Keith, 177
Judgment, existence, 24
Justice, 46, 49, 53, 140, 184
    distributive, 57
    retributive, 57
Justified true belief, 35

Kahn, Richard I., 175
Kant, Immanuel, 158, 159, 176, 202
    arguments against miracles, 132
    axiology, 202
    deontology, 47, 48
    epistemology, 202
    idealism, 8, 161
    metaphysics, 202
    phenomenalism, 30
    skepticism, 131
    social contract theory, 53
    theology, 202
    transcendental analysis of mental faculties, 33
Kantianism, 47
Kenny, Anthony, 106, 107, 172
Keyes, Alan, 178
Keynes, John Maynard, 58, 62, 173, 175
Keynesian economics, 58, 62, 173–175
Khalilzad, Zalmay, 178
Kierkegaard, Søren, 93, 94, 158, 160, 168
Kirzner, Israel, 174
Klein, Lawrence, 174, 175
Knight, Frank, 61, 173, 174
Knowledge
    abstract, 196
    divine, 123, 124, 190
    epistemological theories of, 35, 36
    externalist theories of, 38
    intuitive, 196
    metaphysics of, 29, 36
    a posteriori, 31, 33, 34
    a priori, 31, 33, 34
    representationalism and, 159, 203
    romanticism on, 92
    source of, 30
    value of, 29, 36
Knox, John, 157
Kornblith, Hilary, 38
Kraus, Oskar, 24
Kretzmann, Norman, 107, 122
Kripke, Saul, 119, 167
    causal-historical theory, 74

linguistic essentialism, 65, 70, 80
    modal epistemology, 34
    truth-conditional theory, 75
Kristeva, Julia, 99
Kristol, William, 178
Kuhn, Thomas, 86, 87, 166
Kuyper, Abraham, 177
Kvanvig, Jonathan, 38

Labor, division of, 60
Lacan, Jacques, 98, 118, 163
Lachman, Ludwig, 174
Lactantius, 125, 152
Laissez-faire government, 60
Lakatos, Imre, 85
Lanfranc of Canterbury, 154, 193
Language
    Alvin Plantinga on, 109
    analogical, 111
    analysis, ordinary, 65, 68, 107, 112, 164, 167
    direct reference theory of, 74, 80
    equivocal, 111
    games, 68, 75
    linguistic essentialism and, 65, 70
    logical positivism and, 67
    logical realism and, 66
    metaphorical meaning and, 81
    metaphysics and, 73
    the mind and, 73
    moral, 39, 40
    nature of, 73
    philosophy of, 72–81, 109
    post positivists and physicalists and, 69
    religious, 110–118
    speech act theory of, 68, 75–77
    truth theory of meaning and, 79
    univocal, 111
Lash, Nicolas, 170
Laski, John, 157
La Teoria del Justo Precio (de Molina), 59, 197
Latin apologists, 125, 152
Latin fathers, 152
Law(s)
    areas of, 57
    business, 57
    civil, 140, 184, 203
    constitutional, 57
    of contradictories, 4
    of contraries, 4
    criminal, 57
    divine, 140, 203
    economics and, 57
    eternal, 195
    of the excluded middle, 4
    international, 57
    of logic, 4
    natural, 44, 57, 59, 140, 184, 195
    of non-contradiction, 4
    of opinion or reputation, 203
    philosophy of, 56, 57
    scientific, 83, 84
    social contract theory and, 52
    square of opposition, 4
    of subalternation, 4
    of subcontraries, 4
    temporal and eternal, 139, 140
Laws and Symmetry (van Fraassen), 87
Lefevre, Jacques, 157
Leftow, Brian, 104
Legal positivism, 57
Legislation for a moral community, 48

Leibniz, Gottfried Wilhelm, 8, 13, 90, 158, 159, 201
Leibnizian substance, 11
Lemos, Noah, 24
Leontief, Wassily, 175
Leo XIII, Pope, 103, 106, 172
Lessius, 59, 156
Lettres privinciales (Pascal), 199
Leucippus, 150, 179
Lévinas, Emmanuel, 96, 162, 163
Lévi-Strauss, Claude, 98, 118, 163
Lewis, C. I., 166
Lewis, David, 13, 65, 166, 167
Liberalism, 56, 158, 160, 168, 176, 177
Liberation theology, 118, 168
Libertarians, 56
Lieva, Diego, 156
Lindbeck, George, 168
Linear coherentism, 36
Linguistic essentialism, 65, 70, 80, 167
Linguistic relativism, 98
Linguistic turn in philosophy of religion, 112
Linguistic virtue ethics, 44, 46
Lisska, Anthony, 107
Literature, 55
Loci Communes (Melanchthon), 129
Locke, John
    philosophers influenced by, 204–206
    philosophy of, 6, 11, 30, 36, 158, 159, 176, 177, 203
Locus of value, 24
Locutions, 76, 77
Logic
    British empiricists and, 145
    Continental rationalists and, 146
    formal fallacies in, 2
    informal fallacies, 2, 3
    laws of, 4
    meaning and, 69
    modal, 1, 12
    of science, 82
    as study of arguments, 1
    tems in, 2
Logica (Abelard), 193
Logical fallacy, 2
Logical positivism, 65, 67, 110, 113, 132, 164, 167
Logical realism, 65, 66, 112, 164, 167
Logical truth, 71
Logic of Scientific Discovery, The (Popper), 85
Lombard, Peter, 154
London School of economics, 175
Loomer, Bernard, 105, 171
Love, 46, 116, 139, 140, 195
Lower critical methodologies, 116
Lower criticism of the Bible, 117
Luther, Martin, 129, 157
Lyotard, Jean-Francois, 99

MacDonald, Scott, 107
Machen, J. Gresham, 169
MacIntyre, Alasdair, 44, 46, 172
Mackinnon, Donald, 170
Macquarrie, John, 170
Macro economics, 58
Magna Moralia (Aristotle), 182, 184
Magnus, Albertus, 155
Maimonides, Moses, 110, 155
Malebranche, Nicolas, 90, 159, 199, 206
Man and His Well-being (Spinoza), 200
Mankiw, Gregory, 175
Mansfield, Harvey, 178

Man's state of nature, 52, 53
Manual de confesores y Penitentes (de Azpilcueta), 59
Marcus, Ruth, 70, 74, 166, 167
Marcuse, Herbert, 64, 100, 163
Maritain, Jacques, 103, 106, 172
Marsh, James, 165
Marshall, Alfred, 61, 62, 173, 175
Martyr, Justin, 125, 152
Marx, Karl, 63, 64, 94, 101, 160, 163, 173
Marxism, 58, 63, 101, 168
    analytic, 64, 173
    anti-humanist, 64, 173
Mascall, Eric, 104, 106, 170, 172
Material bodies, 90
Materialism, 88, 91
Mathematics, 1
Maurus, Rhabanus, 153
Mavrodes, George, 103, 108
Mayer, Hans, 174
McInerny, Ralph, 172
McTaggart, John, 18, 161
Meaning
    based on formal logic, 69
    language and, 73, 74
    metaphorical, 81
    of names, 80
    out of facts, 136
    phenomenology and, 95
    pragmatic theory of, 71
    psychological theories of, 75
    reader response and, 118
    speech act theory and, 77
    theories of, 75
    truth-conditional theories of, 75
    truth theory of, 79
    use theory of, 68, 75
    verificationism and, 75
Medieval apologetics, 127, 149
Medieval philosophy, 154, 155
Meditationes Chretiennes (Malebranche), 199
Meditations on First Philosophy (Descartes), 198
Meinong, Alexius, 24
Melanchthon, Philipp, 129, 157
Memorial (Pascal), 199
Memory, 29
Menger, Carl, 61, 173, 174
Menger, Karl, 174
Mental causation, 90
Mental faculties, transcendental analysis of, 33
Mental health, 39, 139–141, 184
Mercier, Cardinal Désiré-Joseph, 106, 172
Mereology
    atomism in, 15, 16
    closure, 16
    fusion principles in, 16
    ground, 16
    principles of, 16
    supplementation principles, 16
    terminology, 15
    types, 15
Merleau-Ponty, Maurice, 93, 96, 162, 163
Merton, Robert, 175
Meta-ethics, 39, 141
Metaphorical meaning, 81
Metaphysics, 5
    Alvin Plantinga on, 109
    Anselm of Canterbury on, 193
    Aristotle on, 24, 28, 182, 183
    Augustine on, 189, 190
    axiology in, 19, 24

Baruch Spinoza on, 200
of beauty, 54
Blaise Pascal on, 199
Boethius on, 192
British empiricists and, 145
Continental rationalists and, 146
cosmology in, 5, 17
David Hume on, 11, 28, 205
doctrines, 14
epicurean, 185
of epistemology, 30
of ethics, 39, 40
Francisco Suarez on, 197
G. W. Leibniz on, 201
George Berkeley on, 204
idealism in, 6–8
Immanuel Kant on, 202
John Duns Scotus on, 196
John Locke on, 203
John Scotus Erigena on, 192
John Stuart Mill on, 207
of knowledge, 29, 36
language and, 73
linguistic essentialism, 70
logical positivism and, 67
logical realism and, 66
Luis de Molina on, 197
mereology in, 15
meta-epistemology and, 29
middle platonist, 186
modality in, 12
of morals, 46, 48, 49, 141, 184
Nicolas Malebranche on, 199
ontology in, 5, 7, 10
ordinary language analysis, 68
particulars in, 5, 7, 10, 11, 13, 181
Peter Abelard on, 193
of Plato, 180, 181
of Plotinus, 187, 188
possible worlds in, 12, 13
postmodernity and, 148
post positivists and physicalists and, 69
property and substance in, 6
realism, 19, 20
René Descartes on, 198
of science, 82, 84
skeptics, 186
stoic, 185
teleology in, 5, 19
terminology, 5
Thomas Aquinas on, 194, 195
Thomas Reid on, 206
truth in, 21, 22
universals in, 5, 7, 9–11, 14
value theory in, 19, 24–28
William of Ockham on, 196
Metaphysics (Aristotle), 182, 184
Metaphysics of Morals (Kant), 202
Methodology of Scientific Research Programs, The (Lakatos), 85
Micro economics, 58
Middle knowledge, 123, 124
Middle platonists, 186
Midrash, 115
Milesians, 150, 179
Mill, James, 207
Mill, John Stuart, 51, 61, 74, 158, 161, 176, 177, 207
Millett, Kate, 97
Mind(s), 7
    /body problem, 89
    Cartesian dualism and, 88, 90

consciousness and, 89, 91, 95
external world and, 89
intentionality and, 89, 91
language and, 73
materialism and, 88, 91
other, 89
philosophy of, 68, 88, 89
unconscious, 101
Minimal epistemic realism, 84
Minimalism
semantic pragmatics and, 76
theory of truth, 22, 23
Minimal psychological realism, 42
Miracles, 132, 205
Mitchell, Basil, 103, 104, 133, 170
Modal epistemology, 34
Modalism, 121
Modality, 12, 80
Modal logic, 1, 12
Modal mereology, 15
Modal realism, 13
Moderate coherentism, 36
Moderate evangelicalism, 169
Moderate foundationalism, 36
Moderate nominalism, 7, 10, 13, 30
Moderate realism, 10, 13, 30
Moderates, political, 56
Modern biblical hermeneutics, 117
Modernity, 144–146, 149
Modern liberals, 56
"Modern Moral Philosophy," 47
Modigliani, Franco, 175
Molinism, 124
Moltmann, Jürgen, 103, 168
Monadology (Leibniz), 201
Monads, 201
Monetarism, 61
Monism
anomalous, 91
value, 26, 27, 29, 38
Monologium (Anselm), 127, 193
Montague, William, 166
Moore, G. E., 32, 161, 164, 167
epistemology and, 30
logical realism and, 65, 66
metaphysics and, 24, 27, 28
philosophy of religion and, 112, 145
Moral constraint and guilt, 101
Moral development, 39, 42
cognitive, 184
internalist, 45
salvation and, 139, 140
Moral epistemology, 39, 41, 49, 51,
139–141, 184
Moral facts, 40
Moral health, 42
Moral internalism, 42, 48, 49, 53, 139, 140
Moral irrealism, 46, 50, 51
Morality
Augustine on, 139
epistemology of, 41, 46
foundations of, 39
intrinsic value and, 26
metaphysics of, 46, 48, 49, 141, 184
nature of, 40
nature of the moral self and, 42
subjectivity and, 93
Moral language, 39, 40
Moral motivation, 39, 42, 48, 50, 51
Moral particularism, 43
Moral properties, 39, 40
Moral psychology, 39, 42, 46, 48, 49, 51,
139–141, 184

Moral realism, 20, 48, 49, 120, 184
graded absolutism and, 142
virtue ethics and, 139, 140
Moral responsibility, 40
Moral skepticism, 30, 41
Morris, Thomas, 103
Motivation
externalism, 50–52
internalism, 46, 49, 184
moral, 39, 42, 48, 50, 51
Murphy, Mark, 172
Music, 55

Naïve simile theory, 81
Names, meaning of, 80
Naming and Necessity (Kripke), 65, 119
Narrative criticism of the Bible, 118
Natural History of Religion (Hume), 131
Naturalism, 13, 14, 19, 82
arguments against miracles, 132
empirical, 71
morality and, 40
Sigmund Freud on, 101
teleology and, 43
value monism and, 27
Naturalistic empiricism, 71
Naturalized epistemology, 35, 38, 41, 69
Natural knowledge, 124
Natural law, 44, 57, 59, 140, 184, 195
Natural ontological attitude, 86
Natural theology, 131
Nature of Necessity, The (Plantinga), 109, 119
Navarrus, 59, 156
Necessity, 2, 5, 12
of God, 120
God as, 135
modal epistemology and, 34
rigid designators and, 80
of truth, 21
Neo-classical economics, 173
Neo-conservatism, 178
Neo-orthodoxy, 103, 160, 168
Neo-Pythagoreans, 186
Neo-realism, 166
Neo-Thomism, 103, 106–107, 172
Neurath, Otto, 65, 67, 113, 164, 167, 174
New Haven Theology, 165
New Industrial State, The (Galbraith), 62
New School Presbyterians, 165
New System of Nature, The (Leibniz), 201
Nicea, 116, 121, 202
Nichomachean Ethics (Aristotle), 182, 184
Niebuhr, H. Richard, 168
Niebuhr, Reinhold, 168
Nietzsche, Friedrich, 30, 94, 158
Nihilism, 40, 54
postmodernity and, 148
No disjunctive universals, 9
Noetic effects of sin, 141, 195
Nominalism
basic, 14
ethical, 40
extreme, 7, 10, 13, 30
metaphysical, 67
moderate, 7, 10, 13, 30
ontology and, 7
realism and, 20
types of value and, 26
value theory and, 25
Noncognitivism, 39, 41, 42, 50–52
Non-consequentialism, 43, 47
Non-contradiction, law of, 4

Nonexistence, principle of, 25
Nonmalificence, 49
Non-naturalism, 27
Nonphysical universals related to physical
universals, 9
Nontrivial essences, 70
Normative economics, 58
Normative epistemology, 29
Normative ethics, 43
Norm expressivism, 41
Noumenal world, 33

Objective idealism, 7, 8
Objectivism, 42, 55
Objects
art, 55
of knowledge, 29
properties of, 6, 203
romanticism and, 92
value, 24
Obstinate designators, 80
Occasionalism, 90, 159
Oecolampadius, Johannes, 157
Ogden, Shubert, 171
Old School Presbyterians, 165
Oligarchy, 56
OLP. *See* Ordinary Language Philosophy
Omnibenevolence of God, 119, 120
Omnipotence of God, 119, 120, 123, 207
Omnipresence of God, 119, 120
Omniscience of God, 119, 120, 123
Omni-temporality of God, 122
On Divine Names (Pseudo Dionysius the
Areopagite), 110
On Law and God the Lawgiver (Suarez), 197
On Liberty (Mill), 207
On Mystical Theology (Pseudo Dionysius the
Areopagite), 110
On Teaching Christian Doctrine (Augustine),
189
*On the Principles of Political Economy and Taxa-
tion* (Ricardo), 61
Ontology, 5, 143, 144, 183
British empiricists and, 145
Continental rationalists and, 146
linguistic essentialism and, 70
of Plato, 181
postmodernity and, 148
universals and, 7, 10
On True Religion (Augustine), 191
Open theism, 123
Opinion, law of, 203
Opuscula (Boethius), 192
Opus Oxoniense (Scotus), 196
Ordinary language analysis, 65, 68, 107,
112, 164, 167
Ordinary Language Philosophy, 78
Organic unities, principle of, 25
Origen of Alexandria, 125, 152
*Origin of Our Knowledge of Right and Wrong,
The* (Brentano), 24
Oswald, James, 161
Over-crossing in mereology, 16
Overlap in mereology, 15, 16
Oxford University, 104, 106, 107, 164, 170,
172

Padgett, Alan, 122
Paganism, 125
Painting, 55
Panentheism, 90, 159, 200

Pannenberg, Wolfhart, 168, 169
Paradox, 2
Parallelism, 90, 159
Parks, Amasa, 165
Parmenides, 179
Parole, 98
Particularism
  epistemological, 66
  moral, 43
Particulars, 5, 7, 10, 11
  concrete, 181, 190, 195
  possible worlds and, 13
  value theory and, 26
Pascal, Blaise, 130, 159, 199
Passions of the Soul (Descartes), 198
Passive Obedience (Berkeley), 204
Patristic apologetics, 125, 149
Patristic philosophy, 152
Payley, William, 133, 136
Pearsall, Marilyn, 97
Pêcheux, Michel, 64
Pelagius, 139
Pensees (Pascal), 130, 199
Perception
  levels of, 200
  metaphysics of epistemology, 30
  modal epistemology and, 34
Perdurantism, 18
Perfect being theology, 119
Perfectionism, 44
Performative theory of truth, 23, 68
Performative utterances, 77
Perichoresis, 121
Perle, Richard, 178
Perlocutions, 76, 77
Perry, Ralph, 166
Persistence through time, 18
Persistent designators, 80
Personal identity, 88, 89
Perspectivism, 37
Peshat, 115
Pesher, 115
Phenomenological theory of truth, 23
Phenomenalism, 30, 33, 95, 96
  Continental rationalists and, 146
Phenomenology, 163
Phenomenology of Perception (Merleau-Ponty), 96
Philo, 151, 152, 155
Philolaus, 179
Philosophers
  modern, 198–207
  premodern, 179–197
  pre-Socratic, 179
  skeptic and middle platonist, 186
  stoic and epicurean, 185
  .See also individual philosophers
Philosophical Analysis in the 20th Century (Soames), 65, 78, 79
Philosophical Fragments (Anselm of Canterbury), 110
Photography, 55
Phronesis, 183
Physicalism, 14, 65, 69, 79, 82, 91, 167
Physics (Aristotle), 5
Pierce, Charles Sanders, 71, 165, 166
Pinker, Steven, 166
Pinnock, Clark, 169
Plantinga, Alvin, 13, 38, 65, 70, 167
  reformed epistemology, 108, 109
  theological essentialism, 103, 109, 119

Plato
  modern philosophers influenced by, 199, 200
  philosophy of, 8, 24, 150–152, 155, 180, 181
  premodern philosophers influenced by, 186
Platonic realism, 7, 10, 13, 70
Platonists, middle, 186
Play, art as, 55
Plotinus, 8, 152, 187, 188
Pluralism
  theoretical scientific, 85
  value, 26, 27, 29, 38
Pluralists, 150, 179
Plutarch of Chaeronea, 186
Political Discourse (Hume), 205
Political philosophy, 56, 97, 173, 174
  .See also Economics
Political Theological Treatise (Spinoza), 117, 132
Political theory, 50
Politics, The (Aristotle), 182, 184
Polity, 56
Polkinghorne, John, 104
Polytheism, 125
Popper, Karl, 83–85, 113, 177
Porphyry, 152, 187, 188
Positive economics, 58
Positivism
  ethics and, 42, 48, 50
  legal, 57
  logical, 65, 67, 110, 113, 132, 164, 167
Possible worlds, 12, 13, 34, 75
  God and, 135
  rigid designators and, 80
Post-conservativism, 169
Post hoc, ergo propter hoc logical fallacies, 3
Post-liberalism, 168
Postmodern biblical interpretation, 118
Postmodernism, 55, 57, 96, 147–149
  Biblical hermeneutics and, 114
Postmodern theology, 103
Postmodern theories of truth, 21, 23
Post positivists, 65, 69, 79
Post-structuralism, 99, 118, 163
Poulantzas, Nicos, 64
Pragmatic instrumentalism, 71
Pragmatic justification theory, 27
Pragmatic(s), 73, 76
  semantic, 66, 76
  theory of meaning, 71, 81
  theory of truth, 20, 22, 23, 30, 71, 114, 118
Pragmatism, 69, 86
  American, 71, 165
  analytic, 166
  Harvard, 166
Predestination, 139
Predicate(s), 5, 9
  nominalism, 10
Premodern biblical hermeneutics, 116
Premodernity, 143, 149
Premodern Old Testament hermeneutics, 115
Premodern philosophers
  Plotinian, 187, 188
  pre-Socratic, 179
  skeptic and middle platonist, 186
  stoic and epicurean, 185
  .See also individual philosophers

Preparation of the Gospel, The (Eusebius), 125
Prescriptivism, 40, 68
Presentism, 17
Pre-Socratic philosophy, 150, 179
Presuppositional apologetics, 133, 138
Prima facie duties, 49
Primary properties of objects, 6, 203
Princeton Theological Seminary, 165
Principia Ethica (Moore), 24, 28
Principle of instantiation, 9
Principle of testability, 85
Principles (Mill), 61
Principles of Economics (Menger), 61
Principles of Human Knowledge (Berkeley), 204
Principles of Nature and Grace (Leibniz), 201
Principles of Philosophy (Spinoza), 200
Private language, 73
Probability theory, 1
Problems of Empiricism (Feyerabend), 85
Process philosophy and theology, 103, 105, 166, 169, 171
Promise keeping, 49
Proof, scientific, 83
Proof of the Gospel, The (Eusebius), 125
Proper functionalism, 35, 38, 41
Proper overlap in mereology, 16
Proper parts principles, 15, 16
Properties, moral, 39, 40
Property
  dualism, 90
  rights, 58, 59, 60
  substance and, 6
Proper underlap in mereology, 16
Prophets, minor, 151
Proportionality, analogy of, 111
Proposition statements, 5
Prosentential theory, 23
Proslogium (Anselm), 127, 193
Protagoras, 150, 179
Prudence, 46, 184
Prudentia, 195
Przeworski, Adam, 64
Pseudo Dionysius the Areopagite, 110, 153, 192
Psychological altruism, 42
Psychological egoism, 42
Psychological theories of meaning, 75
Psychology, moral, 39, 42, 46, 48, 49, 51, 139–141, 184
Psychotherapy, 83
Putnam, Hilary, 22, 71, 74, 75, 166
Pyrhonian skepticism, 41, 186
Pythagoras, 179
Pythagoreans, 150, 179
  neo-, 186

Qualia, 91
Quantum theory, 83
Quasi-realism, 41
Quine, W. V. O., 166, 167
  analytic philosophy and, 65, 69, 71
  epistemology and, 38
  metaphysics and, 23, 28
  on the verification principle, 113
Quinn, Philip, 141
Quodlibet (Scotus), 196

Radicals, liberal, 56
Radical skepticism, 159
Ramm, Bernard, 169

Ramsey, Frank, 23, 65, 67
Ramsey, Ian Thomas, 104, 110, 170
Rashdall, Hastings, 104
Rational altruism, 42
Rational desire theory, 27
Rational egoism, 42
Rationalism, 29, 30
    Continental, 144, 146, 149, 158, 159,
        176, 198–202
Rawls, John, 53
Reactionaries, 56
Reader response and the Bible, 118
Reagan, Ronald, 177
Realism
    aesthetic, 19, 54
    arguments for, 84
    combinatorial, 13
    common sense, 30, 32, 131, 158, 159,
        161, 166
    contemporary, 30
    critical, 166
    epistemic, 29
    epistemological, 143
    extreme, 7, 10, 13, 30
    logical, 65, 66, 112, 164, 167
    metaphysical, 19, 20
    minimal psychological, 42
    modal, 13
    moderate, 10, 13, 30
    moral, 20, 48, 49, 120, 139, 140, 142,
        184
    morality and, 40
    ontology and, 7
    platonic, 7, 10, 13, 70
    quasi-, 41
    scientific, 82–85
    semantic, 84
    types of value and, 26
    value, 20, 25, 66, 70, 143
Reason
    aesthetics and, 54
    British empiricists and, 145
    character and, 45
    faith and, 127, 129
    perception and, 200
    romanticism and, 92
    truth and, 201
Redaction criticism of the Bible, 117
Reductionism, 84
Reduction project, 78
Redundancy theory of truth, 23, 67
Reference(s)
    abstract, 9
    referring and, 74
Referential theory of linguistic meaning, 74
Referring and reference, 74
Reflexivity, 16
Reformation, Protestant, 157
    views of apologetics, 129
Reformed epistemology, 103
Regulative rules, 77
Reid, Thomas, 30, 108, 131, 158, 159, 161
    epistemology, 32, 206
Relativism, linguistic, 98
Relevance theory, 76
Reliabilism, virtue, 37, 38
Religion, philosophy of
    apologetics and, 125–138
    British, 104, 170
    Christian ethics and, 139–142
    linguistic essentialism and, 70
    linguistic turn in, 112

logical positivism and, 67
logical realism and, 66
neo-Thomism in, 103, 106, 107, 172
ordinary language analysis and, 68
philosophical theology and, 119–124
post positivists and physicalists and, 69
process theology, 103, 105
religious language and, 110–118
20th century, 103–104
Religion within the Bounds of Reason Alone
    (Kant), 132, 202
Reorientation, 115
Representationalism, 159, 203
Republic, The (Plato), 180
Reputation, law of, 203
Rescher, Nicholas, 24
Research programs, 85
Resemblance nominalism, 10
Respect for persons, 48
Responsibility
    existentialism and, 93
    moral, 40
Retributive justice, 57
Revealed theology, 131
Rhetoric, 2
Rhetorical criticism of the Bible, 117
Ricardo, David, 61
Richard of St. Victor, 154
Ricouer, Paul, 102, 163
Right and the Good, The (Ross), 49
Rigid designators, 80
Ritschl, Albrecht, 160, 168
Road to Serfdom, The (von Hayek), 61
Roman Catholicism, 168, 171
Romanticism and romanticists, 55, 92, 146,
    159, 160
Rorty, Richard, 22, 71, 166
Roscelin, 154
Ross, W. D., 47, 49
Rossian intuitionism, 47, 49
Rothbard, Murray, 174
Rousseau, Jean Jacques, 52, 176
Royce, Josiah, 165, 166
Ruether, Rosemary R., 103, 118
Ruge, Arnold, 94
Rule(s)
    consequentialism, 43
    non-consequentialism, 43
    speech act theory, 77
    utilitarianism, 51
Russell, Bertrand, 65, 66, 74, 76, 112, 161,
    162, 167
Ryle, Gilbert, 65, 68, 162, 164, 167

Sachs, Jeff, 175
Salamanca School, 156
    of economics, 59
Saltwater School, 175
Salvation
    moral development and, 139, 140
    through Jesus Christ, 130
Samuelson, Paul, 174, 175
Santayana, George, 166
Sapientia, 190
Sartre, Jean Paul, 64, 93, 96, 162
Saussure, Ferdinand, 98, 160, 163
Schelling, F. W. J., 8
Schleiermacher, Friedrich, 102, 117, 136,
    158, 160, 168
Schlick, Moritz, 65, 67, 113, 164, 167
Schmidt, Karl, 94
School of Alexandria philosophy, 152

School of Chartres, 154
School of St. Victor philosophy, 154
Schopenhauer, Arthur, 94, 158, 160
Schumpeter, Joseph, 174, 175
Science
    cognitive, 88
    epistemology of, 84, 86
    Karl Marx on, 101
    limits of, 82
    metaphysics of, 82, 84
    nature of, 82
    philosophy of, 82
    scientific anti-realism and, 82, 83, 86, 87
    scientific method and, 83, 84, 207
    scientific realism and, 82–85
    value theory of, 84, 86
Science of Knowledge (Fichte), 92
Scientia, 190
Scientific anti-realism, 82, 83, 86
Scientific Image, The (van Fraassen), 87
Scientific realism, 82–85
Scotus, John Duns, 110, 122, 127, 141,
    155, 196
Sculpture, 55
Searle, John, 65, 68, 75–77, 81, 164, 167
Secondary properties of objects, 6, 203
Second Sex, The (de Beauvoir), 97
Self-control, 45, 46, 130, 140, 184
Selfhood, 92
Self-improvement, 49
Sellars, Roy, 166
Sellars, Wilfrid, 65, 69, 166, 167
Semantic(s), 73
    ambiguity, 3
    extensional, 79
    intentional, 75, 79
    pragmatics, 66, 76
    realism, 84
    theory of truth, 20, 22, 35, 79
Semiological analysis, 118
Semiology, 98
Semiotics, 73
Sexual Politics (Millett), 97
Short Treatise on God (Spinoza), 200
Sidgwick, Henry, 158, 161, 164
Simons, Henry, 174
Simple foreknowledge, 123
Simplicity
    of God, 119
    test of, 137
Sin, noetic effects of, 141, 195
Situational ethics, 43
Skeptics and skepticism, 30, 41, 131
    classical period, 151
    Humean, 67
    premodern, 186
    pyrhonian, 41
    radical, 159
Skinner, B. F., 91
Slippery slope arguments, 3
Smith, Adam, 58, 60, 61, 173, 176, 177,
    205
Smith, Henry Boynton, 165
Smith, Quentin, 65
Soames, Scott, 65, 78, 79
Social contract theory, 52, 53
Socialism, 58, 63
Socialism (von Mises), 61
Society
    of Jesus, 59, 156
    Marx's theory of, 63, 101
Society of Christian Philosophers, 108

Society of Philosophy of Religion, 108
Socio-critical methodologies, 114, 118
Socrates, 150, 151
Solow, Robert, 175
Sophists, 150, 151, 179
Sosa, Ernest, 37, 38
Soul, the, 187, 188
Source criticism of the Bible, 117
Sowell, Thomas, 174
Space and reality, 17, 195
Space–time continuum, 17
Speech act theory, 68, 75–77
Spencer, Herbert, 161
Spinoza, Baruch, 90, 117, 132, 158, 159, 176, 200
Square of opposition laws, 4
St. Louis University, 107
States of affairs, 5, 10, 11
Stewart, Dugald, 161
Stigler, George, 174
Stirner, Max, 94
Stoics, 150, 151, 185, 186
Strauss, David Friedrich, 94
Strauss, Leo, 178
Straw man arguments, 3
Strawson, P. F., 23, 65, 68, 76, 164, 167
Strong internalism, 42
Strongly rigid designators, 80
Strong physicalism, 14
Strong supplementation in mereology, 16
Structuralism, 98, 118, 160, 163
    Continental rationalists and, 146
    post-, 99, 118, 163
Structuralist theory of truth, 23
Structure of Scientific Revolutions, The (Kuhn), 86, 87
Stuart, Moses, 165
Stump, Eleonore, 107, 122
Suarez, Francisco, 59, 156, 197
Subalternation, law of, 4
Subcontraries, law of, 4
Subjective idealism, 6, 8, 30, 204
Subjectivism, 42, 55
    British empiricists and, 145
    Continental rationalists and, 146
Subjectivity, 93
Subject(s)
    -predicate discourse, 9
    romanticism and, 92
    value, 24
Subordinationism, 121
Subscriber, value, 24
Substance and property, 6
Substantive theories of truth, 21, 22
Substitutionality principle, 79
Substratum, 11
Suchocki, Marjorie, 171
Sufficiency, 2, 115, 116, 117
Sullivan, Andrew, 178
Summa Contra Gentiles (Aquinas), 127, 128
Summa Theologia (Aquinas), 194
Summation, principle of, 25
Summers, Lawrence, 175
Superstring theory, 83
Supervenience, 9, 40
Supplementation principles in mereology, 16
Suspicion, hermeneutic of, 118, 148
Swinburne, Richard, 103, 104, 170
Symbolic logic, 1
Symbolic systems, 73
Syntax, 73
System of Logic (Mill), 207

Tarski's theory of truth, 79
Tatian, 152
Tautology, 2, 33
Taxation, 60
Taylor, Nathaniel William, 165
Teleology, 5, 19, 37, 38, 143
    development, 45
    naturalism and, 43
Television, 148
Temperance, 46, 140, 184
Tertiary properties of objects, 6, 203
Tertullian, 125, 152
Testability, principle of, 85
Testimony, 3, 29
Textual criticism of the Bible, 117
Thales, 150, 179
Thatcher, Margaret, 177
Theater, 55
Theodicy, 120
Theodoric of Chartres, 154
Theologia Christiana (Abelard), 193
Theologia Scholarium (Abelard), 193
Theological essentialism, 103, 119
Theological Political Treatise (Spinoza), 200
Theology, 5, 143, 144
    of Anselm of Canterbury, 193
    of Aristotle, 182
    of Augustine, 189
    of Baruch Spinoza, 200
    of Blaise Pascal, 199
    of Boethius, 192
    epicurean, 185
    of G. W. Leibniz, 201
    of George Berkeley, 204
    of Immanuel Kant, 202
    of John Duns Scotus, 196
    of John Locke, 203
    of John Scotus Erigena, 192
    of John Stuart Mill, 207
    of Luis de Molina, 197
    middle platonist, 186
    of Nicolas Malebranche, 199
    of Peter Abelard, 193
    of Plato, 180
    of Plotinus, 187
    postmodernity and, 148
    of René Descartes, 198
    skeptics, 186
    stoic, 185
    of Thomas Aquinas, 194, 195
    of Thomas Reid, 206
    of William of Ockham, 196
Theophilus of Antioch, 152
Theory of Moral Sentiments, The (Smith), 60
Thomism, 106, 107, 156, 172
Thought of Thomas Aquinas, The (Davies), 107
Three Dialogues between Hylas and Philonus (Berkeley), 204
Three Rival Versions of Moral Enquiry (MacIntyre), 46
Tillich, Paul, 168
Time
    A and B theories of, 17, 18
    cosmology and, 17, 195
    God and, 122
    persistence through, 18
    and space continuum, 17
Timeline charts
    analytic philosophy, 167
    classical liberalism, 176
    classical period, 151
    conservatism, 177

early American philosophy, 165
economics, 173–175
European analytic philosophy, 164
historical overview, 149–178
medieval, 154, 155
modernity, 144–146, 149
neo-conservatism, 178
patristic period, 152
political philosophy, 173, 174
post-Humean British empiricism, 161
postmodernity, 147–149
premodernity, 143, 149
pre-Socratic, 150
process theology, 171
Protestant Reformation, 157
Salamanca School, 156
20thcentury American philosophy, 166
20th century British philosophy of religion, 170
19th century Continental philosophy, 160
20th century Continental philosophy, 162, 163
20th century European philosophy, 162
20th century evangelical theology, 169
20th century theology, 168
20th century Thomistic philosophy of religion, 172
17th–18th century European philosophy, 159
17th–19th century European philosophy, 158
Tobin, James, 175
Token identity theory, 91
Torah, the, 115
Torrance, Thomas F., 104, 170
Torrey, R. A., 169
Totality and Infinity (Lévinas), 96
Traditionalism and truth, 22
Traite de la nature et de la grace (Malebranche), 199
Traite de morale (Malebranche), 199
Transcendence of God, 119, 122, 186
Transcendental idealism, 8
Transcendental Thomism, 172
Transcendental truth, 71
Transitivity, 16
Transworld identification, 80
Treatise Against the Pagans (Athanasius), 125
Treatise Concerning the Principles of Human Knowledge, A (Berkeley), 87
Treatise of Human Nature, A (Hume), 28, 87, 131, 205
Treatise on the Correction of the Understanding (Spinoza), 200
Trible, Phyllis, 97
Trinity, The (Augustine), 189
Trinity, The (Boethius), 192
Trinity Evangelical Divinity School, 169
Tri-theism, 121
Trivial essences, 70
Troeltsch, Ernst, 160
Tropes, 5, 10
True Doctrine (Origen), 125
Trust, hermeneutic of, 143
Truth
    British empiricists and, 145
    coherence theory of, 20, 22, 35, 114, 117, 144
    complex, 71
    correspondence theory of, 22, 66, 70, 114, 115, 143, 196

deflationary theories of, 21, 23, 35
disquotational theory of, 23, 69
God as, 190, 191
language and, 73
logical, 71
modality and, 21
narrative and, 118
perception metaphysics of epistemology and, 30
performative theory of, 23, 68
postmodernity and, 148
postmodern theories of, 21, 23
pragmatic theory of, 20, 22, 71,
114, 118
realism and, 20
reason and, 201
redundancy theory of, 23, 67
semantic theory of, 20, 22, 35
substantive theories of, 21, 22
tests for, 137
theory of meaning, 79
transcendental, 71
types of theories of, 21
universals, 22
value, 77
Truth and Method (Gadamer), 96, 102
Truth-conditional theories of meaning, 75
Truthmakers, 5
"The Two Dogmas of Empiricism"
(Quine), 28, 69, 113
Typology, 115
Tyranny, 56

Unconscious, the, 101
Under-crossing in mereology, 16
Underdetermination, 86
of translation by data, 69
Underlap in mereology, 16
Underlying value, 24
Understanding, belief preceding,
129, 130
Union Seminary, 165
Unitarianism, 165
Universality, 25, 48, 51
Universals
abstract, 181, 183, 190, 195
bare particulars and, 10
defined, 5
key ideas of, 9
nature of, 10
ontology and, 7, 10
realism and nominalism, 14
states of affairs and, 10
truth and, 22
Universe in mereology, 15
University of Chicago, 58, 61, 166,
171
University of Coimbra, Portugal,
59, 156
University of Paris, 155
University of Salamanca, Spain, 59,
156
University of St. Andrews, 107
Univocal language, 111
Unqualified divine temporality of
God, 122

Use theory of meaning, 68, 75
Utilitarianism, 161, 205
act, 50
rule, 51
Utilitarianism (Mill), 207
Utterances, performative, 77

Value
of beauty, 54
of belief, 37
British empiricists and, 145
Continental rationalists and, 146
of knowledge, 29, 36
monism, 26, 27, 29, 38
pluralism, 26, 27, 29, 38
realism, 20, 25, 66, 70, 143
truth, 77
Value in Ethics and Economics (Anderson), 27
Value theory
fact/value dichotomy and, 28
principles of, 25
of science, 84, 86
teleology and, 19
types of value and, 26
Van Fraassen, Bas, 87
Van Til, Cornelius, 133, 169
Verificationism, 75
Verification principle, 67, 110, 112,
113, 132
Vermigli, Peter, 157
Via negativa, 110
Vice, 45, 191
Viner, Jacob, 174
Virtue, 29
Aristotle on, 183
consequentialism, 37, 50
epistemology, 35, 37, 41
ethics, 43, 44, 46, 139, 140, 184
reliabilism, 37, 38
scientific, 84
social contract theory and, 53
Thomas Aquinas on, 195
warrant, 38
Volf, Christian, 202
Voltaire, 176
Voluntarism, theological. *See* Divine
command theory
Von Böhm-Bawerk, Eugen, 174
Von Cieszkowski, August, 94
Von Hayek, Friedrich A., 58, 61,
174, 177
Von Mises, Ludwig, 61, 174
Von Schelling, Friedrich Wilhelm,
92
Von Schlegel, Friedrich, 92
Von Wieser, Friedrich, 174

Walter of St. Victor, 154
Walvoord, John, 169
Warfield, B. B., 165, 169
Warrant
teleological, 38
virtue, 38
Warrant: The Current Debate (Plant-
inga), 108, 109

Warrant and Proper Function (Plant-
inga), 108, 109
Warranted Christian Belief (Plant-
inga), 108, 109
Weak internalism, 42
Weak nominalism, 14
Weak supplementation in mereol-
ogy, 16
Wealth of Nations, The (Smith), 58,
60
Webb, C. C. J., 104, 170
Weiman, Henry Nelson, 171
Welfarism
ethics and, 42, 44, 46, 51, 52
political philosophy and, 57
Westminster Theological Seminary,
169
Whitehead, Alfred North, 103, 105,
161, 171
Wholistic coherentism, 36
Whose Justice, Which Rationality?
(MacIntyre), 46
Will
of God, 47, 141, 196
to power, 94
William of Auvergne, 154, 155
William of Champeaux, 154, 193
William of Conches, 154
William of Ockham, 5, 47, 123,
141, 155, 196
Wisdom, 140
Wisdom, John, 162, 164
Wittgenstein, Ludwig, 110, 113,
162, 164, 167
analytic philosophy and, 65, 66,
68, 107
on ethics, 44, 46
on meaning, 74, 75
semantic pragmatics, 76
Wohlstetter, Albert, 178
Wolf, Christian, 159
Wolfowitz, Paul, 178
Wolterstorff, Nicholas, 103, 108,
122
Women, Knowledge, and Reality (Garry
and Pearsall), 97
Women's Role in Economic Development
(Boserup), 97
Woods, Leonard, 165
Word games, 110
Worlds
actual, 12, 34
God as designer of, 135
language and, 73
noumenal, 33
phenomenal, 33
possible, 12, 13, 34

Xenophanes, 150, 179

Yale University, 108, 165
Young Hegelians, 94, 160

Zagzebski, Linda, 37
Zeno, 150, 179, 185
Zwingli, Ulrich, 157

CPSIA information can be obtained at www.ICGtesting.com
Printed in the USA
LVOW02s0419130115

422543LV00002B/10/P